American Casebook Series
Hornbook Series and Basic Legal Texts
Black Letter Series and Nutshell Series

of

WEST PUBLISHING COMPANY
P.O. Box 64526
St. Paul, Minnesota 55164–0526

Accounting

FARIS' ACCOUNTING AND LAW IN A NUT-SHELL, 377 pages, 1984. Softcover. (Text)

FIFLIS, KRIPKE AND FOSTER'S TEACHING MATERIALS ON ACCOUNTING FOR BUSINESS LAWYERS, Third Edition, 838 pages, 1984. (Casebook)

SIEGEL AND SIEGEL'S ACCOUNTING AND FINANCIAL DISCLOSURE: A GUIDE TO BASIC CONCEPTS, 259 pages, 1983. Softcover. (Text)

Administrative Law

BONFIELD AND ASIMOW'S STATE AND FEDERAL ADMINISTRATIVE LAW, 826 pages, 1989. Teacher's Manual available. (Casebook)

GELLHORN AND LEVIN'S ADMINISTRATIVE LAW AND PROCESS IN A NUTSHELL, Third Edition, approximately 420 pages, 1990. Softcover. (Text)

MASHAW AND MERRILL'S CASES AND MATERIALS ON ADMINISTRATIVE LAW—THE AMERICAN PUBLIC LAW SYSTEM, Second Edition, 976 pages, 1985. (Casebook) 1989 Supplement.

ROBINSON, GELLHORN AND BRUFF'S THE ADMINISTRATIVE PROCESS, Third Edition, 978 pages, 1986. (Casebook)

Admiralty

HEALY AND SHARPE'S CASES AND MATERIALS ON ADMIRALTY, Second Edition, 876 pages, 1986. (Casebook)

MARAIST'S ADMIRALTY IN A NUTSHELL, Second Edition, 379 pages, 1988. Softcover.

(Text)

SCHOENBAUM'S ORNBOOK ON ADMIRALTY AND MARITIME , V, Student Edition, 692 pages, 1987 wit 989 pocket part. (Text)

Agency—Pa)

FESSLER'S A IVES TO INCORPORATION FOR PERSON EST OF PROFIT, Second Edition, 3 s, 1986. Softcover. Teacher's I available. (Casebook)

HENN'S CA MATERIALS ON AGENCY, PARTNERSHI)THER UNINCORPORATED BUSINESS E S, Second Edition, 733 pages, 198 er's Manual available. (Casebook)

REUSCHLEIN AND GREGORY'S HORNBOOK ON THE LAW OF AGENCY AND PARTNERSHIP, Second Edition, 683 pages, 1990. (Text)

SELECTED CORPORATION AND PARTNERSHIP STATUTES, RULES AND FORMS. Softcover. 727 pages, 1989.

STEFFEN AND KERR'S CASES ON AGENCY-PARTNERSHIP, Fourth Edition, 859 pages, 1980. (Casebook)

STEFFEN'S AGENCY-PARTNERSHIP IN A NUTSHELL, 364 pages, 1977. Softcover. (Text)

Agricultural Law

MEYER, PEDERSEN, THORSON AND DAVIDSON'S AGRICULTURAL LAW: CASES AND MATERIALS, 931 pages, 1985. Teacher's Manual available. (Casebook)

Alternative Dispute Resolution

KANOWITZ' CASES AND MATERIALS ON ALTERNATIVE DISPUTE RESOLUTION, 1024 pages,

Alternative Dispute Resolution—Cont'd

1986. Teacher's Manual available. (Casebook) 1990 Supplement.

RISKIN AND WESTBROOK'S DISPUTE RESOLUTION AND LAWYERS, 468 pages, 1987. Teacher's Manual available. (Casebook)

RISKIN AND WESTBROOK'S DISPUTE RESOLUTION AND LAWYERS, Abridged Edition, 223 pages, 1987. Softcover. Teacher's Manual available. (Casebook)

American Indian Law

CANBY'S AMERICAN INDIAN LAW IN A NUTSHELL, Second Edition, 336 pages, 1988. Softcover. (Text)

GETCHES AND WILKINSON'S CASES AND MATERIALS ON FEDERAL INDIAN LAW, Second Edition, 880 pages, 1986. (Casebook)

Antitrust—see also Regulated Industries, Trade Regulation

FOX AND SULLIVAN'S CASES AND MATERIALS ON ANTITRUST, 935 pages, 1989. Teacher's Manual available. (Casebook)

GELLHORN'S ANTITRUST LAW AND ECONOMICS IN A NUTSHELL, Third Edition, 472 pages, 1986. Softcover. (Text)

HOVENKAMP'S BLACK LETTER ON ANTITRUST, 323 pages, 1986. Softcover. (Review)

HOVENKAMP'S HORNBOOK ON ECONOMICS AND FEDERAL ANTITRUST LAW, Student Edition, 414 pages, 1985. (Text)

OPPENHEIM, WESTON AND MCCARTHY'S CASES AND COMMENTS ON FEDERAL ANTITRUST LAWS, Fourth Edition, 1168 pages, 1981. (Casebook) 1985 Supplement.

POSNER AND EASTERBROOK'S CASES AND ECONOMIC NOTES ON ANTITRUST, Second Edition, 1077 pages, 1981. (Casebook) 1984–85 Supplement.

SULLIVAN'S HORNBOOK OF THE LAW OF ANTITRUST, 886 pages, 1977. (Text)

Appellate Advocacy—see Trial and Appellate Advocacy

Architecture and Engineering Law

SWEET'S LEGAL ASPECTS OF ARCHITECTURE, ENGINEERING AND THE CONSTRUCTION PROCESS, Fourth Edition, 889 pages, 1989. Teacher's Manual available. (Casebook)

Art Law

DUBOFF'S ART LAW IN A NUTSHELL, 335 pages, 1984. Softcover. (Text)

Banking Law

LOVETT'S BANKING AND FINANCIAL INSTITUTIONS LAW IN A NUTSHELL, Second Edition, 464 pages, 1988. Softcover. (Text)

SYMONS AND WHITE'S TEACHING MATERIALS ON BANKING LAW, Second Edition, 993 pages, 1984. Teacher's Manual available. (Casebook) 1987 Supplement.

Business Planning—see also Corporate Finance

PAINTER'S PROBLEMS AND MATERIALS IN BUSINESS PLANNING, Second Edition, 1008 pages, 1984. (Casebook) 1990 Supplement.

Statutory Supplement. *See Selected Corporation and Partnership*

SELECTED CORPORATION AND PARTNERSHIP STATUTES, RULES AND FORMS. 727 pages, 1989. Softcover.

Civil Procedure—see also Federal Jurisdiction and Procedure

AMERICAN BAR ASSOCIATION SECTION OF LITIGATION—READINGS ON ADVERSARIAL JUSTICE: THE AMERICAN APPROACH TO ADJUDICATION, 217 pages, 1988. Softcover. (Coursebook)

CLERMONT'S BLACK LETTER ON CIVIL PROCEDURE, Second Edition, 332 pages, 1988. Softcover. (Review)

COUND, FRIEDENTHAL, MILLER AND SEXTON'S CASES AND MATERIALS ON CIVIL PROCEDURE, Fifth Edition, 1284 pages, 1989. Teacher's Manual available. (Casebook)

COUND, FRIEDENTHAL, MILLER AND SEXTON'S CIVIL PROCEDURE SUPPLEMENT. Approximately 450 pages, 1990. Softcover. (Casebook Supplement)

FEDERAL RULES OF CIVIL PROCEDURE—EDUCATIONAL EDITION. Softcover. Approximately 635 pages, 1990.

FRIEDENTHAL, KANE AND MILLER'S HORNBOOK ON CIVIL PROCEDURE, 876 pages, 1985. (Text)

KANE AND LEVINE'S CIVIL PROCEDURE IN CALIFORNIA: STATE AND FEDERAL 498 pages, 1989. Softcover. (Casebook Supplement)

Civil Procedure—Cont'd

KANE'S CIVIL PROCEDURE IN A NUTSHELL, Second Edition, 306 pages, 1986. Softcover. (Text)

KOFFLER AND REPPY'S HORNBOOK ON COMMON LAW PLEADING, 663 pages, 1969. (Text)

MARCUS, REDISH AND SHERMAN'S CIVIL PROCEDURE: A MODERN APPROACH, 1027 pages, 1989. Teacher's Manual available. (Casebook)

MARCUS AND SHERMAN'S COMPLEX LITIGATION–CASES AND MATERIALS ON ADVANCED CIVIL PROCEDURE, 846 pages, 1985. Teacher's Manual available. (Casebook) 1989 Supplement.

PARK'S COMPUTER-AIDED EXERCISES ON CIVIL PROCEDURE, Second Edition, 167 pages, 1983. Softcover. (Coursebook)

SIEGEL'S HORNBOOK ON NEW YORK PRACTICE, 1011 pages, 1978, with 1987 pocket part. (Text)

Commercial Law

BAILEY AND HAGEDORN'S SECURED TRANSACTIONS IN A NUTSHELL, Third Edition, 390 pages, 1988. Softcover. (Text)

EPSTEIN, MARTIN, HENNING AND NICKLES' BASIC UNIFORM COMMERCIAL CODE TEACHING MATERIALS, Third Edition, 704 pages, 1988. Teacher's Manual available. (Casebook)

HENSON'S HORNBOOK ON SECURED TRANSACTIONS UNDER THE U.C.C., Second Edition, 504 pages, 1979, with 1979 pocket part. (Text)

MURRAY'S COMMERCIAL LAW, PROBLEMS AND MATERIALS, 366 pages, 1975. Teacher's Manual available. Softcover. (Coursebook)

NICKLES' BLACK LETTER ON COMMERCIAL PAPER, 450 pages, 1988. Softcover. (Review)

NICKLES, MATHESON AND DOLAN'S MATERIALS FOR UNDERSTANDING CREDIT AND PAYMENT SYSTEMS, 923 pages, 1987. Teacher's Manual available. (Casebook)

NORDSTROM, MURRAY AND CLOVIS' PROBLEMS AND MATERIALS ON SALES, 515 pages, 1982. (Casebook)

NORDSTROM, MURRAY AND CLOVIS' PROBLEMS AND MATERIALS ON SECURED TRANSACTIONS, 594 pages, 1987. (Casebook)

RUBIN AND COOTER'S THE PAYMENT SYSTEM: CASES, MATERIALS AND ISSUES, 885 pages, 1989. (Casebook)

SELECTED COMMERCIAL STATUTES. Softcover. Approximately 1650 pages, 1990.

SPEIDEL'S BLACK LETTER ON SALES AND SALES FINANCING, 363 pages, 1984. Softcover. (Review)

SPEIDEL, SUMMERS AND WHITE'S COMMERCIAL LAW: TEACHING MATERIALS, Fourth Edition, 1448 pages, 1987. Teacher's Manual available. (Casebook)

SPEIDEL, SUMMERS AND WHITE'S COMMERCIAL PAPER: TEACHING MATERIALS, Fourth Edition, 578 pages, 1987. Reprint from Speidel et al., Commercial Law, Fourth Edition. Teacher's Manual available. (Casebook)

SPEIDEL, SUMMERS AND WHITE'S SALES: TEACHING MATERIALS, Fourth Edition, 804 pages, 1987. Reprint from Speidel et al., Commercial Law, Fourth Edition. Teacher's Manual available. (Casebook)

SPEIDEL, SUMMERS AND WHITE'S SECURED TRANSACTIONS: TEACHING MATERIALS, Fourth Edition, 485 pages, 1987. Reprint from Speidel et al., Commercial Law, Fourth Edition. Teacher's Manual available. (Casebook)

STOCKTON'S SALES IN A NUTSHELL, Second Edition, 370 pages, 1981. Softcover. (Text)

STONE'S UNIFORM COMMERCIAL CODE IN A NUTSHELL, Third Edition, 580 pages, 1989. Softcover. (Text)

WEBER AND SPEIDEL'S COMMERCIAL PAPER IN A NUTSHELL, Third Edition, 404 pages, 1982. Softcover. (Text)

WHITE AND SUMMERS' HORNBOOK ON THE UNIFORM COMMERCIAL CODE, Third Edition, Student Edition, 1386 pages, 1988. (Text)

Community Property

MENNELL AND BOYKOFF'S COMMUNITY PROPERTY IN A NUTSHELL, Second Edition, 432 pages, 1988. Softcover. (Text)

VERRALL AND BIRD'S CASES AND MATERIALS

Community Property—Cont'd

ON CALIFORNIA COMMUNITY PROPERTY, Fifth Edition, 604 pages, 1988. (Casebook)

Comparative Law

BARTON, GIBBS, LI AND MERRYMAN'S LAW IN RADICALLY DIFFERENT CULTURES, 960 pages, 1983. (Casebook)

GLENDON, GORDON AND OSAKWE'S COMPARATIVE LEGAL TRADITIONS: TEXT, MATERIALS AND CASES ON THE CIVIL LAW, COMMON LAW AND SOCIALIST LAW TRADITIONS, 1091 pages, 1985. (Casebook)

GLENDON, GORDON AND OSAKWE'S COMPARATIVE LEGAL TRADITIONS IN A NUTSHELL. 402 pages, 1982. Softcover. (Text)

LANGBEIN'S COMPARATIVE CRIMINAL PROCEDURE: GERMANY, 172 pages, 1977. Softcover. (Casebook)

Computers and Law

MAGGS AND SPROWL'S COMPUTER APPLICATIONS IN THE LAW, 316 pages, 1987. (Coursebook)

MASON'S USING COMPUTERS IN THE LAW: AN INTRODUCTION AND PRACTICAL GUIDE, Second Edition, 288 pages, 1988. Softcover. (Coursebook)

Conflict of Laws

CRAMTON, CURRIE AND KAY'S CASES–COMMENTS–QUESTIONS ON CONFLICT OF LAWS, Fourth Edition, 876 pages, 1987. (Casebook)

HAY'S BLACK LETTER ON CONFLICT OF LAWS, 330 pages, 1989. Softcover. (Review)

SCOLES AND HAY'S HORNBOOK ON CONFLICT OF LAWS, Student Edition, 1085 pages, 1982, with 1988–89 pocket part. (Text)

SEIGEL'S CONFLICTS IN A NUTSHELL, 470 pages, 1982. Softcover. (Text)

Constitutional Law—Civil Rights—see also Foreign Relations and National Security Law

ABERNATHY'S CASES AND MATERIALS ON CIVIL RIGHTS, 660 pages, 1980. (Casebook)

BARRON AND DIENES' BLACK LETTER ON CONSTITUTIONAL LAW, Second Edition, 310 pages, 1987. Softcover. (Review)

BARRON AND DIENES' CONSTITUTIONAL LAW IN A NUTSHELL, 389 pages, 1986. Softcover. (Text)

ENGDAHL'S CONSTITUTIONAL FEDERALISM IN A NUTSHELL, Second Edition, 411 pages, 1987. Softcover. (Text)

FARBER AND SHERRY'S HISTORY OF THE AMERICAN CONSTITUTION, 458 pages, 1990. Softcover. Teacher's Manual available. (Text)

GARVEY AND ALEINIKOFF'S MODERN CONSTITUTIONAL THEORY: A READER, 494 pages, 1989. Softcover. (Reader)

LOCKHART, KAMISAR, CHOPER AND SHIFFRIN'S CONSTITUTIONAL LAW: CASES–COMMENTS–QUESTIONS, Sixth Edition, 1601 pages, 1986. (Casebook) 1990 Supplement.

LOCKHART, KAMISAR, CHOPER AND SHIFFRIN'S THE AMERICAN CONSTITUTION: CASES AND MATERIALS, Sixth Edition, 1260 pages, 1986. Abridged version of Lockhart, et al., Constitutional Law: Cases–Comments–Questions, Sixth Edition. (Casebook) 1990 Supplement.

LOCKHART, KAMISAR, CHOPER AND SHIFFRIN'S CONSTITUTIONAL RIGHTS AND LIBERTIES: CASES AND MATERIALS, Sixth Edition, 1266 pages, 1986. Reprint from Lockhart, et al., Constitutional Law: Cases–Comments–Questions, Sixth Edition. (Casebook) 1990 Supplement.

MARKS AND COOPER'S STATE CONSTITUTIONAL LAW IN A NUTSHELL, 329 pages, 1988. Softcover. (Text)

NOWAK, ROTUNDA AND YOUNG'S HORNBOOK ON CONSTITUTIONAL LAW, Third Edition, 1191 pages, 1986 with 1988 pocket part. (Text)

ROTUNDA'S MODERN CONSTITUTIONAL LAW: CASES AND NOTES, Third Edition, 1085 pages, 1989. (Casebook) 1990 Supplement.

VIEIRA'S CONSTITUTIONAL CIVIL RIGHTS IN A NUTSHELL, Second Edition, 322 pages, 1990. Softcover. (Text)

WILLIAMS' CONSTITUTIONAL ANALYSIS IN A NUTSHELL, 388 pages, 1979. Softcover. (Text)

Consumer Law—see also Commercial Law

EPSTEIN AND NICKLES' CONSUMER LAW IN A NUTSHELL, Second Edition, 418 pages,

Consumer Law—Cont'd

1981. Softcover. (Text)

SELECTED COMMERCIAL STATUTES. Softcover. Approximately 1650 pages, 1990.

SPANOGLE AND ROHNER'S CASES AND MATERIALS ON CONSUMER LAW, 693 pages, 1979. Teacher's Manual available. (Casebook) 1982 Supplement.

Contracts

CALAMARI AND PERILLO'S BLACK LETTER ON CONTRACTS, Second Edition, approximately 450 pages, 1990. Softcover. (Review)

CALAMARI AND PERILLO'S HORNBOOK ON CONTRACTS, Third Edition, 1049 pages, 1987. (Text)

CALAMARI, PERILLO AND BENDER'S CASES AND PROBLEMS ON CONTRACTS, Second Edition, 905 pages, 1989. Teacher's Manual Available. (Casebook)

CORBIN'S TEXT ON CONTRACTS, One Volume Student Edition, 1224 pages, 1952. (Text)

FESSLER AND LOISEAUX'S CASES AND MATERIALS ON CONTRACTS—MORALITY, ECONOMICS AND THE MARKET PLACE, 837 pages, 1982. Teacher's Manual available. (Casebook)

FRIEDMAN'S CONTRACT REMEDIES IN A NUTSHELL, 323 pages, 1981. Softcover. (Text)

FULLER AND EISENBERG'S CASES ON BASIC CONTRACT LAW, Fifth Edition, approximately 1100 pages, 1990. (Casebook)

HAMILTON, RAU AND WEINTRAUB'S CASES AND MATERIALS ON CONTRACTS, 830 pages, 1984. (Casebook)

JACKSON AND BOLLINGER'S CASES ON CONTRACT LAW IN MODERN SOCIETY, Second Edition, 1329 pages, 1980. Teacher's Manual available. (Casebook)

KEYES' GOVERNMENT CONTRACTS IN A NUTSHELL, Second Edition, approximately 530 pages, 1990. Softcover. (Text)

SCHABER AND ROHWER'S CONTRACTS IN A NUTSHELL, Third Edition, approximately 438 pages, 1990. Softcover. (Text)

SUMMERS AND HILLMAN'S CONTRACT AND RELATED OBLIGATION: THEORY, DOCTRINE AND PRACTICE, 1074 pages, 1987. Teacher's Manual available. (Casebook)

Copyright—see Patent and Copyright Law

Corporate Finance

HAMILTON'S CASES AND MATERIALS ON CORPORATION FINANCE, Second Edition, 1221 pages, 1989. (Casebook)

Corporations

HAMILTON'S BLACK LETTER ON CORPORATIONS, Second Edition, 513 pages, 1986. Softcover. (Review)

HAMILTON'S CASES AND MATERIALS ON CORPORATIONS—INCLUDING PARTNERSHIPS AND LIMITED PARTNERSHIPS, Fourth Edition, approximately 1250 pages, 1990. (Casebook) 1990 Statutory Supplement.

HAMILTON'S THE LAW OF CORPORATIONS IN A NUTSHELL, Second Edition, 515 pages, 1987. Softcover. (Text)

HENN'S TEACHING MATERIALS ON THE LAW OF CORPORATIONS, Second Edition, 1204 pages, 1986. Teacher's Manual available. (Casebook)

    Statutory Supplement. *See Selected Corporation and Partnership*

HENN AND ALEXANDER'S HORNBOOK ON LAWS OF CORPORATIONS, Third Edition, Student Edition, 1371 pages, 1983, with 1986 pocket part. (Text)

SELECTED CORPORATION AND PARTNERSHIP STATUTES, RULES AND FORMS. Softcover. 727 pages, 1989.

SOLOMON, SCHWARTZ AND BAUMAN'S MATERIALS AND PROBLEMS ON CORPORATIONS: LAW AND POLICY, Second Edition, 1391 pages, 1988. Teacher's Manual available. (Casebook) 1990 Supplement.

    Statutory Supplement. *See Selected Corporation and Partnership*

Corrections

KRANTZ' CASES AND MATERIALS ON THE LAW OF CORRECTIONS AND PRISONERS' RIGHTS, Third Edition, 855 pages, 1986. (Casebook) 1988 Supplement.

KRANTZ' THE LAW OF CORRECTIONS AND PRISONERS' RIGHTS IN A NUTSHELL, Third Edition, 407 pages, 1988. Softcover. (Text)

ROBBINS' CASES AND MATERIALS ON POST-CONVICTION REMEDIES, 506 pages, 1982. (Casebook)

Creditors' Rights

BANKRUPTCY CODE, RULES AND OFFICIAL FORMS, LAW SCHOOL EDITION. Approximately 875 pages, 1990. Softcover.

EPSTEIN'S DEBTOR-CREDITOR RELATIONS IN A NUTSHELL, Third Edition, 383 pages, 1986. Softcover. (Text)

EPSTEIN, LANDERS AND NICKLES' CASES AND MATERIALS ON DEBTORS AND CREDITORS, Third Edition, 1059 pages, 1987. Teacher's Manual available. (Casebook)

LOPUCKI'S PLAYER'S MANUAL FOR THE DEBTOR-CREDITOR GAME, 123 pages, 1985. Softcover. (Coursebook)

NICKLES AND EPSTEIN'S BLACK LETTER ON CREDITORS' RIGHTS AND BANKRUPTCY, 576 pages, 1989. (Review)

RIESENFELD'S CASES AND MATERIALS ON CREDITORS' REMEDIES AND DEBTORS' PROTECTION, Fourth Edition, 914 pages, 1987. (Casebook) 1990 Supplement.

WHITE'S CASES AND MATERIALS ON BANKRUPTCY AND CREDITORS' RIGHTS, 812 pages, 1985. Teacher's Manual available. (Casebook) 1987 Supplement.

Criminal Law and Criminal Procedure—see also Corrections, Juvenile Justice

ABRAMS' FEDERAL CRIMINAL LAW AND ITS ENFORCEMENT, 866 pages, 1986. (Casebook) 1988 Supplement.

AMERICAN CRIMINAL JUSTICE PROCESS: SELECTED RULES, STATUTES AND GUIDELINES. 723 pages, 1989. Softcover.

CARLSON'S ADJUDICATION OF CRIMINAL JUSTICE: PROBLEMS AND REFERENCES, 130 pages, 1986. Softcover. (Casebook)

DIX AND SHARLOT'S CASES AND MATERIALS ON CRIMINAL LAW, Third Edition, 846 pages, 1987. (Casebook)

GRANO'S PROBLEMS IN CRIMINAL PROCEDURE, Second Edition, 176 pages, 1981. Teacher's Manual available. Softcover. (Coursebook)

HEYMANN AND KENETY'S THE MURDER TRIAL OF WILBUR JACKSON: A HOMICIDE IN THE FAMILY, Second Edition, 347 pages, 1985. (Coursebook)

ISRAEL, KAMISAR AND LAFAVE'S CRIMINAL

PROCEDURE AND THE CONSTITUTION: LEADING SUPREME COURT CASES AND INTRODUCTORY TEXT. Approximately 725 pages, 1990 Edition. Softcover. (Casebook)

ISRAEL AND LAFAVE'S CRIMINAL PROCEDURE—CONSTITUTIONAL LIMITATIONS IN A NUTSHELL, Fourth Edition, 461 pages, 1988. Softcover. (Text)

JOHNSON'S CASES, MATERIALS AND TEXT ON CRIMINAL LAW, Fourth Edition, approximately 790 pages, 1990. Teacher's Manual available. (Casebook)

JOHNSON'S CASES AND MATERIALS ON CRIMINAL PROCEDURE, 859 pages, 1988. (Casebook) 1990 Supplement.

KAMISAR, LAFAVE AND ISRAEL'S MODERN CRIMINAL PROCEDURE: CASES, COMMENTS AND QUESTIONS, Seventh Edition, 1593 pages, 1990. (Casebook) 1990 Supplement.

KAMISAR, LAFAVE AND ISRAEL'S BASIC CRIMINAL PROCEDURE: CASES, COMMENTS AND QUESTIONS, Seventh Edition, 792 pages, 1990. Softcover reprint from Kamisar, et al., Modern Criminal Procedure: Cases, Comments and Questions, Seventh Edition. (Casebook) 1990 Supplement.

LAFAVE'S MODERN CRIMINAL LAW: CASES, COMMENTS AND QUESTIONS, Second Edition, 903 pages, 1988. (Casebook)

LAFAVE AND ISRAEL'S HORNBOOK ON CRIMINAL PROCEDURE, Student Edition, 1142 pages, 1985, with 1989 pocket part. (Text)

LAFAVE AND SCOTT'S HORNBOOK ON CRIMINAL LAW, Second Edition, 918 pages, 1986. (Text)

LANGBEIN'S COMPARATIVE CRIMINAL PROCEDURE: GERMANY, 172 pages, 1977. Softcover. (Casebook)

LOEWY'S CRIMINAL LAW IN A NUTSHELL, Second Edition, 321 pages, 1987. Softcover. (Text)

LOW'S BLACK LETTER ON CRIMINAL LAW, Revised First Edition, approximately 430 pages, 1990. Softcover. (Review)

SALTZBURG'S CASES AND COMMENTARY ON AMERICAN CRIMINAL PROCEDURE, Third Edition, 1302 pages, 1988. Teacher's Manual available. (Casebook) 1990 Supplement.

Criminal Law and Criminal Procedure— Cont'd

UVILLER'S THE PROCESSES OF CRIMINAL JUSTICE: INVESTIGATION AND ADJUDICATION, Second Edition, 1384 pages, 1979. (Casebook) 1979 Statutory Supplement. 1986 Update.

VORENBERG'S CASES ON CRIMINAL LAW AND PROCEDURE, Second Edition, 1088 pages, 1981. Teacher's Manual available. (Casebook) 1990 Supplement.

Decedents' Estates—see Trusts and Estates

Domestic Relations

CLARK'S HORNBOOK ON DOMESTIC RELATIONS, Second Edition, Student Edition, 1050 pages, 1988. (Text)

CLARK AND GLOWINSKY'S CASES AND PROBLEMS ON DOMESTIC RELATIONS, Fourth Edition. Approximately 1125 pages, 1990. Teacher's Manual available. (Casebook)

KRAUSE'S BLACK LETTER ON FAMILY LAW, 314 pages, 1988. Softcover. (Review)

KRAUSE'S CASES, COMMENTS AND QUESTIONS ON FAMILY LAW, Third Edition, 1433 pages, 1990. (Casebook)

KRAUSE'S FAMILY LAW IN A NUTSHELL, Second Edition, 444 pages, 1986. Softcover. (Text)

KRAUSKOPF'S CASES ON PROPERTY DIVISION AT MARRIAGE DISSOLUTION, 250 pages, 1984. Softcover. (Casebook)

Economics, Law and—see also Antitrust, Regulated Industries

GOETZ' CASES AND MATERIALS ON LAW AND ECONOMICS, 547 pages, 1984. (Casebook)

MALLOY'S LAW AND ECONOMICS: A COMPARATIVE APPROACH TO THEORY AND PRACTICE, Approximately 152 pages, 1990. Softcover. (Text)

Education Law

ALEXANDER AND ALEXANDER'S THE LAW OF SCHOOLS, STUDENTS AND TEACHERS IN A NUTSHELL, 409 pages, 1984. Softcover. (Text)

Employment Discrimination—see also Women and the Law

ESTREICHER AND HARPER'S CASES AND

MATERIALS ON THE LAW GOVERNING THE EMPLOYMENT RELATIONSHIP, 962 pages, 1990. Teacher's Manual available. (Casebook) Statutory Supplement.

JONES, MURPHY AND BELTON'S CASES AND MATERIALS ON DISCRIMINATION IN EMPLOYMENT, (The Labor Law Group). Fifth Edition, 1116 pages, 1987. (Casebook) 1990 Supplement.

PLAYER'S FEDERAL LAW OF EMPLOYMENT DISCRIMINATION IN A NUTSHELL, Second Edition, 402 pages, 1981. Softcover. (Text)

PLAYER'S HORNBOOK ON EMPLOYMENT DISCRIMINATION LAW, Student Edition, 708 pages, 1988. (Text)

PLAYER, SHOBEN AND LIEBERWITZ' CASES AND MATERIALS ON EMPLOYMENT DISCRIMINATION LAW, Approximately 810 pages, 1990. (Casebook)

Energy and Natural Resources Law—see also Oil and Gas

LAITOS' CASES AND MATERIALS ON NATURAL RESOURCES LAW, 938 pages, 1985. Teacher's Manual available. (Casebook)

SELECTED ENVIRONMENTAL LAW STATUTES—EDUCATIONAL EDITION. Softcover. Approximately 1040 pages, 1990.

Environmental Law—see also Energy and Natural Resources Law; Sea, Law of

BONINE AND McGARITY'S THE LAW OF ENVIRONMENTAL PROTECTION: CASES—LEGISLATION—POLICIES, 1076 pages, 1984. Teacher's Manual available. (Casebook)

FINDLEY AND FARBER'S CASES AND MATERIALS ON ENVIRONMENTAL LAW, Second Edition, 813 pages, 1985. (Casebook) 1988 Supplement.

FINDLEY AND FARBER'S ENVIRONMENTAL LAW IN A NUTSHELL, Second Edition, 367 pages, 1988. Softcover. (Text)

RODGERS' HORNBOOK ON ENVIRONMENTAL LAW, 956 pages, 1977, with 1984 pocket part. (Text)

SELECTED ENVIRONMENTAL LAW STATUTES—EDUCATIONAL EDITION. Softcover. Approximately 1040 pages, 1990.

Equity—see Remedies

Estate Planning—see also Trusts and Estates; Taxation—Estate and Gift

LYNN'S AN INTRODUCTION TO ESTATE PLANNING IN A NUTSHELL, Third Edition, 370 pages, 1983. Softcover. (Text)

Evidence

BROUN AND BLAKEY'S BLACK LETTER ON EVIDENCE, 269 pages, 1984. Softcover. (Review)

BROUN, MEISENHOLDER, STRONG AND MOSTELLER'S PROBLEMS IN EVIDENCE, Third Edition, 238 pages, 1988. Teacher's Manual available. Softcover. (Coursebook)

CLEARY, STRONG, BROUN AND MOSTELLER'S CASES AND MATERIALS ON EVIDENCE, Fourth Edition, 1060 pages, 1988. (Casebook)

FEDERAL RULES OF EVIDENCE FOR UNITED STATES COURTS AND MAGISTRATES. Softcover. Approximately 380 pages, 1990.

GRAHAM'S FEDERAL RULES OF EVIDENCE IN A NUTSHELL, Second Edition, 473 pages, 1987. Softcover. (Text)

LEMPERT AND SALTZBURG'S A MODERN APPROACH TO EVIDENCE: TEXT, PROBLEMS, TRANSCRIPTS AND CASES, Second Edition, 1232 pages, 1983. Teacher's Manual available. (Casebook)

LILLY'S AN INTRODUCTION TO THE LAW OF EVIDENCE, Second Edition, 585 pages, 1987. (Text)

McCORMICK, SUTTON AND WELLBORN'S CASES AND MATERIALS ON EVIDENCE, Sixth Edition, 1067 pages, 1987. (Casebook)

McCORMICK'S HORNBOOK ON EVIDENCE, Third Edition, Student Edition, 1156 pages, 1984, with 1987 pocket part. (Text)

ROTHSTEIN'S EVIDENCE IN A NUTSHELL: STATE AND FEDERAL RULES, Second Edition, 514 pages, 1981. Softcover. (Text)

Federal Jurisdiction and Procedure

CURRIE'S CASES AND MATERIALS ON FEDERAL COURTS, Fourth Edition, approximately 1125 pages, 1990. (Casebook)

CURRIE'S FEDERAL JURISDICTION IN A NUTSHELL, Third Edition, approximately 260 pages, 1990. Softcover. (Text)

FEDERAL RULES OF CIVIL PROCEDURE—EDUCATIONAL EDITION. Softcover. Approxi-

mately 635 pages, 1990.

REDISH'S BLACK LETTER ON FEDERAL JURISDICTION, 219 pages, 1985. Softcover. (Review)

REDISH'S CASES, COMMENTS AND QUESTIONS ON FEDERAL COURTS, Second Edition, 1122 pages, 1989. (Casebook) 1990 Supplement.

VETRI AND MERRILL'S FEDERAL COURTS PROBLEMS AND MATERIALS, Second Edition, 232 pages, 1984. Softcover. (Coursebook)

WRIGHT'S HORNBOOK ON FEDERAL COURTS, Fourth Edition, Student Edition, 870 pages, 1983. (Text)

Foreign Relations and National Security Law

FRANCK AND GLENNON'S FOREIGN RELATIONS AND NATIONAL SECURITY LAW, 941 pages, 1987. (Casebook)

Future Interests—see Trusts and Estates

Health Law—see Medicine, Law and

Human Rights—see International Law

Immigration Law

ALEINIKOFF AND MARTIN'S IMMIGRATION PROCESS AND POLICY, Second Edition, approximately 1100 pages, October, 1990 (Casebook)

Statutory Supplement. *See Immigration and Nationality Laws*

IMMIGRATION AND NATIONALITY LAWS OF THE UNITED STATES: SELECTED STATUTES, REGULATIONS AND FORMS. Softcover. Approximately 400 pages, 1990.

WEISSBRODT'S IMMIGRATION LAW AND PROCEDURE IN A NUTSHELL, Second Edition, 438 pages, 1989, Softcover. (Text)

Indian Law—see American Indian Law

Insurance Law

DEVINE AND TERRY'S PROBLEMS IN INSURANCE LAW, 240 pages, 1989. Softcover. Teacher's Manual available. (Coursebook)

DOBBYN'S INSURANCE LAW IN A NUTSHELL, Second Edition, 316 pages, 1989. Softcover. (Text)

KEETON'S CASES ON BASIC INSURANCE LAW,

Insurance Law—Cont'd

Second Edition, 1086 pages, 1977. Teacher's Manual available. (Casebook)

KEETON'S COMPUTER-AIDED AND WORKBOOK EXERCISES ON INSURANCE LAW, 255 pages, 1990. Softcover. (Coursebook)

KEETON AND WIDISS' INSURANCE LAW, Student Edition, 1359 pages, 1988. (Text)

WIDISS AND KEETON'S COURSE SUPPLEMENT TO KEETON AND WIDISS' INSURANCE LAW, 502 pages, 1988. Softcover. (Casebook)

WIDISS' INSURANCE: MATERIALS ON FUNDAMENTAL PRINCIPLES, LEGAL DOCTRINES AND REGULATORY ACTS, 1186 pages, 1989. (Casebook)

YORK AND WHELAN'S CASES, MATERIALS AND PROBLEMS ON GENERAL PRACTICE INSURANCE LAW, Second Edition, 787 pages, 1988. Teacher's Manual available. (Casebook)

International Law—see also Sea, Law of

BUERGENTHAL'S INTERNATIONAL HUMAN RIGHTS IN A NUTSHELL, 283 pages, 1988. Softcover. (Text)

BUERGENTHAL AND MAIER'S PUBLIC INTERNATIONAL LAW IN A NUTSHELL, Second Edition, 275 pages, 1990. Softcover. (Text)

FOLSOM, GORDON AND SPANOGLE'S INTERNATIONAL BUSINESS TRANSACTIONS—A PROBLEM-ORIENTED COURSEBOOK, 1160 pages, 1986. Teacher's Manual available. (Casebook) 1989 Documents Supplement.

FOLSOM, GORDON AND SPANOGLE'S INTERNATIONAL BUSINESS TRANSACTIONS IN A NUTSHELL, Third Edition, 509 pages, 1988. Softcover. (Text)

HENKIN, PUGH, SCHACHTER AND SMIT'S CASES AND MATERIALS ON INTERNATIONAL LAW, Second Edition, 1517 pages, 1987. (Casebook) Documents Supplement.

JACKSON AND DAVEY'S CASES, MATERIALS AND TEXT ON LEGAL PROBLEMS OF INTERNATIONAL ECONOMIC RELATIONS, Second Edition, 1269 pages, 1986. (Casebook) 1989 Documents Supplement.

KIRGIS' INTERNATIONAL ORGANIZATIONS IN THEIR LEGAL SETTING, 1016 pages, 1977. Teacher's Manual available. (Casebook) 1981 Supplement.

WESTON, FALK AND D'AMATO'S INTERNATIONAL LAW AND WORLD ORDER—A PROBLEM-ORIENTED COURSEBOOK, Second Edition, approximately 1305 pages, 1990. Teacher's Manual available. (Casebook) Documents Supplement.

Interviewing and Counseling

BINDER AND PRICE'S LEGAL INTERVIEWING AND COUNSELING, 232 pages, 1977. Teacher's Manual available. Softcover. (Coursebook)

BINDER, BERGMAN AND PRICE'S LAWYERS AS COUNSELORS: A CLIENT CENTERED APPROACH, Approximately 400 pages, October, 1990 Pub. Softcover. (Coursebook)

SHAFFER AND ELKINS' LEGAL INTERVIEWING AND COUNSELING IN A NUTSHELL, Second Edition, 487 pages, 1987. Softcover. (Text)

Introduction to Law—see Legal Method and Legal System

Introduction to Law Study

HEGLAND'S INTRODUCTION TO THE STUDY AND PRACTICE OF LAW IN A NUTSHELL, 418 pages, 1983. Softcover. (Text)

KINYON'S INTRODUCTION TO LAW STUDY AND LAW EXAMINATIONS IN A NUTSHELL, 389 pages, 1971. Softcover. (Text)

Judicial Process—see Legal Method and Legal System

Jurisprudence

CHRISTIE'S JURISPRUDENCE—TEXT AND READINGS ON THE PHILOSOPHY OF LAW, 1056 pages, 1973. (Casebook)

Juvenile Justice

FOX'S CASES AND MATERIALS ON MODERN JUVENILE JUSTICE, Second Edition, 960 pages, 1981. (Casebook)

FOX'S JUVENILE COURTS IN A NUTSHELL, Third Edition, 291 pages, 1984. Softcover. (Text)

Labor and Employment Law—see also Employment Discrimination, Social Legislation

FINKIN, GOLDMAN AND SUMMERS' LEGAL PROTECTION OF INDIVIDUAL EMPLOYEES, (The La-

Labor and Employment Law—Cont'd

bor Law Group). 1164 pages, 1989. (Casebook)

GORMAN'S BASIC TEXT ON LABOR LAW—UNIONIZATION AND COLLECTIVE BARGAINING, 914 pages, 1976. (Text)

LESLIE'S LABOR LAW IN A NUTSHELL, Second Edition, 397 pages, 1986. Softcover. (Text)

NOLAN'S LABOR ARBITRATION LAW AND PRACTICE IN A NUTSHELL, 358 pages, 1979. Softcover. (Text)

OBERER, HANSLOWE, ANDERSEN AND HEINSZ' CASES AND MATERIALS ON LABOR LAW—COLLECTIVE BARGAINING IN A FREE SOCIETY, Third Edition, 1163 pages, 1986. (Casebook) Statutory Supplement.

RABIN, SILVERSTEIN AND SCHATZKI'S LABOR AND EMPLOYMENT LAW: PROBLEMS, CASES AND MATERIALS IN THE LAW OF WORK, (The Labor Law Group). 1014 pages, 1988. Teacher's Manual available. (Casebook) 1988 Statutory Supplement.

Land Finance—Property Security—see Real Estate Transactions

Land Use

CALLIES AND FREILICH'S CASES AND MATERIALS ON LAND USE, 1233 pages, 1986. (Casebook) 1988 Supplement.

HAGMAN AND JUERGENSMEYER'S HORNBOOK ON URBAN PLANNING AND LAND DEVELOPMENT CONTROL LAW, Second Edition, Student Edition, 680 pages, 1986. (Text)

WRIGHT AND GITELMAN'S CASES AND MATERIALS ON LAND USE, Third Edition, 1300 pages, 1982. Teacher's Manual available. (Casebook) 1987 Supplement.

WRIGHT AND WRIGHT'S LAND USE IN A NUTSHELL, Second Edition, 356 pages, 1985. Softcover. (Text)

Legal History—see also Legal Method and Legal System

PRESSER AND ZAINALDIN'S CASES AND MATERIALS ON LAW AND JURISPRUDENCE IN AMERICAN HISTORY, Second Edition, 1092 pages, 1989. Teacher's Manual available. (Casebook)

Legal Method and Legal System—see also Legal Research, Legal Writing

ALDISERT'S READINGS, MATERIALS AND CASES IN THE JUDICIAL PROCESS, 948 pages, 1976. (Casebook)

BERCH AND BERCH'S INTRODUCTION TO LEGAL METHOD AND PROCESS, 550 pages, 1985. Teacher's Manual available. (Casebook)

BODENHEIMER, OAKLEY AND LOVE'S READINGS AND CASES ON AN INTRODUCTION TO THE ANGLO-AMERICAN LEGAL SYSTEM, Second Edition, 166 pages, 1988. Softcover. (Casebook)

DAVIES AND LAWRY'S INSTITUTIONS AND METHODS OF THE LAW—INTRODUCTORY TEACHING MATERIALS, 547 pages, 1982. Teacher's Manual available. (Casebook)

DVORKIN, HIMMELSTEIN AND LESNICK'S BECOMING A LAWYER: A HUMANISTIC PERSPECTIVE ON LEGAL EDUCATION AND PROFESSIONALISM, 211 pages, 1981. Softcover. (Text)

KEETON'S JUDGING, 842 pages, 1990. Softcover. (Coursebook)

KELSO AND KELSO'S STUDYING LAW: AN INTRODUCTION, 587 pages, 1984. (Coursebook)

KEMPIN'S HISTORICAL INTRODUCTION TO ANGLO-AMERICAN LAW IN A NUTSHELL, Third Edition, approximately 302 pages, 1990. Softcover. (Text)

REYNOLDS' JUDICIAL PROCESS IN A NUTSHELL, 292 pages, 1980. Softcover. (Text)

Legal Research

COHEN'S LEGAL RESEARCH IN A NUTSHELL, Fourth Edition, 452 pages, 1985. Softcover. (Text)

COHEN, BERRING AND OLSON'S HOW TO FIND THE LAW, Ninth Edition, 716 pages, 1989. (Text)

COHEN, BERRING AND OLSON'S FINDING THE LAW, 570 pages, 1989. Softcover reprint from Cohen, Berring and Olson's How to Find the Law, Ninth Edition. (Coursebook)

Legal Research Exercises, 3rd Ed., for use with Cohen, Berring and Olson, 229 pages, 1989. Teacher's Manual available.

ROMBAUER'S LEGAL PROBLEM SOLVING—

Legal Research—Cont'd

ANALYSIS, RESEARCH AND WRITING, Fourth Edition, 424 pages, 1983. Teacher's Manual with problems available. (Coursebook)

STATSKY'S LEGAL RESEARCH AND WRITING, Third Edition, 257 pages, 1986. Softcover. (Coursebook)

TEPLY'S LEGAL RESEARCH AND CITATION, Third Edition, 472 pages, 1989. Softcover. (Coursebook)

Student Library Exercises, 3rd ed., 391 pages, 1989. Answer Key available.

Legal Writing

CHILD'S DRAFTING LEGAL DOCUMENTS: MATERIALS AND PROBLEMS, 286 pages, 1988. Softcover. Teacher's Manual available. (Coursebook)

DICKERSON'S MATERIALS ON LEGAL DRAFTING, 425 pages, 1981. Teacher's Manual available. (Coursebook)

FELSENFELD AND SIEGEL'S WRITING CONTRACTS IN PLAIN ENGLISH, 290 pages, 1981. Softcover. (Text)

GOPEN'S WRITING FROM A LEGAL PERSPECTIVE, 225 pages, 1981. (Text)

MELLINKOFF'S LEGAL WRITING—SENSE AND NONSENSE, 242 pages, 1982. Softcover. Teacher's Manual available. (Text)

PRATT'S LEGAL WRITING: A SYSTEMATIC APPROACH, 422 pages, 1989. Teacher's Manual available. (Coursebook)

RAY AND RAMSFIELD'S LEGAL WRITING: GETTING IT RIGHT AND GETTING IT WRITTEN, 250 pages, 1987. Softcover. (Text)

SQUIRES AND ROMBAUER'S LEGAL WRITING IN A NUTSHELL, 294 pages, 1982. Softcover. (Text)

STATSKY AND WERNET'S CASE ANALYSIS AND FUNDAMENTALS OF LEGAL WRITING, Third Edition, 424 pages, 1989. Teacher's Manual available. (Text)

TEPLY'S LEGAL WRITING, ANALYSIS AND ORAL ARGUMENT, 576 pages, 1990. Softcover. Teacher's Manual available. (Coursebook)

WEIHOFEN'S LEGAL WRITING STYLE, Second Edition, 332 pages, 1980. (Text)

Legislation

DAVIES' LEGISLATIVE LAW AND PROCESS IN A NUTSHELL, Second Edition, 346 pages, 1986. Softcover. (Text)

ESKRIDGE AND FRICKEY'S CASES AND MATERIALS ON LEGISLATION: STATUTES AND THE CREATION OF PUBLIC POLICY, 937 pages, 1988. Teacher's Manual available. (Casebook) 1990 Supplement.

NUTTING AND DICKERSON'S CASES AND MATERIALS ON LEGISLATION, Fifth Edition, 744 pages, 1978. (Casebook)

STATSKY'S LEGISLATIVE ANALYSIS AND DRAFTING, Second Edition, 217 pages, 1984. Teacher's Manual available. (Text)

Local Government

FRUG'S CASES AND MATERIALS ON LOCAL GOVERNMENT LAW, 1005 pages, 1988. (Casebook)

MCCARTHY'S LOCAL GOVERNMENT LAW IN A NUTSHELL, Third Edition, approximately 400 pages, 1990. Softcover. (Text)

REYNOLDS' HORNBOOK ON LOCAL GOVERNMENT LAW, 860 pages, 1982, with 1990 pocket part. (Text)

VALENTE'S CASES AND MATERIALS ON LOCAL GOVERNMENT LAW, Third Edition, 1010 pages, 1987. Teacher's Manual available. (Casebook) 1989 Supplement.

Mass Communication Law

GILLMOR, BARRON, SIMON AND TERRY'S CASES AND COMMENT ON MASS COMMUNICATION LAW, Fifth Edition, 947 pages, 1990. (Casebook)

GINSBURG'S REGULATION OF BROADCASTING: LAW AND POLICY TOWARDS RADIO, TELEVISION AND CABLE COMMUNICATIONS, 741 pages, 1979 (Casebook) 1983 Supplement.

ZUCKMAN, GAYNES, CARTER AND DEE'S MASS COMMUNICATIONS LAW IN A NUTSHELL, Third Edition, 538 pages, 1988. Softcover. (Text)

Medicine, Law and

FURROW, JOHNSON, JOST AND SCHWARTZ' HEALTH LAW: CASES, MATERIALS AND PROBLEMS, 1005 pages, 1987. Teacher's Manual available. (Casebook) 1989 Supplement.

HALL AND ELLMAN'S HEALTH CARE LAW AND

Medicine, Law and—Cont'd

ETHICS IN A NUTSHELL, 401 pages, 1990. Softcover (Text)

KING'S THE LAW OF MEDICAL MALPRACTICE IN A NUTSHELL, Second Edition, 342 pages, 1986. Softcover. (Text)

SHAPIRO AND SPECE'S CASES, MATERIALS AND PROBLEMS ON BIOETHICS AND LAW, 892 pages, 1981. (Casebook)

SHARPE, BOUMIL, FISCINA AND HEAD'S CASES AND MATERIALS ON MEDICAL LIABILITY, Approximately 500 pages, September, 1990 Pub. (Casebook)

Military Law

SHANOR AND TERRELL'S MILITARY LAW IN A NUTSHELL, 378 pages, 1980. Softcover. (Text)

Mortgages—see Real Estate Transactions

Natural Resources Law—see Energy and Natural Resources Law, Environmental Law

Negotiation

GIFFORD'S LEGAL NEGOTIATION: THEORY AND APPLICATIONS, 225 pages, 1989. Softcover. (Text)

WILLIAMS' LEGAL NEGOTIATION AND SETTLEMENT, 207 pages, 1983. Softcover. Teacher's Manual available. (Coursebook)

Office Practice—see also Computers and Law, Interviewing and Counseling, Negotiation

HEGLAND'S TRIAL AND PRACTICE SKILLS IN A NUTSHELL, 346 pages, 1978. Softcover (Text)

STRONG AND CLARK'S LAW OFFICE MANAGEMENT, 424 pages, 1974. (Casebook)

Oil and Gas—see also Energy and Natural Resources Law

HEMINGWAY'S HORNBOOK ON OIL AND GAS, Second Edition, Student Edition, 543 pages, 1983, with 1989 pocket part. (Text)

KUNTZ, LOWE, ANDERSON AND SMITH'S CASES AND MATERIALS ON OIL AND GAS LAW, 857 pages, 1986. Teacher's Manual available. (Casebook) Forms Manual. Revised.

LOWE'S OIL AND GAS LAW IN A NUTSHELL,

Second Edition, 465 pages, 1988. Softcover. (Text)

Partnership—see Agency—Partnership

Patent and Copyright Law

CHOATE, FRANCIS AND COLLINS' CASES AND MATERIALS ON PATENT LAW, INCLUDING TRADE SECRETS, COPYRIGHTS, TRADEMARKS, Third Edition, 1009 pages, 1987. (Casebook)

MILLER AND DAVIS' INTELLECTUAL PROPERTY—PATENTS, TRADEMARKS AND COPYRIGHT IN A NUTSHELL, Second Edition, approximately 440 pages, 1990. Softcover. (Text)

NIMMER'S CASES AND MATERIALS ON COPYRIGHT AND OTHER ASPECTS OF ENTERTAINMENT LITIGATION ILLUSTRATED—INCLUDING UNFAIR COMPETITION, DEFAMATION AND PRIVACY, Third Edition, 1025 pages, 1985. (Casebook) 1989 Supplement.

Products Liability

FISCHER AND POWERS' CASES AND MATERIALS ON PRODUCTS LIABILITY, 685 pages, 1988. Teacher's Manual available. (Casebook)

NOEL AND PHILLIPS' CASES ON PRODUCTS LIABILITY, Second Edition, 821 pages, 1982. (Casebook)

PHILLIPS' PRODUCTS LIABILITY IN A NUTSHELL, Third Edition, 307 pages, 1988. Softcover. (Text)

Professional Responsibility

ARONSON, DEVINE AND FISCH'S PROBLEMS, CASES AND MATERIALS IN PROFESSIONAL RESPONSIBILITY, 745 pages, 1985. Teacher's Manual available. (Casebook)

ARONSON AND WECKSTEIN'S PROFESSIONAL RESPONSIBILITY IN A NUTSHELL, 399 pages, 1980. Softcover. (Text)

MELLINKOFF'S THE CONSCIENCE OF A LAWYER, 304 pages, 1973. (Text)

PIRSIG AND KIRWIN'S CASES AND MATERIALS ON PROFESSIONAL RESPONSIBILITY, Fourth Edition, 603 pages, 1984. Teacher's Manual available. (Casebook)

ROTUNDA'S BLACK LETTER ON PROFESSIONAL RESPONSIBILITY, Second Edition, 414 pages, 1988. Softcover. (Review)

SCHWARTZ AND WYDICK'S PROBLEMS IN LE-

Professional Responsibility—Cont'd

GAL ETHICS, Second Edition, 341 pages, 1988. (Coursebook)

SELECTED STATUTES, RULES AND STANDARDS ON THE LEGAL PROFESSION. Softcover. Approximately 600 pages, 1990.

SMITH AND MALLEN'S PREVENTING LEGAL MALPRACTICE, 264 pages, 1989. Reprint from Mallen and Smith's Legal Malpractice, Third Edition. (Text)

SUTTON AND DZIENKOWSKI'S CASES AND MATERIALS ON THE PROFESSIONAL RESPONSIBILITY FOR LAWYERS, 839 pages, 1989. Teacher's Manual available. (Casebook)

WOLFRAM'S HORNBOOK ON MODERN LEGAL ETHICS, Student Edition, 1120 pages, 1986. (Text)

Property—see also Real Estate Transactions, Land Use, Trusts and Estates

BERNHARDT'S BLACK LETTER ON PROPERTY, 318 pages, 1983. Softcover. (Review)

BERNHARDT'S REAL PROPERTY IN A NUT-SHELL, Second Edition, 448 pages, 1981. Softcover. (Text)

BOYER'S SURVEY OF THE LAW OF PROPERTY, Third Edition, 766 pages, 1981. (Text)

BROWDER, CUNNINGHAM, NELSON, STOEBUCK AND WHITMAN'S CASES ON BASIC PROPERTY LAW, Fifth Edition, 1386 pages, 1989. Teacher's Manual available. (Casebook)

BRUCE, ELY AND BOSTICK'S CASES AND MATERIALS ON MODERN PROPERTY LAW, Second Edition, 953 pages, 1989. Teacher's Manual available. (Casebook)

BURKE'S PERSONAL PROPERTY IN A NUT-SHELL, 322 pages, 1983. Softcover. (Text)

CUNNINGHAM, STOEBUCK AND WHITMAN'S HORNBOOK ON THE LAW OF PROPERTY, Student Edition, 916 pages, 1984, with 1987 pocket part. (Text)

DONAHUE, KAUPER AND MARTIN'S CASES ON PROPERTY, Second Edition, 1362 pages, 1983. Teacher's Manual available. (Casebook)

HILL'S LANDLORD AND TENANT LAW IN A NUTSHELL, Second Edition, 311 pages, 1986. Softcover. (Text)

KURTZ AND HOVENKAMP'S CASES AND

MATERIALS ON AMERICAN PROPERTY LAW, 1296 pages, 1987. Teacher's Manual available. (Casebook) 1988 Supplement.

MOYNIHAN'S INTRODUCTION TO REAL PROPERTY, Second Edition, 239 pages, 1988. (Text)

Psychiatry, Law and

REISNER AND SLOBOGIN'S LAW AND THE MENTAL HEALTH SYSTEM, CIVIL AND CRIMINAL ASPECTS, Second Edition, approximately 1127 pages, 1990. (Casebook)

Real Estate Transactions

BRUCE'S REAL ESTATE FINANCE IN A NUT-SHELL, Second Edition, 262 pages, 1985. Softcover. (Text)

MAXWELL, RIESENFELD, HETLAND AND WARREN'S CASES ON CALIFORNIA SECURITY TRANSACTIONS IN LAND, Third Edition, 728 pages, 1984. (Casebook)

NELSON AND WHITMAN'S BLACK LETTER ON LAND TRANSACTIONS AND FINANCE, Second Edition, 466 pages, 1988. Softcover. (Review)

NELSON AND WHITMAN'S CASES ON REAL ESTATE TRANSFER, FINANCE AND DEVELOPMENT, Third Edition, 1184 pages, 1987. (Casebook)

NELSON AND WHITMAN'S HORNBOOK ON REAL ESTATE FINANCE LAW, Second Edition, 941 pages, 1985 with 1989 pocket part. (Text)

Regulated Industries—see also Mass Communication Law, Banking Law

GELLHORN AND PIERCE'S REGULATED INDUSTRIES IN A NUTSHELL, Second Edition, 389 pages, 1987. Softcover. (Text)

MORGAN, HARRISON AND VERKUIL'S CASES AND MATERIALS ON ECONOMIC REGULATION OF BUSINESS, Second Edition, 666 pages, 1985. (Casebook)

Remedies

DOBBS' HORNBOOK ON REMEDIES, 1067 pages, 1973. (Text)

DOBBS' PROBLEMS IN REMEDIES. 137 pages, 1974. Teacher's Manual available. Softcover. (Coursebook)

DOBBYN'S INJUNCTIONS IN A NUTSHELL, 264 pages, 1974. Softcover. (Text)

Remedies—Cont'd

FRIEDMAN'S CONTRACT REMEDIES IN A NUT-SHELL, 323 pages, 1981. Softcover. (Text)

LEAVELL, LOVE AND NELSON'S CASES AND MATERIALS ON EQUITABLE REMEDIES, RESTI-TUTION AND DAMAGES, Fourth Edition, 1111 pages, 1986. Teacher's Manual available. (Casebook)

MCCORMICK'S HORNBOOK ON DAMAGES, 811 pages, 1935. (Text)

O'CONNELL'S REMEDIES IN A NUTSHELL, Second Edition, 320 pages, 1985. Softcover. (Text)

SCHOENBROD, MACBETH, LEVINE AND JUNG'S CASES AND MATERIALS ON REMEDIES: PUBLIC AND PRIVATE, Approximately 807 pages, 1990. Teacher's Manual available. (Case-book)

YORK, BAUMAN AND RENDLEMAN'S CASES AND MATERIALS ON REMEDIES, Fourth Edition, 1029 pages, 1985. Teacher's Manual available. (Casebook)

Sea, Law of

SOHN AND GUSTAFSON'S THE LAW OF THE SEA IN A NUTSHELL, 264 pages, 1984. Soft-cover. (Text)

Securities Regulation

HAZEN'S HORNBOOK ON THE LAW OF SECURI-TIES REGULATION, Second Edition, Student Edition, approximately 1000 pages, 1990. (Text)

RATNER'S MATERIALS ON SECURITIES REGULA-TION, Third Edition, 1000 pages, 1986. Teacher's Manual available. (Casebook) 1989 Supplement.

    Statutory Supplement. *See Selected Se-curities Regulation*

RATNER'S SECURITIES REGULATION IN A NUT-SHELL, Third Edition, 316 pages, 1988. Softcover. (Text)

SELECTED STATUTES, REGULATIONS, RULES, DOCUMENTS AND FORMS ON SECURITIES REGU-LATION. Softcover. 1272 pages, 1990.

Social Legislation

HOOD, HARDY AND LEWIS' WORKERS' COM-PENSATION AND EMPLOYEE PROTECTION LAWS IN A NUTSHELL, Second Edition, 361 pages, 1990. Softcover. (Text)

LAFRANCE'S WELFARE LAW: STRUCTURE AND ENTITLEMENT IN A NUTSHELL, 455 pages, 1979. Softcover. (Text)

MALONE, PLANT AND LITTLE'S CASES ON WORKERS' COMPENSATION AND EMPLOYMENT RIGHTS, Second Edition, 951 pages, 1980. Teacher's Manual available. (Casebook)

Sports Law

SCHUBERT, SMITH AND TRENTADUE'S SPORTS LAW, 395 pages, 1986. (Text)

Tax Practice and Procedure

GARBIS, STRUNTZ AND RUBIN'S CASES AND MATERIALS ON TAX PROCEDURE AND TAX FRAUD, Second Edition, 687 pages, 1987. (Casebook)

MORGAN'S TAX PROCEDURE AND TAX FRAUD IN A NUTSHELL, Approximately 382 pages, 1990. Softcover. (Text)

Taxation—Corporate

KAHN AND GANN'S CORPORATE TAXATION, Third Edition, 980 pages, 1989. Teacher's Manual available. (Casebook)

WEIDENBRUCH AND BURKE'S FEDERAL INCOME TAXATION OF CORPORATIONS AND STOCKHOLD-ERS IN A NUTSHELL, Third Edition, 309 pages, 1989. Softcover. (Text)

Taxation—Estate & Gift—see also Estate Planning, Trusts and Estates

MCNULTY'S FEDERAL ESTATE AND GIFT TAX-ATION IN A NUTSHELL, Fourth Edition, 496 pages, 1989. Softcover. (Text)

PENNELL'S CASES AND MATERIALS ON INCOME TAXATION OF TRUSTS, ESTATES, GRANTORS AND BENEFICIARIES, 460 pages, 1987. Teacher's Manual available. (Casebook)

Taxation—Individual

DODGE'S THE LOGIC OF TAX, 343 pages, 1989. Softcover. (Text)

GUNN AND WARD'S CASES, TEXT AND PROB-LEMS ON FEDERAL INCOME TAXATION, Second Edition, 835 pages, 1988. Teacher's Man-ual available. (Casebook) 1990 Supple-ment.

HUDSON AND LIND'S BLACK LETTER ON FED-ERAL INCOME TAXATION, Third Edition, ap-proximately 390 pages, 1990. Softcover. (Review)

Taxation—Individual—Cont'd

KRAGEN AND MCNULTY'S CASES AND MATERIALS ON FEDERAL INCOME TAXATION—INDIVIDUALS, CORPORATIONS, PARTNERSHIPS, Fourth Edition, 1287 pages, 1985. (Casebook)

MCNULTY'S FEDERAL INCOME TAXATION OF INDIVIDUALS IN A NUTSHELL, Fourth Edition, 503 pages, 1988. Softcover. (Text)

POSIN'S HORNBOOK ON FEDERAL INCOME TAXATION, Student Edition, 491 pages, 1983, with 1989 pocket part. (Text)

ROSE AND CHOMMIE'S HORNBOOK ON FEDERAL INCOME TAXATION, Third Edition, 923 pages, 1988, with 1989 pocket part. (Text)

SELECTED FEDERAL TAXATION STATUTES AND REGULATIONS. Softcover. Approximately 1650 pages, 1991.

SOLOMON AND HESCH'S PROBLEMS, CASES AND MATERIALS ON FEDERAL INCOME TAXATION OF INDIVIDUALS, 1068 pages, 1987. Teacher's Manual available. (Casebook)

Taxation—International

DOERNBERG'S INTERNATIONAL TAXATION IN A NUTSHELL, 325 pages, 1989. Softcover. (Text)

KAPLAN'S FEDERAL TAXATION OF INTERNATIONAL TRANSACTIONS: PRINCIPLES, PLANNING AND POLICY, 635 pages, 1988. (Casebook)

Taxation—Partnership

BERGER AND WIEDENBECK'S CASES AND MATERIALS ON PARTNERSHIP TAXATION, 788 pages, 1989. Teacher's Manual available. (Casebook)

Taxation—State & Local

GELFAND AND SALSICH'S STATE AND LOCAL TAXATION AND FINANCE IN A NUTSHELL, 309 pages, 1986. Softcover. (Text)

HELLERSTEIN AND HELLERSTEIN'S CASES AND MATERIALS ON STATE AND LOCAL TAXATION, Fifth Edition, 1071 pages, 1988. (Casebook)

Torts—see also Products Liability

CHRISTIE AND MEEKS' CASES AND MATERIALS ON THE LAW OF TORTS, Second Edition, 1264 pages, 1990. (Casebook)

DOBBS' TORTS AND COMPENSATION—PERSONAL ACCOUNTABILITY AND SOCIAL RESPONSIBILITY FOR INJURY, 955 pages, 1985. Teacher's Manual available. (Casebook) 1990 Supplement.

KEETON, KEETON, SARGENTICH AND STEINER'S CASES AND MATERIALS ON TORT AND ACCIDENT LAW, Second Edition, 1318 pages, 1989. (Casebook)

KIONKA'S BLACK LETTER ON TORTS, 339 pages, 1988. Softcover. (Review)

KIONKA'S TORTS IN A NUTSHELL: INJURIES TO PERSONS AND PROPERTY, 434 pages, 1977. Softcover. (Text)

MALONE'S TORTS IN A NUTSHELL: INJURIES TO FAMILY, SOCIAL AND TRADE RELATIONS, 358 pages, 1979. Softcover. (Text)

PROSSER AND KEETON'S HORNBOOK ON TORTS, Fifth Edition, Student Edition, 1286 pages, 1984 with 1988 pocket part. (Text)

ROBERTSON, POWERS AND ANDERSON'S CASES AND MATERIALS ON TORTS, 932 pages, 1989. Teacher's Manual available. (Casebook)

Trade Regulation—see also Antitrust, Regulated Industries

MCMANIS' UNFAIR TRADE PRACTICES IN A NUTSHELL, Second Edition, 464 pages, 1988. Softcover. (Text)

OPPENHEIM, WESTON, MAGGS AND SCHECHTER'S CASES AND MATERIALS ON UNFAIR TRADE PRACTICES AND CONSUMER PROTECTION, Fourth Edition, 1038 pages, 1983. Teacher's Manual available. (Casebook) 1986 Supplement.

SCHECHTER'S BLACK LETTER ON UNFAIR TRADE PRACTICES, 272 pages, 1986. Softcover. (Review)

Trial and Appellate Advocacy—see also Civil Procedure

APPELLATE ADVOCACY, HANDBOOK OF, Second Edition, 182 pages, 1986. Softcover. (Text)

BERGMAN'S TRIAL ADVOCACY IN A NUTSHELL, Second Edition, 354 pages, 1989. Softcover. (Text)

BINDER AND BERGMAN'S FACT INVESTIGATION: FROM HYPOTHESIS TO PROOF, 354 pages, 1984. Teacher's Manual available. (Coursebook)

Trial and Appellate Advocacy—Cont'd

CARLSON AND IMWINKELRIED'S DYNAMICS OF TRIAL PRACTICE: PROBLEMS AND MATERIALS, 414 pages, 1989. Teacher's Manual available. (Coursebook)

GOLDBERG'S THE FIRST TRIAL (WHERE DO I SIT? WHAT DO I SAY?) IN A NUTSHELL, 396 pages, 1982. Softcover. (Text)

HAYDOCK, HERR, AND STEMPEL'S FUNDAMENTALS OF PRE-TRIAL LITIGATION, 768 pages, 1985. Softcover. Teacher's Manual available. (Coursebook)

HEGLAND'S TRIAL AND PRACTICE SKILLS IN A NUTSHELL, 346 pages, 1978. Softcover. (Text)

HORNSTEIN'S APPELLATE ADVOCACY IN A NUTSHELL, 325 pages, 1984. Softcover. (Text)

JEANS' HANDBOOK ON TRIAL ADVOCACY, Student Edition, 473 pages, 1975. Softcover. (Text)

LISNEK AND KAUFMAN'S DEPOSITIONS: PROCEDURE, STRATEGY AND TECHNIQUE, Law School and CLE Edition. 250 pages, 1990. Softcover. (Text)

MARTINEAU'S CASES AND MATERIALS ON APPELLATE PRACTICE AND PROCEDURE, 565 pages, 1987. (Casebook)

NOLAN'S CASES AND MATERIALS ON TRIAL PRACTICE, 518 pages, 1981. (Casebook)

SONSTENG AND HAYDOCK'S TRIAL: THEORIES, TACTICS, TECHNIQUE, Approximately 650 pages, 1990. Softcover. (Text)

SONSTENG, HAYDOCK AND BOYD'S THE TRIALBOOK: A TOTAL SYSTEM FOR PREPARATION AND PRESENTATION OF A CASE, 404 pages, 1984. Softcover. (Coursebook)

WHARTON, HAYDOCK AND SONSTENG'S CALIFORNIA CIVIL TRIALBOOK, Law School and CLE Edition. Approximately 300 pages, 1990. Softcover. (Text)

Trusts and Estates

ATKINSON'S HORNBOOK ON WILLS, Second Edition, 975 pages, 1953. (Text)

AVERILL'S UNIFORM PROBATE CODE IN A NUTSHELL, Second Edition, 454 pages, 1987. Softcover. (Text)

BOGERT'S HORNBOOK ON TRUSTS, Sixth Edition, Student Edition, 794 pages, 1987. (Text)

CLARK, LUSKY AND MURPHY'S CASES AND MATERIALS ON GRATUITOUS TRANSFERS, Third Edition, 970 pages, 1985. (Casebook)

DODGE'S WILLS, TRUSTS AND ESTATE PLANNING–LAW AND TAXATION, CASES AND MATERIALS, 665 pages, 1988. (Casebook)

KURTZ' PROBLEMS, CASES AND OTHER MATERIALS ON FAMILY ESTATE PLANNING, 853 pages, 1983. Teacher's Manual available. (Casebook)

MCGOVERN'S CASES AND MATERIALS ON WILLS, TRUSTS AND FUTURE INTERESTS: AN INTRODUCTION TO ESTATE PLANNING, 750 pages, 1983. (Casebook)

MCGOVERN, KURTZ AND REIN'S HORNBOOK ON WILLS, TRUSTS AND ESTATES–INCLUDING TAXATION AND FUTURE INTERESTS, 996 pages, 1988. (Text)

MENNELL'S WILLS AND TRUSTS IN A NUTSHELL, 392 pages, 1979. Softcover. (Text)

SIMES' HORNBOOK ON FUTURE INTERESTS, Second Edition, 355 pages, 1966. (Text)

TURANO AND RADIGAN'S HORNBOOK ON NEW YORK ESTATE ADMINISTRATION, 676 pages, 1986. (Text)

UNIFORM PROBATE CODE, OFFICIAL TEXT WITH COMMENTS. 615 pages, 1989. Softcover.

WAGGONER'S FUTURE INTERESTS IN A NUTSHELL, 361 pages, 1981. Softcover. (Text)

WATERBURY'S MATERIALS ON TRUSTS AND ESTATES, 1039 pages, 1986. Teacher's Manual available. (Casebook)

Water Law—see also Energy and Natural Resources Law, Environmental Law

GETCHES' WATER LAW IN A NUTSHELL, Second Edition, approximately 441 pages, 1990. Softcover. (Text)

SAX AND ABRAMS' LEGAL CONTROL OF WATER RESOURCES: CASES AND MATERIALS, 941 pages, 1986. (Casebook)

TRELEASE AND GOULD'S CASES AND MATERIALS ON WATER LAW, Fourth Edition, 816 pages, 1986. (Casebook)

AMERICAN BAR ASSOCIATION
SECTION OF LITIGATION

READINGS ON ADVERSARIAL JUSTICE: THE AMERICAN APPROACH TO ADJUDICATION

By

Stephan Landsman
Professor of Law
Cleveland-Marshall College of Law

Produced under the Sponsorship of the American Bar Association Section of Litigation

AMERICAN CASEBOOK SERIES

WEST PUBLISHING CO.
ST. PAUL, MINN., 1988

American Casebook Series, the key symbol appearing on the front
cover and the WP symbol are registered trademarks of West Publishing
Co. Registered in U.S. Patent and Trademark Office.

COPYRIGHT © 1988 By WEST PUBLISHING CO.
                              50 West Kellogg Boulevard
                              P.O. Box 64526
                              St. Paul, Minnesota 55164–0526

Library of Congress Cataloging-in-Publication Data

Landsman, Stephan.
  Adversarial justice.

  (American casebook series)
  Includes index.
  1. Adversary system (Law)—Unites States.   I. Title.
KF384.A7L36   1988   347.73   88–258
ISBN 0–314–36115.4   347.307

ISBN 0–314–36115–4

Landsman—Adversarial Justice ACB
1st Reprint—1990

Preface

This text grew out of the work of the American Bar Association Section of Litigation Task Force on Training the Advocate. It was prepared to help meet the Task Force's goal of promoting a clearer understanding and appreciation of the adversary system. It is designed for use as a supplement in any first year course, as well as any course that concerns itself with issues arising out of litigation. While this volume was produced under the sponsorship and with the support of the American Bar Association Section of Litigation all views expressed are those of the author.

Case and statute citations, as well as footnotes, of the courts and commentators have been omitted without so specifying; other omissions are indicated by asterisks or by brackets. Numbered footnotes are from the original materials; lettered footnotes are mine.

STEPHAN LANDSMAN

February 1988

*

Summary of Contents

———————

Table of Contents

*

READINGS ON ADVERSARIAL JUSTICE: THE AMERICAN APPROACH TO ADJUDICATION

*

Chapter I

INTRODUCTION TO THE ADVERSARY SYSTEM

SECTION A. THE ADVERSARY SYSTEM DEFINED

For more than 250 years American courts have relied upon neutral and passive factfinders to resolve lawsuits on the basis of evidence presented by contending litigants during formal adjudicatory proceedings. This method of resolving disputes is generally referred to as the adversary system. The adversarial approach is viewed by both friend and foe alike as a fundamental attribute of our adjudicatory process. The United States Supreme Court has determined that the Constitution mandates an adversarial form of procedure, at least in criminal cases. As it found in *Faretta v. California* [a], the Sixth Amendment

> rights to notice, confrontation, and compulsory process, when taken together, guarantee that a criminal charge may be answered in a manner now considered fundamental to the fair administration of American justice—through the calling and interrogation of favorable witnesses, the cross-examination of adverse witnesses, and the orderly introduction of evidence. In short, the Amendment constitutionalizes the right in an adversary criminal trial to make a defense as we know it.

While no such broad-ranging proposition has been stated with respect to civil matters, it is safe to say that under the rubric of Due Process much the same sort of procedure is required.

As many of the readings in the following materials demonstrate, criticism of the adversary system is widespread. Calls for its reform have been made by a significant number of influential members of both bench and bar. Before these criticisms and proposals can be evaluated it is necessary to understand the nature and values of the adversary system. It is to that end that this introductory essay and, indeed, this whole volume are addressed.

a. 422 U.S. 806, 818, 95 S.Ct. 2525, 2532, 45 L.Ed.2d 562, 572 (1975).

The adversary process should not be viewed as a single technique or collection of techniques; it is a unified concept that works by use of a number of interconnecting procedures, each of real importance to the process as a whole. The central precept of the adversary process is that out of the sharp clash of proofs presented by adversaries in a highly structured forensic setting is most likely to come the information upon which a neutral and passive decision maker can base the resolution of a litigated dispute acceptable to both the parties and society. This formulation is advantageous not only because it expresses the overarching adversarial concept, but also because it identifies the method to be utilized in adjudication (the sharp clash of proofs in a highly structured setting), the actors essential to the process (two adversaries and a decision maker), the nature of their functions (presentation of proofs and adjudication of disputes, respectively), and the goal of the entire endeavor (the resolution of disputes in a manner acceptable to the parties and to society).

Like any brief definition of a complex subject the foregoing description of the adversary system fails to indicate some of the most important principles and practices inherent in adversary methodology. The key elements in the system—utilization of a neutral and passive fact finder, reliance on party presentation of evidence, and use of a highly structured forensic procedure—must be more fully discussed to present an accurate picture. This additional information will also be of particular importance in helping to assess the value and shortcomings of the adversary process.

1. NEUTRAL AND PASSIVE DECISION MAKER

The adversary system relies on a neutral and passive decision maker to adjudicate disputes after they have been aired by the adversaries in a contested proceeding. The decision maker is expected to refrain from making any judgments until the conclusion of the contest and is prohibited from becoming actively involved in the gathering of evidence or the settlement of the case. Adversary theory suggests that if the decision maker strays from the passive role, she runs a serious risk of prematurely committing herself to one or another version of the facts and of failing to appreciate the value of all the evidence.

Adversary theory further suggests that neutrality and passivity are essential not only to ensure an evenhanded consideration of each case, but also to convince society at large that the judicial system is trustworthy. When a decision maker becomes an active questioner or otherwise participates in a case, she is likely to be perceived as· partisan rather than neutral. Judicial passivity helps to ensure the appearance of fairness.

The judicial process is generally used to satisfy two objectives: first, the search for material truth, and second, the resolution of disputes between contending parties. Although most court systems seek to accomplish both these goals, the procedural mechanisms best suited to the achievement of each are different. Where judges are assigned an active, inquisitorial part in the litigation process, they will be expected to undertake an uninhibited search for truth. Perhaps the best examples of this approach are to be found in the justice systems of the Socialist states of Eastern Europe. Where judges are assigned a neutral and passive function, however, they will, in all likelihood, be expected to devote their energies to resolving the disputes framed by the litigants. One of the most significant implications of the American adoption of the principles of neutrality and passivity is that it tends to commit the adversary system to the objective of resolving disputes rather than searching for material truth.

Another major implication of insistence on the neutrality and passivity of the decision maker is that it favors the use of lay juries rather than professional judges. Judges are deeply involved in the management of lawsuits. They are constantly being called upon to make rulings and otherwise oversee the contest. Their passivity and neutrality are likely to be strained as they perform these functions. Except in cases of unusual notoriety, juries are unlikely to face similar strains or to become embroiled in the contest. Further, the members of the jury are likely to be free of those predispositions judges develop because of their training and daily experience in the handling of legal matters. In addition, because the jury comprises a number of individuals, the prejudices of a single juror are not likely to destroy the capacity of the group to render a fair decision. This is to be contrasted with the situation of the solitary judge whose biases can easily influence the decisions she renders. Finally, potential jurors can be questioned before they are permitted to take a seat on the jury and can be excluded if biased. There is no similar mechanism to ensure judicial neutrality. For all these reasons the jury is more likely than the judge to meet adversarial expectations of neutrality and passivity and is therefore favored in adversarial proceedings.

2. PARTY PRESENTATION OF EVIDENCE

Intimately connected with the requirements of decision maker passivity and neutrality is the procedural principle that the parties are responsible for producing all the evidence upon which the decision will be based. This principle insulates the adjudicator from involvement in the contest. It also encourages the adversaries to find and present their most persuasive evidence. Adherence to this principle affords the decision maker the advantage of seeing what each litigant believes to be his most consequential proof. It also focuses the litigation upon the questions of greatest importance to the parties, making more likely a decision tailored to their needs. The benefits of such an approach may be measured in economic terms. A judge-dominated procedure increases the likelihood that the needs of the litigants will not be fully appreciated or satisfied. When this is the case "impositional costs" (those caused by an unbargained for and poorly tailored solution) are substantially increased. Such costs can, in large measure, be avoided in a system relying on participant direction and control.

Because of the potential complexity of legal questions and the intricacy of the legal mechanism, parties generally cannot manage their own lawsuits. Rather, they, and the adversary system, have come to rely upon a class of skilled professional advocates to assemble and to present the testimony upon which decisions will be based. The advocates are expected to provide the forensic talents necessary to organize the evidence and to formulate the legal issues. If the lawyers fail to carry out their duty, development of the case will be impeded, and the adversary process may be undermined. Additionally, the inadequacy of counsel may draw the judge into the contest either in search of material truth or in an attempt to ensure a balanced presentation. Such intervention may impair judicial neutrality.

3. HIGHLY STRUCTURED FORENSIC PROCEDURE

Elaborate sets of rules to govern the pretrial and posttrial periods (rules of procedure), the trial itself (rules of evidence), and the behavior of counsel (rules of ethics) are all important to the adversary system. Rules of procedure serve at least two functions in the adversary scheme. First, they structure litigation to produce a climactic confrontation between the parties in a single trial session or set of trial sessions. Such a confrontation yields the evidence upon which the decision will be based and diminishes the opportunity for the decision maker to undertake a potentially biasing independent investigation. Second, adversarial rules of procedure help to ensure the fairness of the contest by affording each litigant an equal opportunity to make the best possible case. The primary mechanism for ensuring equality is pretrial discovery, a technique allowing each party to examine his opponent's proof.

The trial or evidence rules protect the integrity of the testimonial segment of adversary proceedings. They prohibit the use of evidence that is likely to be unreliable and thereby insulate the trier from misleading information. The evidence rules also prohibit the use of evidence that poses a serious threat of exciting unfair prejudice against one of the parties. Rather than allow the use of such information the adversary system seeks to preserve the neutrality and passivity of the decision maker by a strictly enforced prohibition. Rules of evidence also enhance the power of the attorney to control the presentation of facts by providing him with a precisely formulated set of principles to measure the admissibility of every piece of evidence. In this way the rules confine the authority of the judge in managing the proceedings. Judges are not free to pick and choose the evidence they think most appropriate; rather, they are bound to obey previously fixed evidentiary prescripts.

Since the rough-and-tumble of adversary procedure exacerbates the natural tendency of advocates to seek to win by any means available, the adversary system employs rules of ethics to control the behavior of counsel. To ensure the integrity of the process certain tactics are forbidden, including those designed to harass or to intimidate an opponent as well as those intended to mislead or to prejudice the trier of fact. In addition to their prohibitory function, the rules of ethics are designed to promote vigorous adversarial contests by requiring that each attorney zealously represent his client's interests at all times. To ensure zeal, attorneys are required to give their undivided loyalty to their clients.

Reliance on elaborate sets of rules to structure the adversary process also helps to promote the use of appellate courts. These courts see to it that litigants and judges comply with mandated rules and procedures. Appellate judges review the records of trial proceedings and determine whether the law's requirements have been obeyed. If error is found, the appellate courts are free to use any one of a number of remedies to redress the harm done. Appellate review also encourages attorneys and judges at the trial level to adhere to the requirements of the law in order to avoid reversal on appeal.

SECTION B. THE HISTORY OF ADVERSARIAL ADJUDICATION

1. MEDIEVAL PROCEDURE

The adversary method of resolving disputes did not appear, fully formed, at a precise moment in history. Rather, it is one of the products of the slow evolution of English and American judicial procedure. To understand how the adversary system arose, one must go back at least to the eleventh century and examine the ancient precursors to present-day judicial practice.

(a) Trial by Battle

The forensic clash of the parties in the adversary system seems so like combat, it is tempting to suggest that the real source of the adversary process was the ancient mode of resolving disputes referred to as trial by battle. Historical evidence does not, however, support this proposition.

Trial by battle was a means of settling conflicts that required the disputants or their champions to engage in physical combat until one side or the other yielded (by speaking the word "craven"), was decisively defeated or, in certain serious criminal matters, was slain. Judicial officers oversaw the battle, which commenced after each of the combatants had taken a solemn oath that his cause was just, had invoked the judgment of God, and had declared that he had made no use of sorcery or enchantment.

Trial by battle was in common use throughout most of northern Europe in the early Middle Ages. It was not employed in England, however, until after the Norman Conquest in 1066. The fact of its late introduction into Britain, its Norman sponsorship, its potentially drastic consequences, and its bias in favor of the rich, who either had martial skills or could hire those with such skills, have led most commentators to surmise that it was never a popular or influential form of adjudication in England.

(b) Alternatives to Battle

Battle was generally the last resort of the medieval English courts, and there were several alternatives to it. The two most important alternative means of resolving disputes were wager of law and ordeal. In wager of law, one of the litigants swore a precisely prescribed oath that his claims were true. He was then obliged to produce a certain number of other persons, usually referred to as compurgators, to support his oath by means of oaths of their own. If all the oaths were properly presented, the oath taker won his case. Historian Theodore Plucknett described the wager of law as a "character test" in which the oath taker established his case by demonstrating his good standing in the community.[b]

The ordeal was a form of adjudication popular throughout medieval Europe. It was premised upon the idea that God would intervene and by miraculous sign indicate which litigant was in the right. A priest usually administered an oath before the ordeal, and, quite frequently, the ordeal was conducted on church grounds. Plucknett indicates that in England the primary forms of ordeal called for the litigant to carry a red-hot iron bar, to place an arm in boiling water, or to be immersed in deep water. In the first two instances, if the litigant's burns did not fester after a prescribed period, he was held to be in the right. In the latter case, the litigant was declared innocent if he briefly sank rather than floated.

(c) Elements in Common

In most cases more than one form of trial might be applicable. A crucial function of the medieval court was to decide which method to employ. This was usually done after the plaintiff had orally stated his claim to the court and had supported it with various proofs, sometimes logically persuasive evidence, more often oaths from individuals not directly involved in the litigation. The defendant was limited to a single defense, denial of the plaintiff's claim. Based upon these preliminary proceedings the court would enter a "medial judgment" fixing the form of trial and designating the party required to make the proof. Being permitted to make the proof was generally considered an advantage because the maker (especially in cases of wager of law and ordeal) was likely to succeed. The outcome of the wager, ordeal, or battle was the exclusive basis upon which the dispute was resolved, and no other evidence would be considered on the ultimate issue of the case.

b. Plucknett, *A Concise History of the Common Law* 115 (1956).

All medieval methods of trial were premised upon divine intervention. Direct heavenly intercession was postulated with respect to ordeal and battle, while eternal damnation was supposed to enforce the oath-taking mechanism. Emphasis was clearly on the judgment of God rather than that of man (though the medial judgment procedure suggests some tempering of this idea). As befitted such a system, there was very little use of evidence. The process was not orally contentious. There was no need for any sort of fact finding because no facts were to be deduced from evidence. Activity in the courts was, to an overwhelming degree, carried on by the parties rather than by advocates and the sorts of activities advocates could undertake were strictly limited. Because the court relied on divine revelation, there was no appellate process.

(d) Relationship to the Adversary Process

Although none of the medieval methods was even remotely adversarial, medieval forms of procedure appear to have contributed to the formulation of adversarial concepts in at least two ways. First, they helped to establish the principle that the parties to a dispute are to play the preeminent part in the procedure leading to its resolution. This idea of active party participation is fundamental to the adversary system and is continuously present in English law from the medieval period onwards. Second, medieval practice circumscribed the part to be played by judicial officials. Although judges would eventually gain a far more important role in resolving disputes, the early restraints on judicial activity at least helped to establish a tradition restricting judicial control of litigation.

(e) Demise of Medieval Procedure

By the middle of the thirteenth century all the medieval procedures had been either banned or seriously criticized. In 1215 the Fourth Lateran Council prohibited church involvement in trials by ordeal. This prohibition effectively ended the practice because participation by priests had been a fundamental component of the process. At about the same time, canon and lay critics began a sustained attack on wager of law and trial by battle. The decline of the medieval methods led to the development of new judicial practices between the thirteenth and seventeenth centuries. These practices formed the foundation upon which the adversary system was erected in the eighteenth and nineteenth centuries.

2. THE RISE OF THE JURY

Without doubt the most important new practice was the use of the jury to resolve disputes in English courts. The origins of the jury have not been authoritatively established. Most historians now support a continental genesis (Plucknett, for example, points to France during the reign of Louis the Pious, circa 829 A.D.).[c] However it originally arose, by the end of the twelfth century the jury had been incorporated into the English judicial process. Its acceptance at that time was undoubtedly linked to the decline of the medieval forms of procedure. As ordeal, battle, and wager shrank in significance, trial by jury expanded to replace them.

(a) The Early History of Trial by Jury

Sir William Holdsworth and Theodore Plucknett suggest that criminal and civil jury practice evolved along separate though related lines during the formative period from the end of the twelfth century to the middle of the fifteenth century.[d] The first kind of criminal jury to appear was the jury of presentment, or grand jury. This jury consisted of a group of prominent citizens called together at royal insistence to report on the misdeeds of local residents and to prepare indictments for the prosecution of accused malefactors. In the early days indicted defendants were tried either by ordeal or by wager of law. (Battle could only be used in privately initiated criminal cases.) As ordeal and wager fell into disuse, the judiciary naturally gravitated toward the use of a second jury (often containing several members of the original presentment jury) to decide the question of guilt or innocence. (In the case of privately pursued criminal actions, the defendant, as early as the twelfth century, could purchase from the king the opportunity to be tried by a jury rather than to engage in battle.) Although criminal jury procedure was quite variable during the thirteenth and fourteenth centuries, the size of the trial jury eventually came to be fixed at twelve men. From the earliest times the jurors had to be drawn from the neighborhood in which the crime had taken place.

On the civil side, Henry II, in the late part of the twelfth century, introduced the assize as a means of settling certain disputes concerning the ownership of land. As had been the case with the criminal jury, the assize was composed of a group of prominent citizens from the community in which the dispute arose. Members of the assize were selected by the king's officers and were charged with the responsibility of deciding disputes upon the basis of their personal knowledge. Gradually, such groups came to be used to resolve conflicts other than those concerning the ownership of land. The popularity of this form of adjudication led to its ever expanding use, and it eventually became the procedure of choice for virtually every civil cause of action.

The early juries were not the neutral and passive fact-finding mechanism they eventually became when incorporated within the adversary system. At first, the jury was little more than another sort of formal and inscrutable trial, like ordeal or wager of law. In its early days the jury heard no evidence and rendered its decision on no rational basis. Apparently, divine guidance was relied upon to produce

c. Plucknett, *A Concise History of the Common Law* 109–10 (1956).

d. Holdsworth, I *A History of English Law* 321–32 (1956); Plucknett, *A Concise History of the Common Law* 107 (1956).

the proper result. Yet, even in its earliest avatars, the jury was an improvement over the medieval methods of proof. Jurors were selected from the locality in which the dispute arose and almost always included among their number some persons with knowledge of the events that were the focus of the litigation. As the jury mechanism matured, jurors were allowed as much as two weeks notice before jury trials. During the period between notice and trial, jurors were allowed to "certify" themselves of the facts in dispute by talking to the litigants and making private inquiries in the community. All of this tended to ensure that jurors would be, to some degree, informed of the facts in issue and therefore likely to make a reasoned decision.

The use of jurors from the neighborhood and reliance upon each juror's personal knowledge marked early jury procedure as inquisitorial rather than adversarial. The jury did not act as a neutral and passive fact finder, but as an active and inquiring body searching for material truth. Although the jury was not by its nature intrinsically adversarial, certain of its procedures and much of its early development paved the way for the later growth of the adversary process. From 1300 to 1500 the jury developed many of the characteristics that would result in its becoming a neutral and passive adjudicator. By the middle of the 1300s, prospective jurors could be challenged by the parties and potentially biased jurors removed from the panel. Toward the end of the 1300s or in the early 1400s, contacts between litigants and jurors during the pendency of a case were significantly curtailed, thereby reducing the possibility of prejudice. By 1470 Fortesque in his famous volume, *In Praise of the Laws of England,* was able to describe jurors as impartial men who came to court with open minds.[e] In addition, from at least the fifteenth century on jurors began to rely upon what was presented in court as the basis for their decision. Sources of in-court information included the arguments of counsel (often treated as the equivalent of testimony given under oath) and the testimony of witnesses. The use of a considerable volume of evidence had the effect of subtly shifting the function of the jury from active inquiry to passive review and analysis.

(b) The Rise of Jury Independence

The juries assembled by the king's representatives in the twelfth and thirteenth centuries were quite clearly under the control of the government. They were specially selected by royal officials for the purpose of answering questions propounded on behalf of the sovereign. Eventually, however, the jury evolved into an independent entity unconnected with the objectives of the king. One of the most important steps in this process came in 1670 in *Bushell's Case,* a *habeas corpus* proceeding brought to free a juror who was imprisoned for refusing to pay a fine imposed by a trial judge when he and his fellow jurors acquitted William Penn and William Mead of trespass, contempt, and

e. Fortesque, *De Laudibus Legum Anglie* 57, 59 (Chrimes trans. 1942).

unlawful assembly. There, Chief Justice Vaughan flatly rejected the idea that the judiciary could control juries by the imposition of sanctions, like fines or jailing. The effect of this ruling was to make the jury an independent agency capable of resisting government control. (Plucknett suggests that evidence of the political independence of the jury may be found as early as 1544 when a jury refused to convict Throckmorton despite clear evidence of his involvement in Wyatt's rebellion.) [f]

(c) Jury as a Bulwark Against Inquisitorial Procedure

The rise of the jury not only laid the groundwork for adversary procedure, it also inhibited the development of the inquisitorial process. In England, the vacuum created by the Fourth Lateran Council's ban on ordeals in 1215 was filled by jury trial. On the continent a very different form of procedure was adopted, most frequently referred to as the Roman-canon system. This system was the product of the combination of certain aspects of ancient Roman law with judicial principles developed in European ecclesiastical circles. By the end of thirteenth century this amalgamation of the Roman and canon approaches had replaced the ordeal and other forms of medieval adjudication throughout much of Europe.

The Roman-canon system placed fundamental emphasis on active inquiry by the judge to uncover truth. He was charged with the duty of investigating the case, gathering the proof, and rendering the decision. He was obviously the central figure in the litigation, and his actions determined the outcome. The judge's powers were so extensive (and such a radical departure from the ordeal, which purported to rely on the judgment of God) that it was thought prudent, at least in the criminal context, to limit judicial authority by means of strict evidentiary requirements for the establishment of guilt. The judge could not find a defendant guilty unless two eyewitnesses were produced who had observed the gravamen of the crime. If two such witnesses were not available, conviction could only be obtained if the defendant confessed. Circumstantial evidence was never sufficient, in itself, to warrant conviction. The effect of these evidentiary rules was to make it impossible to obtain convictions in many cases unless the defendant was willing to confess. To extract the necessary confessions, Roman-canon process authorized the use of torture. Torture became a tool of judicial inquiry and was used to generate the evidence upon which the defendant would be condemned.

Rather than adopt the Roman-canon approach the English elected to rely upon the jury. By so doing Britain rejected the straitjacketing evidentiary rules of the ecclesiastical courts, the active and inquiring judicial officer, and the use of torture to obtain confessions. The jury made England resistant to Roman-canon ideas and thereby opened

f. Plucknett, *A Concise History of the Common Law* 134 (1956).

English courts at an early date to a broad spectrum of evidence to be assessed by an increasingly neutral and passive fact finder. The English chose to utilize an existing form of procedure to meet the needs of society. They thereby maintained traditional protections and avoided the adoption of a new and, in significant ways, oppressive alternative.

3. DEVELOPMENT OF PREADVERSARIAL LEGAL INSTITUTIONS BETWEEN 1200 AND 1700

(a) Counsel

Between the thirteenth and seventeenth centuries a number of legal institutions besides the jury underwent changes that paved the way for adversarial procedure. Lawyers rose to prominence both as advocates and as judicial officers. In the early 1300s requirements were established concerning the education and conduct of those who would be allowed to argue cases in the king's courts. In time these advocates formed special organizations for the training and governance of the bar called the Inns of Court. The Inns produced lawyers highly skilled in court procedure and disputation. These men formed the nucleus of a legal profession that would eventually assert control over the judicial machinery.

As the jury's investigative role diminished, the advocates' trial responsibilities increased. Lawyers undertook the job of supplying the jury with evidence upon which decisions would be based. By 1600, lawyers had established their special status as masters of the evidentiary process. One recognition of this status was the adoption of the concept of attorney-client privilege around 1577. Lawyers were granted a special exemption from the obligation to provide evidence if it was originally provided to them by their clients. Although the privilege was first premised upon the dignity of the attorney, the rule clearly facilitated the lawyer's freewheeling search for evidence by insulating him from compulsion to disclose information obtained from his client. Seldom could anyone else claim such protection.

(b) The Judiciary

Lawyers came to dominate not only the advocacy process but the judiciary as well. By the thirteenth century, English law and procedure had become sufficiently technical to warrant the designation of full-time judges. At first, the judges were drawn from among the king's retainers. These men functioned as civil servants and traced their allegiance directly to the sovereign. But by the close of the thirteenth century the legal profession had wrested control of the judiciary away from civil servants. From 1300 on, judges would be appointed only from the ranks of serjeants, a small group that constituted the elite of the bar. This placed the judiciary firmly in the hands of lawyers and linked judicial concerns to advocate interests.

The professionalization of the judiciary led to ever more complex law and procedure. Technicality had the effect of isolating the judges and their work from the rest of the government. While this isolation was eventually to have negative consequences (a rigid preoccupation with form and excessive tolerance of delay), it did foster judicial independence. Reliance on a small group of elite judges also had the effect of inhibiting the establishment of any sizable judicial bureaucracy. Such a bureaucracy in several European countries had facilitated the adoption of methods dependent on extensive judicial inquiry rather than on party presentation. Its absence in England made inquisitorial methods impractical.

(c) Live Testimony

The transformation of the jury and the legal profession was accompanied by important changes in the English attitude toward witnesses and the value of their testimony. Through the fifteenth century the testimony of witnesses was not highly valued. Voluntary testimony was viewed with suspicion, and witnesses could not be compelled to testify against their will. In the sixteenth century, however, the presentation of testimonial evidence grew dramatically. In accordance with the Marian statutes of 1554–1555, justices of the peace were assigned the task of securing evidence and testimony in criminal proceedings. Professor John Langbein of the University of Chicago Law School has argued that the designation of the justice of the peace as an evidence-gathering prosecutorial officer was of critical importance to the survival of jury procedure in criminal cases. He notes that, for unknown reasons, by the start of the sixteenth century juries had ceased to be self-informing. Without the justice of the peace to provide a steady flow of information to the jury, the usefulness of that body would have been thoroughly undermined.[g] In the early 1560s the enactment of legislation allowing courts to compel witnesses to testify also helped to alter English attitudes toward witnesses. This legislation placed a stamp of approval on oral testimony as a source of information for the increasingly passive and uninformed jury. Both developments helped open the way to adversarial evidentiary procedure. They shifted attention from each juror's private knowledge toward witness testimony given in open court.

(d) Rules of Evidence

To facilitate the evaluation of testimonial and other proof, the English courts, after the enactment of the Marian statutes, accelerated their efforts to fashion rules of evidence. The judiciary developed rules prohibiting the use of certain sorts of misleading and untrustworthy material (for example, the testimony of proven perjurers). Other types of protective rules were advanced, including limitations upon the use of a wife's testimony against her husband. At the same time, previously

g. Langbein, *Prosecuting Crime in the Renaissance* 22 (1974).

established evidentiary rules were being refined, including the "best evidence" rule (limiting use of secondary sources to prove the contents of a writing), the opinion rule (controlling the use of opinion testimony), and the hearsay rule (barring the use of certain out-of-court statements). These rules did not prohibit the introduction of all misleading evidence, nor did they seriously address the problem of evidence that might be so prejudicial as to distract the jurors from their task. The rules did, however, demonstrate the growing judicial awareness of evidence problems and opened the way for the creation of a full set of adversarial rules of evidence in the eighteenth and nineteenth centuries.

(e) Adversarial Shortcomings Before 1700

Although the legal mechanism developed between the thirteenth and seventeenth centuries provided the foundation upon which adversarial process was built, judicial activity during this period was not truly adversarial. In 1565, Sir Thomas Smith in his book *De Republica Anglorum* provided a description of the typical criminal felony trial of his day.[h] According to Smith the trial began with the defendant's being brought before the court and asked how he pleaded. Almost invariably the defendant entered a formal plea that he be tried by jury. (The penalty for refusing to plead was severe and persuaded all but the most obdurate defendants to choose the jury.) Local citizens were then called one at a time and seated as members of the jury unless the defendant objected to their participation in the case. After twelve jurors had been seated they were sworn and the hearing commenced.

Usually, the case was prosecuted by a justice of the peace who began his presentation by reading from a written account of his interrogations of the accused and of various witnesses. Next, the victim and other witnesses were produced and questioned. The questioning was initiated by the judge, and as it proceeded, questions were put to the defendant as well as to the witnesses. The questioning most frequently led to a freewheeling discussion, or in Smith's word "altercation," among the witnesses, defendant, and judge. When the judge was satisfied that he had heard enough he called an end to the "altercation," summarized the case for the jury, and charged them to decide it. Frequently, the jury was asked to hear evidence in a number of cases before retiring to deliberate. Once the jury had retired, its members were not allowed to eat or drink until a decision had been rendered.

In Smith's day the judge was clearly an active enquirer (perhaps even prosecutor) rather than a neutral arbiter. The defendant was not represented by counsel and, indeed, was specifically prohibited from having legal assistance. The defendant was not allowed to call witnesses, conduct any real cross-examination, or develop an affirmative case. All sorts of evidence could be used in the proceedings, including

h. Smith, II *De Republica Anglorum* 94–104 (Alston ed. 1906).

potentially misleading and prejudicial material like the out-of-court statements read by the justice of the peace. Although the jury was ostensibly neutral and passive, its deliberations were strongly influenced by the judge's remarks and instructions. The judge was free to urge a verdict upon the jury, and, until 1670, jurors who refused to follow the judge's directions could be jailed or fined. Finally, there was no appellate procedure by which the litigants could secure review of the decision. While the germ of the adversarial process may be seen in such proceedings—because they were orally contentious, decided upon the evidence of witnesses, and judged by an arguably neutral and passive jury—they cannot be classified as truly adversarial.

The courtroom routine was more adversarial in the sixteenth and seventeenth centuries in civil litigation than it was in criminal litigation. Even in civil cases, however, the emphasis was not upon adversarial presentation of evidence. Rather, lawyers of that age devoted most of their energy to the fabrication and presentation of pleadings designed to reduce the case to a single, certain, and material question of fact. In order to arrive at this tightly constricted jury question, counsel were compelled by the rules of procedure to refine ever more narrowly their claims by means of a series of writs, motions, and court rulings. At first this winnowing process was conducted before the courts at oral hearings, but in the latter part of the fifteenth century the pleading process came to be based primarily upon written materials. The legal papers involved were measured by the most exacting technical standards and were treated as the most important facet of the case.

The development of legal principles, not the discovery of evidence upon which to resolve disputes between litigants, was of central concern to the bench and bar during this era. The system was not truly adversarial because it dramatically shifted focus away from factual disputes to be resolved by examination of evidence presented in open court. The system was designed to satisfy an astonishing array of formal requirements rather than to address the substance of the parties' claims. It confined the proof-presenting process to the narrowest corner of judicial activity. In addition, as in the case of criminal proceedings, the judge played a very active role, there was little protection against misleading or prejudicial evidence, and appellate review was seldom available. With respect to this last point, the only way jury action could be reviewed was by means of a quasi-criminal prosecution of the jurors. This mechanism was woefully inadequate to correct any but the grossest errors or misdeeds. Where appellate review was available it was conceptualized as a challenge to the judge rather than as a continuation of the case or the correction of an error. Further, review was premised on a record that generally did not include the trial proceedings. In sum, there was seldom an effective means by which to appeal adverse factual determinations or breaches of the rules governing trial.

As a final matter it should be noted that between the fifteenth and seventeenth centuries certain judicial mechanisms fundamentally at odds with adversary principles flourished. Most important among these was the Star Chamber created in the late 1400s to decide noncapital criminal matters (especially political cases) and to punish misbehaving jurors. Star Chamber practice was based upon the judicial examination of witnesses *in camera*. Cases were frequently commenced with secret judicial examination of the defendant under oath. Thereafter, other witnesses would be called and privately examined. At the end of the questioning, records of the examinations were provided to the judges and used as the basis for the court's decision. One can see in the procedures of the Star Chamber the spirit of an era not yet guided by adversary principles. The legislation dismantling the Star Chamber in the 1640s, while motivated by the politics of the time, may be taken as the announcement of a change in English sensibilities and a turning toward adversarial tenets.

4. THE ESTABLISHMENT OF THE ADVERSARY SYSTEM

(a) Neutral and Passive Fact Finders

Political turmoil engulfed England in the second half of the seventeenth century and triggered dramatic changes. From the 1640s onward, the full range of adversarial mechanisms began to grow, and by the end of the the 1700s the adversary system had become firmly established not only in England but in America as well.

During this period both judge and jury came to conform fairly closely to the ideals of neutrality and passivity. The jury was placed firmly on the road to neutrality in *Bushell's Case* in 1670. Although that decision left jurors free to use extrajudicial knowledge to decide a case, the notion of active jury inquiry was on the wane well before 1670. By 1700, decisions rendered at *nisi prius* (civil cases tried by circuit-riding representatives of the central English courts) could be reversed and a new trial ordered if the judge believed the evidence was insufficient to warrant the verdict. The availability of a new trial in these circumstances bespeaks judicial confidence that the great bulk of the evidence was being heard in open court rather than gathered in private. The new trial mechanism was effectively extended to all cases by Lord Mansfield after 1756.

By the eighteenth century the jury came to be seen not only as neutral and passive toward the factual issues in the case but also as a fundamental check on governmental and judicial despotism. Cases like the famous New York trial of Peter Zenger on charges of seditious libel in 1734 and *Bushell's Case* illustrate this trend. In both cases jurors at some personal risk resisted government efforts to use the judicial mechanism to punish political opponents. It is not surprising that when the Constitution of the United States was fashioned in the 1780s there was widespread insistence that it specifically incorporate the right to jury trial as a check on the other institutions of government.

Judicial neutrality and passivity took a longer time to develop. In England the struggle between the principles of royal prerogative and impartial adjudication raged throughout the seventeenth century. The reign of the Stuart kings was marked by repeated royal attempts to manipulate the judiciary and by the frequent removal of judges for political reasons. (The most famous incident of this sort was the removal of Chief Justice Coke by King James I in 1616.) It was not until 1701, when Parliament passed the Act of Settlement, that judges were assured tenure during good behavior. About that time, Lord Holt became chief justice of King's Bench and significantly altered judicial attitudes toward criminal defendants. Under Holt the court began to recognize an obligation to protect defendants and to ensure fair trials. The rise of judicial independence and even-handedness in criminal cases together set the courts firmly on the road to judical neutrality.

In the United States the struggle for judicial neutrality occurred primarily in the early 1800s. Until then judges might be expected to be political partisans who openly advertised their attitudes in court. After Jefferson was elected, his supporters attempted to remove a number of incompetent or partisan Federalist judges from office by impeachment and conviction. In 1804 John Pickering was removed in this manner, and, shortly thereafter, Supreme Court Justice Samuel Chase was impeached. After a turbulent trial, Chase was acquitted by a single vote in the Senate. Chase's prosecution served as a powerful warning against strident political activity by judges. The neutral posture adopted by Supreme Court Chief Justice John Marshall came to be accepted as the standard by which to measure the propriety of judicial behavior. After 1800 tighter controls were also imposed on the courtroom activity of American judges. Judicial conduct was controlled by applying strict rules of evidence and by placing exacting limits on the remarks that could be made at the close of the case. All of this moved American judges toward neutrality and passivity.

(b) Expanding Role of the Trial Bar

While judges and juries were evolving into neutral and passive fact finders, attorneys were expanding their responsibilities as purveyors of evidence and managers of litigation. The rules of procedure and evidence that facilitated this expansion will be discussed later in this section. In addition to procedural changes, the strength and importance of the legal profession increased significantly throughout the eighteenth century. In England, counsel came to have a decisive part to play in both criminal and civil processes. Defendants accused of treason were allowed attorneys in 1695, and throughout the 1700s lawyers were given widening responsibility in felony cases. By 1837 felony defendants were allowed attorneys for all purposes in British courts.

The English bar was highly skilled and well established even before the eighteenth century. Its position was simply enhanced during the era. In the United States the bar was not as well established, but its growth in the 1700s was impressive. Professor Lawrence Friedman, in his book *A History of American Law,* suggests that in 1700 there were few attorneys in America, but that by 1750 there was a competent and successful bar in virtually every major American community.[i] This pattern of growth continued throughout the succeeding two centuries, particularly after 1850. As the number and authority of attorneys increased, so apparently did the vigor of their advocacy. By the first half of the nineteenth century flamboyant courtroom advocacy was the main avenue to success. Lawyers rose to prominence because of their forensic skills, and this aspect of the attorney's work took on paramount importance.

(c) Modern Rules of Procedure and Evidence

Changes in procedure introduced in the eighteenth and nineteenth centuries shifted legal focus away from elaborate pleadings and debates about fine points of law toward resolution of disputes on the merits. Lord Mansfield was one of those responsible for reform. He worked to reduce use of the rules of procedure as a device for avoiding adjudication on the merits. He fashioned simpler rules where possible and elsewhere sought to persuade litigants to consent voluntarily to the use of streamlined practices. The reforms begun by Mansfield were carried forward by both English and American legislatures. Throughout the nineteenth century the legislatures acted to reduce the technicality and complexity of the legal process. Among the outstanding achievements of this legislative effort were the Field Code adopted by New York in 1848 and the Judicature Acts adopted by the English Parliament in 1851 and 1873. These reforms encouraged advocates to devote their energies to the resolution of disputes by the presentation of evidence in open court.

With the growth in importance of the courtroom presentation came heightened sensitivity to evidentiary problems. The law of evidence developed in two directions in the 1700s and 1800s. First, rules were shaped that increased the availability of evidence. Proscriptions incapacitating various witnesses were overthrown. Parties to litigation had, for several centuries, been barred from testifying. After repeated attacks by Jeremy Bentham and others, the rule of party incapacity was abandoned. (The English law on this question was revised in 1851.) Even earlier, Mansfield took the lead in toppling other witness disqualifications including those concerning non-Christians, Quakers (who refused to take an oath), and nonparty witnesses who were in some way interested in the outcome of the litigation. Judicial authority to compel testimony was enhanced during the period. In 1804 English common law courts were given the power, by writ of *habeas corpus ad testificandum,* to require the appearance of any witness. Beginning in 1806 witnesses could no longer refuse to answer questions

i. Friedman, *A History of American Law* 81–84 (1973).

on the ground that response might lead to civil liability. The effect of all these changes was to open the courts to the testimony of virtually every witness and to increase the burden on the trier of fact to sift and to analyze conflicting testimony.

The second development in the law of evidence in the 1700s and 1800s was the expansion of rules designed to safeguard the neutrality and passivity of the fact finder. Included were regulations intended to insulate the decision maker from misleading or prejudicial material and others designed to prevent the trial judge from taking too active a part in the prosecution of the case. Fundamental to the effort to ensure the integrity of the evidence was an emphasis on cross-examination. Attorneys were encouraged to test virtually every piece of evidence by rigorous questioning. Where evidence could not be tested in this way, as in the case of out-of-court affidavits, rules were established to bar use of the evidence in most circumstances. Exclusionary rules were fashioned not only to ensure cross-examination but also to prevent the use of questionable materials. The opinion and hearsay rules were refined as a means of achieving this objective. Where the newly expanded rules of evidence were violated, reversal and retrial could be expected. This sort of enforcement of the rules coupled with limitations on judicial questioning and comment helped to curtail judicial activism. The rules of evidence developed during this period provided a framework within which a truly adversarial contest could be conducted.

(d) Adversarial Code of Ethics

The regulation of the practice of law had begun long before the eighteenth century. In the 1200s, rules governing the conduct of advocates were already common. An adversarial code, however, emphasizing zealous representation of each client and loyalty to his cause was the product of the 1700s and 1800s. As proceedings became more adversarial, conflicting ethical demands were exerted upon lawyers. (This was especially likely as attorneys became more frequently involved in criminal cases.) On the one hand, attorneys were expected to be officers of the court and to seek the truth. On the other, they were expected to be keen advocates on behalf of their clients.

These conflicting duties were highlighted in a series of hotly contested trials in the late eighteenth and early nineteenth centuries. One of the most famous involved the prosecution of Queen Caroline on a charge of adultery in 1821. During the course of the proceedings the queen's attorney, Lord Brougham, declared that regardless of personal and political risk he had but a single duty, to represent his client zealously. While this doctrine of single-minded zeal was never officially adopted, it became a fundamental tenet of the adversary lawyer's code. Serving as a counterbalance to this principle was a series of rules curtailing underhanded practices, forbidding tactics designed to harass or to intimidate an opponent, and barring behavior intended to mislead or to prejudice the fact finder. In America, Judge George Sharswood, in a series of lectures given in 1854 at the University of Pennsylvania, delineated a set of ethical precepts placing primary emphasis on zeal and loyalty. These precepts were the model upon which the American canons of professional conduct were based.

(e) Appellate Review

The final component of the adversary system to take shape during the eighteenth and nineteenth centuries was appellate review. Until the 1700s there was little review of trial proceedings. Thereafter, two procedures, the new trial motion and bill of exceptions, grew to maturity and provided a sound basis for review. Coupled with the expansion of appeals was the development, in the nineteenth century, of courts that did nothing but decide appellate cases. These courts were committed to a careful search of the record to determine if there was error warranting reversal. The emphasis on the search for error may have been what led nineteenth century courts to a preoccupation with technical nicety.

Although the precise reasons for appellate technicality in the 1800s are not known, the development of adversarial principles may have had much to do with it. As appellate courts began to see themselves as guardians of a system with precise rules concerning evidence, procedure, passivity, and neutrality, they may have concluded that strict enforcement by means of reversal was the only way to ensure compliance with the new principles. Old habits may have died hard in the lower courts, causing the appellate judges to be even more vigorous in their review. Whatever the cause of strict review, it did help to establish the adversarial principle that trial activity would have to conform to the rules vesting the litigants with control of the process and securing the neutrality and passivity of the fact finder.

5. REASONS FOR THE DEVELOPMENT OF THE ADVERSARY SYSTEM

Although it is not clear why the adversary process came into its own during the eighteenth and nineteenth centuries, there are a variety of social and economic considerations that may have influenced developments. The 1700s and 1800s were a time of intense social and economic ferment. They were the centuries of the American and French revolutions and of dramatic industrialization. The traditional bases of wealth and power in English society, real property and aristocratic position, were steadily undermined by growing profits from trade and manufacture. Those who profited in the new industries swelled the ranks of the middle class. As this class grew in size and strength, its champions (including Jeremy Bentham, Lord Brougham, and Adam Smith) argued that fundamental changes should be made in the organization of society. Among the changes sought was a significant extension of the franchise. The democratization of the electorate during this era accelerated the shift of power from the landed gentry to urban, energetic, nonaristocratic groups.

The same forces that sought voting rights also pressed for expansion of political and economic freedoms. Freedom of speech, of assembly, and of petition were all vigorously asserted and given ever wider recognition. On the economic scene, freedom was associated with the dissolution of social restraints on wages, prices, and profits and with the principle of freedom of contract, allowing each man the right to enter into whatever agreements he thought proper. Economic competition and social change rather than stability became the hallmarks of society. Disappearance of the old restraints released forces that transformed society. Those who could function effectively in the marketplace, like the entrepreneurs and the business corporations, grew in prominence while individual laborers faced greater privation and suffering than they had ever known.

The demise of stability led to a new legal situation. The numbers and sorts of disputes that were brought to the courts grew significantly. Amidst all the conflict and change it is likely that a desire arose for a legal mechanism that could meet the problems of the day and yet preserve some continuity with the more stable past. The adversary mechanism met these requirements. It was an outgrowth of procedures that had been used for hundreds of years in England and America. The idea of a neutral and passive fact finder was not a radical departure but rather the extension of trusted and traditional methods. At the same time, the adversary courts were receptive to new claims. They allowed the parties to define the issues and the evidence. They thereby provided a forum for questions that no other institution in society would hear or resolve.

The special needs of eighteenth and nineteenth century society accentuated the adversarial aspects of Anglo–American judicial procedure. Because there were more participants in the legal process and because they were affiliated with different social and economic classes, a demonstrably neutral mechanism was needed. The best means to demonstrate neutrality was by using a disinterested and passive fact finder. The jury readily filled this need. Respect for the principle of neutrality made the courts a credible mechanism for resolving disputes. It also tended to make the courts an open forum to which each new social group could come seeking vindication of its rights. This tradition of openness to new claims of right has continued into the twentieth century.

The element of party control of proceedings apparent in English procedure from the earliest times was also attractive to the intensely individualistic polity of the eighteenth and nineteenth centuries. The English and American judicial process made increasing allowances for each party to run his lawsuit as he saw fit, to voice his claims, and to select his evidence. The judicial decision was directly tied to the presentations of the parties. It is not surprising that these facets of procedure were accentuated in an age preoccupied with the establishment of individual political and economic rights.

These tendencies toward adversarial procedure were further sharpened by the judges and lawyers who controlled the legal system. Members of the bench and bar in both England and the United States were practical men with broad experience. They knew their society and shared the social and economic values it was coming to adopt. Doubtless, in their legal activity they attempted to respond to the needs they perceived. Further, adversarial process was in the interest of lawyers as a group. It created ever more work for attorneys, as increasing numbers of potential litigants sought legal advice. It also provided a dramatic public outlet for lawyers' forensic skills. Adversary procedure was the right procedure for the times. It did not pose a threat of radical change, but could credibly accommodate the demands of the forces of change at work in England and America.

6. NONADVERSARIAL REFORMS

In a number of settings, courts in the United States have abandoned adversarial techniques. This trend did not begin recently. It has grown out of social and economic forces that have been building for a long time. The individualistic adversarial approach is, to a significant degree, inconsistent with what Max Weber has described as the fundamental requirements of modern "bureaucratic" government and industry, that official business be dispatched with "utmost speed, precision, definiteness and continuity." [j] Adversarial process, as will later be discussed, is slower and more individualized than some other procedures. These characteristics, among others, have made adversary procedure a target of reformers both inside and outside the judiciary.

Historically, reformers have sought to alter the adversary system in several ways. First, the kinds of cases courts will hear have been limited. In the latter half of the nineteenth century the courts were inundated with suits involving job-related worker injuries and did not prove adept at handling such claims. Their procedures were slow and their solutions unsatisfactory. Often, injured workers received absolutely no compensation. Legislation eventually took most such claims out of the hands of the courts and assigned them to workmen's compensation boards to decide. These boards relied on streamlined administrative methods rather than on full-blown adversary proceedings. In recent times, similar action has been taken with respect to labor disputes, automobile accidents, and medical malpractice claims. Influential commentators, including a number of prominent judges and attorneys, have urged a further narrowing of jurisdiction by the exclusion of cases involving prisoner's rights, antitrust, and civil rights questions.

The number of cases heard has been limited not only by the narrowing of jurisdiction, but also by increasing the pressure for settlement rather than adjudication on the merits. It should be noted

j. Weber, *Max Weber on Law in Economy and Society* 350 (1954).

that settlement is not necessarily antithetical to the adversary process. In fact, a high percentage of settlements has long been a trait of adversary systems of justice. Today well over 90 percent of all criminal and civil cases are settled or otherwise resolved short of trial, and the percentage of such resolutions seems to be growing. The Supreme Court has specifically endorsed the movement toward more settlements in criminal cases. In a series of cases decided in the early 1970s, the Court sanctioned plea bargaining agreements (transactions in which the defendant pleads guilty in order to secure a reduced sentence or some other benefit). Although the propriety of such agreements has been hotly debated, the Supreme Court viewed them as essential in dealing with the high volume of criminal work.

The trend toward settlement has created some concern among commentators. Professors Zeisel, Kalven, and Buchholz have argued that there is a "core of cases" that should be tried either because of the nature of the issues involved or because a certain number of trials is needed to ensure the continuing credibility of the system.[k] If the number of litigated cases shrinks too drastically, the continuing efficacy of the system may be called into question.

Another sort of reform employed to deal with demands for "speed, precision, definiteness and continuity" has been to reduce judicial reliance on adversary principles in conducting the business of the courts. Basic components of the adversary system including judicial passivity, advocate responsibility for the development of the case, jury primacy, traditional rules of procedure and evidence, and thoroughgoing appellate review have all been modified. Judicial passivity has been undermined in a number of ways. In the name of efficiency, judges have been admonished to take charge of settlement negotiations at the earliest moment, to supervise the bargaining process, to render opinions concerning issues not yet litigated (as a means of persuading counsel to settle), and to settle as many lawsuits as possible. A large number of judges have adopted these and similar practices without focusing significant attention on the apparent conflict between this approach to settlement and the principle of passivity, which holds that judges should limit their involvement in the compromise of cases lest they become embroiled in the merits and committed to a specified outcome notwithstanding the weight of the proof.

Judicial passivity has come under attack not only in the settlement context but also with respect to the management of litigation. The judge who passively awaits the development of the evidence by the parties is said to be incapable of properly protecting the proceedings from delay and distortion caused by unskilled or excessively contentious counsel. She is also said to be ill-equipped to meet the challenge of complex litigation. To redress these perceived weaknesses the managerial powers of the trial judge have been radically expanded. In

k. Zeisel, Kalven, & Buchholz, *Delay in the Court* 108 (1959).

recent years, judges have been freed to take an active part in both the preparation and presentation of lawsuits. Judges regularly use tools such as the pretrial conference and pretrial order to determine not only the pace but the content and direction of litigation. Rules regulating judicial involvement in the trial have been steadily liberalized. Judges have been ceded extensive authority to question witnesses called by the parties as well as to call witnesses on their own. The practice of judicial summary of and comment upon the evidence has increased. These changes have appreciably altered the adversary process by encouraging judicial management at the expense of party control of proceedings.

As judicial power has increased, the primacy of the jury in adversary proceedings has been reduced. The right to trial by jury has not, in itself, been altered because Article III as well as the Sixth and Seventh Amendments to the United States Constitution guarantee the right to jury trial in a wide variety of circumstances. Procedures regulating the way in which jury trials are run, however, have been substantially modified.

For centuries it was agreed that the jury was to comprise twelve members and was to render a unanimous verdict. These principles have been substantially altered. In two famous cases, *Williams v. Florida*[l] and *Colgrove v. Battin*,[m] the Supreme Court rejected the rule that the jury is required to have twelve members. In each case the Court approved the use of as few as six jurors. (In *Ballew v. Georgia*,[n] the Court drew the line at six, holding that five-person juries were of insufficient size to perform the adjudicatory function.) In two more important cases, *Johnson v. Louisiana*[o] and *Apodaca v. Oregon*,[p] the Supreme Court held that a unanimous verdict was not required in state court criminal trials. In arriving at these conclusions the Supreme Court did not consider the effect of change on the jury as a neutral and passive decision maker. In fact, empirical analysis has demonstrated that changes regarding jury size and unanimity have reduced the neutrality of juries. Research indicates that smaller juries are less likely to engage in reliable deliberations and are less likely to consider minority points of view.[q] These changes have reduced the attractiveness of the jury to litigants and have effectively narrowed its utility in the adjudicatory process.

The procedural and evidentiary rules governing the adversarial process have also been the target of reformers. A wide range of reforms have been adopted that sacrifice adversarial principles. Per-

---

l.   399 U.S. 78, 90 S.Ct. 1893, 26 L.Ed.2d 446 (1970).

m.   413 U.S. 149, 93 S.Ct. 2448, 37 L.Ed.2d 522 (1973).

n.   435 U.S. 223, 98 S.Ct. 1029, 55 L.Ed.2d 234 (1978).

o.   406 U.S. 356, 92 S.Ct. 1620, 32 L.Ed.2d 152 (1972).

p.   406 U.S. 404, 92 S.Ct. 1628, 32 L.Ed.2d 184 (1972).

q.   For a summary of this research see Lempert, *Uncovering 'Nondiscernible' Differences: Empirical Research and the Jury–Size Cases*, 73 Mich.L.Rev. 644 (1975).

haps the most significant is the large number of rules that enhance the discretionary powers of the trial judge. Professor Maurice Rosenberg of the Columbia Law School has estimated that in as many as forty procedural situations the Federal Rules of Civil Procedure have been construed to allow for the exercise of judicial discretion.[r] This sort of expansion of judicial discretion undermines the judge's passivity and reduces the ability of the advocates to direct the proceedings. Judicial discretion has also been expanded in the Federal Rules of Evidence. Material previously banned as prejudicial may now be admitted at the court's discretion. Further, changes in the evidence rules cede the trial judge increased power to control fundamental processes like cross-examination, determination of preliminary questions of fact, and the use of hearsay evidence.

Finally, the likelihood of thoroughgoing appellate review has been subject to significant limitation. Although an absolute right to review has never been established, it is generally agreed that, at least in criminal cases, the defendant will be allowed a minimum of one appeal. The Supreme Court helped to ensure this result by guaranteeing indigent criminal defendants appointed counsel to press their first appeal, by requiring that indigents be provided transcripts if a written record is necessary for appeal, and by requiring the waiver of fees that would otherwise bar the impecunious from filing a criminal appeal. These decisions are now so firmly rooted that it seems unlikely appellate review in criminal matters will be directly curtailed. By contrast, the Court has limited appellate review in the last few years by endorsing rules that limit access to appeal in civil cases (by upholding the requirement of a filing fee with respect to civil appeals), reduce the scope of appeal in all cases (by approving the ever expanding application of the doctrine of "harmless error," which states that no judgment shall be reversed unless the error or defect *substantially* affects the rights of a party), and diminish the availability of review beyond the first appeal (by holding that criminal defendants have no right to the appointment of counsel beyond the first appeal).

In summary, although the predominant means of resolving disputes in American courts is the adversary system, a variety of nonadversarial mechanisms have been incorporated into the judicial process. In recent years a steadily increasing number of nonadversarial techniques have been adopted in all sorts of cases.

SECTION C. CRITICISMS OF THE
ADVERSARY METHOD CONSIDERED

Critics have, in recent years, vigorously attacked the adversary system, claiming that it is seriously flawed. These attacks have profoundly affected the debate concerning retention of adversary proce-

r. Rosenberg, *Appellate Review of Trial Court Discretion,* 79 F.R.D. 173 (1978).

dure and have greatly facilitated the adoption of nonadversarial methods. The two most frequently voiced criticisms are that the adversary process is too slow to serve the needs of modern society adequately and that it sets too low a value on the discovery of material truth.

1. THE PACE OF ADJUDICATION

It must be admitted at the outset that adversary procedure relies on mechanisms that appreciably slow adjudication. Adversary theory requires the judge to remain passive until the conclusion of the advocates' presentations. She is not free to conduct an independent inquiry or otherwise accelerate the pace of the proceedings. The judge's passivity undoubtedly slows adjudication. When a jury is used as decision maker, proceedings are even slower because of the extra time spent selecting the jurors and presenting the case.

Although the requirement of passivity slows the judicial process, important considerations justify this result. The decision maker's passivity is relied upon in the adversary system to ensure that the trier will remain neutral until she renders her decision. Neutrality, in turn, tends to ensure the integrity of adversary deliberations. In this context, as well as a number of others, the adversary system sacrifices speed to protect the probity of the process.

The rules of procedure that regulate the adversary contest also slow the pace of litigation. Adversary procedure assures each party ample opportunity to prepare and to present his case. This preparation and presentation time, dependent as it is on the vagaries of legal practice and advocate efficiency, does not lead to nearly so swift a decision as would a process primarily concerned with judicial inquiry rather than party presentation. By allowing both sides to be heard in full, however, the adversary process tends to expand the pool of information available to the fact finder. This arguably increases the likelihood the trier will be able to render a decision that satisfies the needs of the litigants.

The use of a strict set of rules of evidence to prevent the introduction of prejudicial or misleading information also slows the adversary process. Before evidence may be introduced, it's source and trustworthiness must be stipulated or demonstrated. Testimony from witnesses may be elicited only through a series of precisely formulated questions. These procedures invite careful scrutiny of each question and each answer. This careful control of the fact-gathering process undoubtedly slows the tempo of proceedings. Again, the adversary approach rejects celerity to improve the quality of deliberations.

Finally, the adversary process relies upon appellate review to ensure obedience to the codes regulating litigation. In effect, the appellate mechanism gives each party a chance to be heard at least twice. Appellate review undercuts the finality of judgment and thereby allows litigants to prolong the adjudicatory process substantially.

Here, as in the previous examples, the adversary method sacrifices speed to enhance the integrity of deliberations.

Almost every procedure in the adversary process moves at a measured pace rather than at maximum speed. Delay, or perhaps more accurately, deliberation, has been built into every aspect of the adversary system. If one adopts the view that any diminution in speed is a serious danger, then every part of the adversary process is open to challenge. The problem with this sort of challenge is that it fails to focus on the most important question, whether there is a need for a process that is careful, deliberative, and committed to airing the claims of each litigant fully rather than one that proceeds at maximum speed. As will be argued in the following section, there is a real need for a legal mechanism controlled by the litigants and devoted to the resolution of their claims. A deliberate pace is valuable because it encourages the careful scrutiny of each claim and increases party involvement in and control of the judicial process.

Moreover, there is little evidence that adversary procedures cause greater delay than nonadversary alternatives. A recent study conducted by Thomas Church, Jr., for the National Center for State Courts, found that courts exercising the greatest effort to avoid adversarial trials by inducing settlements were also the courts in which litigants were most likely to experience long delays in getting their cases resolved.[s] Similarly, Professor Hans Zeisel and his associates, in their classic study of court delay, found that the use of adversarial juries actually speeded cases to final resolution in many circumstances.[t] Analyses like these suggest that adversary mechanisms may not be a fundamental cause of unnecessary delay in adjudication.

2. THE DISCOVERY OF MATERIAL TRUTH

The second frequently voiced criticism of the adversary system is that it sets too low a value on the discovery of material truth. At the heart of this criticism is the notion that various parts of the adversary mechanism inhibit the development of a historically accurate picture of what happened on the relevant occasion and that this is likely to deter the fact finder from reaching a just decision. The three facets of the adversary system most strongly condemned as inhibitors of the discovery of truth are party control of the information-gathering process, zealous and single-minded representation of each litigant by his attorney, and evidentiary rules that circumscribe the types of information available to the decision maker.

(a) General Observations

Before reviewing these specific criticisms, three general points should be considered. First, although the first section of this essay suggests that the adversary process places somewhat more emphasis on

---

s. Church, *Justice Delayed: The Pace of Litigation in Urban Trial Courts* 32 (1978).

t. Zeisel, Kalven, & Buchholz, *Delay in the Court* 4 (1959).

the resolution of disputes than on the discovery of material truth, it need not be conceded that the process is inept at finding truth. The adversary process is open to an extremely broad range of information. Indeed, adversary courts probably hear more detailed and divergent testimony than courts using judge-centered methods of inquiry. Justice Benjamin Kaplan of the Massachusetts Supreme Judicial Court, formerly a professor at Harvard Law School, compared the fact-gathering efforts of American and West German courts.[u] He concluded that America's party-controlled courts receive significantly more information than West Germany's judge-directed courts because the adversary courts hear at least two distinct versions of the facts in every case. Further, these versions are likely to be the product of intensive pretrial investigation. (Pretrial inquiry is quite limited in Germany and in other civil law countries.) Considering the information-gathering potential of the parties, it is debatable whether the adversary approach is any less effective at uncovering truth than is a judge-centered alternative.

Second, one must keep human limitations in mind when defining judicial objectives. The weakness of human perception, memory, and expression will often render the discovery of material truth impossible. To become preoccupied with truth may be both naive and futile. It is to the advantage of the adversary system that it does not define its objectives in such an absolute and unrealistic fashion.

Third, a preoccupation with material truth may be not only futile but dangerous to society as well. If the exclusive objective of the judicial process were the disclosure of facts, then any technique that increases the prospect of gathering facts would be permissible. Spouses could be compelled to testify against one another, psychoactive drugs could be used to loosen the tongues of reluctant witnesses, and even torture could be employed in certain situations. Between 1300 and 1800 the inquisitorial judges of Europe functioned within a system of criminal procedure that placed special emphasis on the discovery of truth. The outcome of this approach was wholesale reliance on torture. Today no Western judicial system accepts such methods. Truth is not the end the courts seek. Truth is nothing more than a means of achieving the end, justice. The disclosure of material facts is not the only means of achieving justice, and to treat it as the end is to open the way to unsavory abuses.

(b) Party Control of Litigation

Critics of the adversary system argue that parties should not be allowed to control the information-gathering process because they cannot be trusted to present all the relevant evidence. Rather, the parties are likely to provide only the information that they think helps their cause. This sort of presentation is said to skew the proof in ways that

u. Kaplan, *Civil Procedure—Reflections on the Comparison of Systems,* 9 Buffalo L.Rev. 409 (1960).

undermine the accuracy of the final determination. Litigant control is also criticized because it allows each party to confer freely with all the witnesses and to assist witnesses in preparing their testimony. This investigation and preparation procedure is said to pose two sorts of threats: first, the subtle transmutation of testimony by means of psychological suggestion; second, the subornation of perjury.

In response it should be remarked that party control is necessary to preserve the neutrality of the fact finder. If the judge is assigned the task of making factual inquiry, both theoretical analysis and empirical data suggest that her biases are likely to be intensified and her decisions opened to prejudicial influence. This loss of neutrality is arguably as significant a problem as any skewing caused by party control.

Litigant direction yields benefits besides neutrality. Psychological experiments have indicated that when parties in an adversary system find themselves at a factual disadvantage, they will expend significant effort to improve their position.[v] This tends to bring the proof presented at trial into balance and to ensure a decision based upon more complete information than would otherwise be the case. Another advantage of party control is that it is likely to reduce "impositional costs" by minimizing the chances that judges will render uneconomical decisions poorly fitted to the needs of the litigants.[w]

While there is solid evidence to support the principle of party control of the witness selection and examination process *at trial,* caution may be warranted with respect to endorsement of rules allowing the adversaries to interrogate freely and to prepare all witnesses *before trial.* Recent psychological studies by Professor Elizabeth Loftus of the University of Washington suggest that the testimony of eyewitnesses and other disinterested informants may be substantially altered by the manner in which they are interrogated before trial.[x] There may be substantial danger in allowing uninhibited pretrial interrogation not only because it will influence the witness's story but because later cross-examination is not likely to demonstrate that new material has been insinuated into the witness's recollections. (Not even the witness is likely to recognize that this has occurred.)

The solution to this problem is far from clear. On the one hand, parties need the freedom to make thorough inquiry in order to prepare their cases. On the other hand, thorough inquiry may cause irremediable taint. The answer lies in limiting pretrial interrogation while allowing parties to gather the information they need. (One solution would be to allow the parties pretrial access to all witnesses but only when opposing counsel is present.) Whatever the precise answer may

v. Thibaut & Walker, *Procedural Justice, A Psychological Analysis* (1975).

w. Lea & Walker, *Efficient Procedure,* 57 N.Car.L.Rev. 361 (1979).

x. Loftus, *Eyewitness Testimony* 88–109 (1979).

be, this problem is not so serious as to warrant the overthrow of the system.

(c) Zealous Representation of Each Litigant

Attorneys have, from the earliest times, been viewed as obstructors of truth. The basis for this view is not hard to identify. Attorneys are skilled advocates. Their facility with words and procedure gives them the means of manipulating the information-gathering process. When the advocate lends his talents to the single-minded pursuit of the goals of his client, it is not hard to understand why onlookers might consider him the enemy of veracity. The ethical rule that compels the attorney zealously to represent his client officially reinforces loyalty at the expense of commitment to the search for truth.

In response it should first be noted that attorney zeal is directly linked to party control of proceedings and that the arguments in favor of party control also support zealous representation of the litigant. This is so because the complexity of legal proceedings makes it virtually impossible for parties to proceed without counsel. It has frequently been suggested that the attorney can serve his client and, at the same time, ensure that the truth is disclosed. This position fails to preserve attorney zeal and loyalty because it requires the attorney to act as an agent of the court whenever there is a potential conflict between the client's interests and the pursuit of material information. The likely results of casting the attorney in this impossible situation are unethical conduct if the lawyer chooses to act on behalf of his client in a doubtful case or substantial discouragement of client candor, cooperation, and trust if the lawyer chooses to act on behalf of the court.

This does not mean that an attorney can never be required to act in ways that oppose his client's wishes. When a client asks his lawyer to aid him in the commission of a crime or in the perpetration of a fraud, the attorney can and must reject such overtures. The situations in which the attorney must reject his client's wishes should be clearly and narrowly defined, however, otherwise a chill will be cast over the relationship and over the entire adversary process.

(d) Strict Evidentiary Code

The rules of evidence prohibit a wide range of information from being presented to the fact finder. No matter how useful or important certain items may be, if they fall afoul of the evidence rules they cannot be considered. This applies to most words spoken out of court (frequently classified as hearsay) as well as to such information as a party's criminal record or the existence of insurance. In all this the critics see a substantial barrier to the disclosure of important facts and, hence, an impediment to the discovery of truth.

As in the case of attorney zeal, the rules of evidence serve, at least in part, to preserve party control of litigation. They achieve this result by curtailing judicial power over the admission and exclusion of evidence. The rules also directly protect the neutrality of the fact finder. While each rule may not be defensible on this ground, the general thrust of the rules is to insulate the decision maker from unreliable or prejudicial evidence. The protective function is of special importance when lay jurors decide cases. Protection also takes on added importance in the American adversary system because facts are presented only once, at the trial level. In these circumstances insulation from misleading material seems crucial because taint cannot be overcome by a *de novo* hearing on appeal.

3. ACCESS TO THE JUDICIAL SYSTEM

Critics have advanced a number of other objections to the adversary system. They have argued that the American system fails to allow any but the wealthy and powerful access to counsel and the courts. The cost of litigation is said to be so great that the vast majority of Americans cannot afford to participate in the system. Substantial evidence indicates that cost does exclude some from participating in the justice system. Exclusion does not, however, result from any characteristic intrinsic to the adversary method but rather to the means by which it is presently implemented in the United States. Because the problem is not inherent in an adversarial system, it does not warrant the scrapping of the system. What is required is reform of the social and economic conditions that exclude a sizable segment of the population from access to the courts.

Recent American legal history contains a significant number of examples of efforts to expand the availability of legal services. The United States Supreme Court, in a number of precedent-setting decisions, starting with *Gideon v. Wainwright*,[y] has required that every criminal defendant who faces the prospect of jail be provided an attorney and the means to prepare his defense adequately. This mandate has measurably increased participation in the process. While it would be unrealistic to claim that *Gideon* has solved all the problems in the criminal setting, it is clear that progress has been made.

Access has been facilitated in civil as well as criminal litigation. The development of the contingency fee as a means of financing litigation has opened the courts in many cases. (In such cases the attorney proceeds without a fee in the hope of sharing in the fruits of victory.) The creation of the Legal Services Corporation appreciably expanded the availability of low-cost legal assistance to the poor. The courts themselves have helped to improve access to judicial remedies by allowing litigants to proceed on behalf of others as well as themselves in cases in which individual claims might not justify the expense of litigation. Class actions and cases involving institutional reform have provided at least a partial remedy to the market failures involved when litigants with serious claims cannot afford to press their grievances.

y. 372 U.S. 335, 83 S.Ct. 792, 9 L.Ed.2d 799 (1963).

None of these mechanisms has been problem-free, but each has helped to lessen the exclusionary effect of the cost of litigation. Much remains to be done to improve access in civil cases. The American Bar Association and other bar groups appear to be moving in the proper direction with their proposals to increase each lawyer's obligation to undertake *pro bono* work.

The problem of exclusion is not unique to adversarial systems. Professor Inga Markovits of the University of Texas has suggested that the didactic and collectivistic attitudes of East European Socialist judicial systems greatly inhibit citizens from pursuing various individual claims.[z] This observation suggests that very different judicial systems can pose practical problems of exclusion for significant classes of claimants. The problem of exclusion may be beyond complete remedy. What is of importance is a willingness to recognize that the problem exists and to undertake efforts to ameliorate it whenever possible. So long as a society works to improve access to its judicial mechanism, criticsm based on exclusion does not justify radical change.

4. THE POWER OF THE ATTORNEY

A number of perceptive critics have argued that the attorneys upon whom the adversary system relies have become too dominant a force in the litigation they prosecute. The value of the adversary system is, in large part, attributable to party involvement in the litigation process. When the attorney comes to play too decisive a role, he can short-circuit the benefits of party control. In such circumstances the parties are likely to feel that they have not had a hand in the adjudication of the case and that they are not bound by the mandates of the court. Attorney domination can also cause an increase in "impositional costs" by focusing the litigation on the lawyer's interests rather than on the client's needs.

At present, it does not appear that the problem of attorney control is so grave as to threaten the integrity of the adversary system. Further, corrective mechanisms within the adversary framework help to ensure that the attorney will serve his client's interests. Perhaps most significant are the ethical rules governing attorney behavior. These compel the attorney to solicit and to obey his client's instructions with respect to settlement and crucial strategic decisions during the course of litigation. While it is uncertain whether attorneys will obey such rules, the heightened awareness of the lawyer's ethical responsibilities created by the Watergate scandal and reinforced by the American Bar Association's continuing activism in the ethics field provide a basis for optimism. In cases of serious deviation from a client's instructions, the injured litigant can seek damages in a malpractice action. The expanding scope of attorney malpractice liability has had the beneficial

z. Markovits, *Law and Order—Constitutionalism and Legality in Eastern Europe,* 34 Stan.L.Rev. 513 (1982).

effect of providing a means of enforcing the ethical rules regulating consultation and control.

5. CONFLICTING JUDICIAL RESPONSIBILITIES

A final criticism of the adversary system warranting discussion is that it places the trial judge in the untenable position of having to perform inconsistent or conflicting tasks. Judge Marvin Frankel devotes a chapter of his book *Partisan Justice* to one aspect of this problem.[a] He asserts that because the judge is obliged to control the litigation and the litigants, it is extremely difficult for her to remain neutral and passive. According to Frankel the judge is likely to become the "target" of one or both of the parties as soon as she exercises her authority. They will attempt to lure the judge into committing reversible error as a means of ensuring victory on appeal if they are not successful in the trial court. As a defense, argues Frankel, the judge becomes "adversarial," and loses the neutrality and passivity upon which the system depends.

The accuracy of Frankel's description of the judicial situation is not beyond challenge. A significant body of literature supports the proposition that judges in the adversary system generally do not view their situation as adversarial and do not allow themselves to be drawn into the contest. The sensitive judicial officer may indeed feel some strain. This is not surprising in a system designed to control tightly the judge's discretion and to place significant power in the hands of the parties. It would appear, however, that judges generally do not allow such personal feelings to override their professional obligation to deal dispassionately with the cases that come before them. To help maintain equilibrium in the courtroom the adversary system relies on the jury rather than on the judge as fact finder. The interposition of this neutral body of laymen tends to reduce the likelihood of clashes between judges and lawyers.

A second aspect of the problem of conflicting judicial responsibilities involves the judge's duties as lawmaker. One of the primary functions of the judge in the adversary system is to fix the legal rules that will be applied in resolving each case. With some frequency, the legal rules to be applied are so vague, unformed, or out of date that the judge must take it upon herself to fashion the law. Critics argue that this sort of active lawmaking is in conflict with the principles of judicial neutrality and passivity. In point of fact, the law-fixing function does not conflict with neutrality or passivity. The history of the adversary system suggests that judges took a significant step *toward* neutrality when they placed the fact-finding function in the hands of the jury and began to devote their energies to the development of legal doctrine.

Despite this historical evidence, one could maintain that there is a difference between *declaring* law for the benefit of the fact finder and

a. Frankel, *Partisan Justice* 39–58 (1980).

making law. In the latter context, one could argue that the judge becomes an active advocate committed to vindicating her newly coined legal doctrine. The Anglo–American common law system has never relied on an all-inclusive code of legal principles. Instead the law has been developed on a case-by-case basis, establishing only those rules necessary to resolve the litigated issue. This choice, one of ancient and honorable lineage, makes it inevitable that judges will be lawmakers as well as law declarers. While there is some danger that judges may come to see themselves as advocates on behalf of the legal principles they fashion, the system has established certain controls to limit this prospect. Foremost is appellate review. The courts of appeals in the adversary system are the primary lawmakers. Their review checks judicial excess at the trial level and fixes legal principles that serve as an authoritative guide to trial judges.

Although several of the most frequently advanced criticisms of the adversary system are not well founded, the system is not without its faults. Upon examination, however, it appears that none of these is so serious as to warrant the abandonment of adversary procedure. The following section will consider the special worth of the adversary system and the defects in the judge-dominated system most likely to be offered as an alternative.

SECTION D. DEFENSE OF THE ADVERSARIAL PROCESS

A fundamental lesson of Anglo–American legal history is that traditional methods of resolving disputes have served as a rampart against government tyranny. In light of this insight, reform of the judicial machinery should be approached with caution. The historical evidence will not support a flat refusal to change (innovation has been an important element in English and American law since the medieval period), but it does counsel caution where significant departures from previous practices are contemplated. Therefore, even if there were little good to say about the adversary system, those who argue for change would still face a significant burden of persuasion.

1. BENEFITS OF PARTY CONTROL OF LITIGATION

A number of reasons, apart from the historical, warrant reliance on adversarial methods. The adversary process provides litigants with the means to control their lawsuits. The parties are preeminent in choosing the forum, designating the proofs, and running the process. The courts, as a general rule, pursue the questions the parties propound. Ultimately, the whole procedure yields results tailored to the litigants' needs and in this way reinforces individual rights. As already noted, this sort of procedure also enhances the economic efficiency of adjudication by sharply reducing impositional costs.

Party control yields other benefits as well. Perhaps most important, it promotes litigant and societal acceptance of decisions rendered by the courts. Adversary theory holds that if a party is intimately involved in the adjudicatory process and feels that he has been given a fair opportunity to present his case, he is likely to accept the results whether favorable or not. Assuming this theory is correct, the adversary process will serve to reduce post-litigation friction and to increase compliance with judicial mandates.

Adversary theory identifies litigant control as important to satisfy not only the parties but society as well. When litigants direct the proceedings, there is little opportunity for the judge to pursue her own agenda or to act on her biases. Because the judge seldom takes the lead in conducting the proceedings, she is unlikely to appear to be partisan or to become embroiled in the contest. Her detachment preserves the appearance of fairness as well as fairness itself. In legal proceedings, as the United States Supreme Court stated in *Offutt v. United States,* "justice must satisfy the appearance of justice." [b] When it fails to do so, social credibility is eroded and distrust introduced. There is little direct evidence of the extent of personal or societal acceptance of adversarial processes as contrasted with other adjudicatory methodologies. A number of multinational surveys, however, including those conducted by Professors John Thibaut and Laurens Walker, have found that a majority of subjects will designate adversary procedure as the fairest for resolving disputes. [c] This finding lends support to the argument that adversary procedures are perceived as fairest and are more likely to satisfy litigants and onlookers than nonadversary alternatives.

Thibaut and Walker have provided empirical evidence that litigant control produces other sorts of benefits. [d] First, it tends to encourage desirable conduct on the part of litigants and their counsel. Psychological experimentation has shown that an advocate working in an adversarial context who finds his client at a factual disadvantage will expend significant effort to improve his client's position. This is to be contrasted with the behavior of the advocate working in an inquisitorial setting who will seldom undertake an extensive search for better evidence to bolster a weak case. The adversary process appears to encourage advocates to protect parties facing an initial disadvantage and hence to improve the overall quality of the evidence upon which adjudication will be based.

Thibaut and Walker have also found that adversarial emphasis on party presentation tends to counteract the bias of the decision maker more effectively than does an approach requiring the active participation of the trier in marshaling the proof. [e] This finding provides tangible support for the theoretical assertion that the best decision maker is one whose *sole function* is adjudication. Because the adversa-

b. 348 U.S. 11, 14, 75 S.Ct. 11, 13, 99 L.Ed. 11, 16 (1954).

c. Thibaut & Walker, *Procedural Justice, A Psychological Analysis* 77–80, 94–96 (1975).

d. Thibaut & Walker, supra 38–39.

e. Thibaut & Walker, supra, 49–51.

ry process assigns the prosecutorial function to the parties, it serves to increase the likelihood that the trier will be able to devote her full attention to the neutral adjudication of the case.

The adversary process assigns each participant a single function. The judge is to serve as neutral and passive arbiter. Counsel are to act as zealous advocates. According to adversary theory, when each actor performs only a single function the dispute before the court will be resolved in the fairest and most efficient way. The strength of such a division of labor is that individual responsibilities are clear. The possibility that a participant in the system will face conflicting responsibilities is minimized. Each knows what is expected of him and can work conscientiously to achieve a specifically defined goal. When participants in the judicial process are confronted with conflicting obligations, it becomes difficult for them to discharge any of their duties satisfactorily. The more frequently they face conflict, the more likely it is that they will not perform their assigned part or will not perform it in a way that minimizes conflict rather than fully discharging their responsibilities. Among the greatest dangers in this regard are that the judge will abandon neutrality if encouraged to search for material truth and that the attorney will compromise his client's interests if compelled to serve as an officer of the court rather than as an advocate. In either case the probity of the process is seriously undermined.

Party control has another beneficial effect as well. It affirms human individuality. It mandates respect for the opinions of each party rather than those of his attorney, of the court, or of society at large. It provides the litigant a neutral forum in which to air his views and promises that those views will be heard and considered. The individualizing effect of adversary procedure has important implications besides those involving individual satisfaction. The receptiveness of adversary procedure to individual claims implies that an adversarial court will take a sympathetic view of the claims of individuals against the state. The prospects for sympathetic hearing are increased because the judge and, to an even greater extent, the jury are beyond governmental control and cannot be taken to task for their decisions.

These propositions concerning the receptiveness of adversarial courts to the claims of individual citizens are, at least in part, borne out by historical evidence. For centuries adversarial courts have served as a counterbalance to official tyranny and have worked to broaden the scope of individual rights. The steady expansion of doctrines protecting minorities both in England and in the United States reflects this fact. When adversarial process has been ignored in the operation of the courts, as in the days of the Star Chamber, human rights diminished and governmental repression increased.

We live in an era of expanding government power. The urgency of social problems, including the scarcity of resources and the exigencies of national defense, tends to lead the government to exert pressure on the citizenry to cooperate in ensuring the efficient operation of society as a whole. This pressure poses a keen threat to the maintenance of individual rights. In these circumstances, there is a need to preserve the kind of institution that will sympathetically review claims based on individual rights rather than on governmental necessity or the common good. Because the adversarial courts are primarily committed to hearing and to upholding the claims of individuals, they are most likely to be capable of handling this task.

2. CONSTITUTIONAL RECOGNITION OF ADVERSARIAL PROCEDURES

Any defense of the American adversary system would be incomplete if it did not consider the constitutional status of adversarial procedure. The adversary process has not, as a whole, been made the immutable law of the land by incorporation in the Constitution. Significant parts of the adversarial mechanism, however, are recognized in the Constitution or have been held by the Supreme Court to be constitutionally required. The text of the Constitution does not specify what form of judicial procedure shall be used in the courts of the United States. It does, however, incorporate a great deal of adversarial machinery. Article III of the Constitution specifies that judges "shall hold their Offices during good Behaviour, and shall at stated Times, receive for their Services a Compensation, which shall not be diminished during their Continuance in Office." This provision does not protect an exclusively adversarial mechanism, but it does help to ensure an independent judiciary, a key element in any adversarial system. Article III also specifies that the trial of crimes shall be by jury. Again, the text does not require adversary procedure, but helps to encourage it, at least in criminal cases, by mandating the use of the most neutral and passive of fact finders.

The most important constitutional recognition of adversary procedure is to be found in the Sixth and Seventh Amendments to the Constitution. The Sixth Amendment requires that a jury be available in all criminal cases and that the accused have the right "to be confronted with the Witnesses against him, to have compulsory process for obtaining witnesses in his favor, and to have the Assistance of Counsel for his defence." Taken together these requirements go a long way toward establishing adversary procedure in criminal cases.

The Supreme Court has held that implicit in the confrontation requirement is a strong predisposition in favor of the cross-examination of witnesses in open court and a preference for live testimony in general. The compulsory process clause adds to these requirements the principle that the defendant has the right to present a defense. These rights together seem to call for an adversarial process in which each litigant is given an opportunity to present his case. The right to counsel takes this idea one step further. It has been construed to require the state to make counsel available to all defendants, thereby increasing their effectiveness as litigants. The mandate for counsel has other implications as well. When considered together with other requirements of the Sixth Amendment, it has been held to bar states from controlling the order in which the accused presents his proof at trial and to guarantee that the defendant be granted an opportunity to make closing argument.

The Seventh Amendment, which addresses civil litigation, does not specify nearly so much as does the Sixth. It does, however, preserve the right to jury trial in civil cases and specifies that "no fact tried by jury, shall be otherwise re-examined in any Court of the United States, than according to the rules of the common law." This latter requirement seems to envision a process of adjudication and review of the sort utilized in adversarial proceedings.

In addition to these specific prescriptions, the Fifth and Fourteenth Amendments state that no person shall be deprived "of life, liberty, or property, without due process of law." These words have been viewed as requiring a fair trial in a fair forum in both civil and criminal cases. To what extent this mandate compels adversary procedure is open to question. In criminal cases, the Supreme Court has viewed the due process requirement as fixing the principle of judicial neutrality. Even the appearance of partiality has been condemned. Further, the due process clauses have been held, in association with the requirements of the Sixth Amendment, to protect a defendant's right to make a full defense. Although no right of appeal has been discovered, either in the due process clauses or elsewhere, the Fifth and Fourteenth Amendments have been construed to require states that do provide a criminal appeals process to open it to the poor as well as to the rich. This requirement has gone a long way toward establishing a criminal appellate system.

Civil litigation has been less affected by the due process clauses than has criminal litigation. Beyond the basic mandate of fairness just what process is "due" has never been specified. At a minimum, judicial neutrality, some opportunity to present evidence, and the right, at one's own expense, to be represented by counsel seem to be protected.[f]

The determination that the Constitution requires an array of adversarial mechanisms, especially in criminal proceedings, suggests that our courts and perhaps the framers of the Constitution have viewed adversary process (or at least its essential components) as fundamental to a fair judicial system. Constitutional endorsement of the adversary system makes change particularly inappropriate.

f. See, e.g., *Mullane v. Central Hanover Bank & Trust Co.*, 339 U.S. 306, 70 S.Ct. 652, 94 L.Ed. 865 (1950) (right to reasonable notice); *Brinkerhoff–Faris Trust & Savings Co. v. Hill*, 281 U.S. 673, 50 S.Ct. 451, 74 L.Ed. 1107 (1930) (right to be heard).

3. COMPARISON OF ADVERSARIAL AND INQUISITORIAL PROCESSES

To compare adversary procedure with its most likely replacement will help in assessing the value of the adversary system. Without doubt, the most likely substitute for adversary procedure is some variant of the judge-centered inquisitorial process used in most European countries. The first step toward understanding such a procedure is to identify its attributes. The key actor in the inquisitorial process is the judge. It is her duty to investigate the facts and interrogate the witnesses as well as to formulate the decision. The entire adjudicatory process revolves around the judge. Because she is so important, lay juries are not favored. For the same reason party control of the proceedings is minimized. Generally, the parties initiate the proceedings and participate in the inquiry, but they are never allowed to control the fact-gathering process. Lawyers play a far less important role than they do in the adversary system. As one might expect, the inquisitorial process is firmly committed to the search for material truth.

Since the objective of the inquisitorial process is likely to be material truth, few technical rules of evidence or procedure are recognized. The judge is relatively free to conduct the inquiry as she sees fit. She can ask for virtually any sort of information (except for items protected because of extrajudicial concerns like those expressed in the marital or priest-penitent privileges). Proceedings are run in the most informal fashion, more like an American pretrial conference than an evidentiary hearing. The proceedings are not recorded in a verbatim transcript. Rather, the judge extracts what she thinks is important and records it. On appeal, all issues in the case, both legal and factual, are open to review, and new evidence can be submitted on all points. This is in marked contrast to Anglo–American procedure, which narrowly circumscribes review of factual determinations and seldom allows the introduction of new evidence on appeal. Finally, the inquisitorial process relies on a rather large judicial bureaucracy arranged in a hierarchical structure. Judicial responsibilities at each level of the system are specified in detail, and strict conformity is required. Innovation or variation is generally not tolerated.

An inquisitorial approach to adjudication is open to several criticisms. First, the inquiring judge is more likely to act upon her biases than is her adversarial counterpart. The late Professor Lon Fuller of Harvard Law School described what generally occurs:

> At some early point a familiar pattern will seem to emerge from the evidence; an accustomed label is waiting for the case and, without waiting further proofs, this label is promptly assigned to it. It is a mistake to suppose that this premature cataloguing must necessarily result from impatience, prejudice or mental sloth. Often it proceeds from a very understandable desire to bring the hearing into some order and coherence, for without some tentative theory of the case there is

no standard of relevance by which testimony may be measured. But what starts as a preliminary diagnosis designed to direct the inquiry tends, quickly and imperceptibly, to become a fixed conclusion, as all that confirms the diagnosis makes a strong imprint on the mind, while all that runs counter to it is received with diverted attention.[g]

Second, the inquisitorial approach is less sensitive to claims concerning individual rights. It is committed to material truth. This commitment was so strong between 1300 and 1800 that judicial officers felt warranted in using torture to pursue the facts in the criminal litigation before them. Modern inquisitorial process has clearly rejected such methods, but the emphasis on material truth remains. This emphasis relegates questions of individual rights to a subsidiary position in the litigation.

Generally, the inquisitorial process will not serve as a check on government power. Inquisitorial judges (at least throughout Europe) are bureaucrats who identify with the government and whose advancement in the judicial hierarchy depends on accommodation rather than confrontation. Such officials are not likely to identify novel rights against the government or expand rights previously established. Further, inquisitorial judges are not likely to be inclined toward the creative use of judicial authority in any context. Advancement in the bureaucracy is not won by creative activity but rather by conformity to the rules of the organization. The successful inquisitorial judge is the one who confines her conduct within the previously established organizational boundaries.

The proud history and constitutional status of the adversary system as well as the benefits to be derived from its individualizing effect are strong reasons for its retention. Adversary procedure has served as a guardian of individual liberty since its inception. It has facilitated the extension of personal rights to a wide range of minority groups. Given these facts and the absence of a clearly superior alternative, the American commitment to the adversary system ought to be maintained.

g. Fuller, *The Adversary System,* in Berman, ed., Talks on American Law 38–39 (1961) (quoting from the *Report of the Joint Conference on Professional Responsibility of the American Bar Association,* 1958).

Chapter 2

OTHER VIEWS OF THE
ADVERSARY SYSTEM

Since at least the turn of the century there has been a lively debate about the value of the adversary process. The following materials include classic statements both in favor of and opposed to the adversarial method of adjudication. The debate waxes as hot today as it did in 1906 when Roscoe Pound first challenged the "sporting theory of justice." While the debate has not been concluded, succeeding chapters will demonstrate that the critics' attacks have led to significant changes in the American legal mechanism. The shape of reform has, to a large extent, been predicated upon the criticisms and responses reproduced here.

SECTION A. AN INTRODUCTION—ONE JUDGE'S VIEW OF THE SYSTEM

HERBERT STERN—JUDGMENT IN BERLIN

358–75 (1984).
Reprinted with permission of the author, copyright ©1984. Herbert Stern.

[On August 30, 1978, Hans Detlef Alexander Tiede, an East German citizen, hijacked a Polish airliner on a flight to East Berlin and forced it to land at Tempelhof Airport in the United States Sector of West Berlin. He was accompanied on this flight by a young East German woman, Ingrid Ruske, and her daughter, Sabine. The three were taken into custody by American officials and held without bail, charge and counsel while authorities attempted to determine what should be done with them.

International treaty commitments require that hijackers either be prosecuted or extradited. In the *Tiede* case extradition to Poland was viewed by both Americans and West Germans as politically unpalatable. Hence, the question became who would prosecute the hijacker and in what sort of court. The West Germans were exceedingly reluctant to assume this task and prevailed upon the United States to shoulder the political burden. The German Federal Republic, however, agreed to pay all expenses arising out of the prosecution.

Among its rights as an occupying power after the Second World War, the United States was ceded extensive legislative and judicial authority with respect to its sector of Berlin. In 1955 the United States had exercised its authority to create the United States Court for Berlin. This court had been little more than a hollow shell until the *Tiede* case came along. The United States then resolved to activate the court in Berlin to try the matter.

After a number of false starts, Herbert Stern, a United States federal district court judge, agreed to hear the case. To the surprise and consternation of American officials, Judge Stern insisted that Tiede be treated in almost precisely the same manner as a defendant in an American federal court. Over State Department protests that the judge had only such authority *as American officials chose to give him,* Judge Stern insisted upon a jury trial and the full range of constitutionally required protections for defendant Tiede. Eventually, a group of German residents from West Berlin was called for jury duty. Twelve heard the case and found Tiede guilty of hijacking. Throughout these proceedings American officials attempted to entice Tiede to waive his "rights" so that no precedent would be set in connection with Judge Stern's rulings about the applicability of constitutional protections. The judge was eventually informed of these arguably improper efforts.

The following excerpt is drawn from the conclusion of Judge Stern's book about the affair. The *Tiede* case had arrived at the moment for sentencing. After an opening citation to a remark by Cyrus Vance, one time American Secretary of State, Judge Stern describes his reaction to the government's behavior throughout the *Tiede* case and to its assertion that he was nothing more than a government employee bound to follow State Department orders.]

As I have traveled around the world and observed other nations, I have been struck by the fact that the strength of our great nation lies importantly in our unique federal judicial system, a system which is marked by a strong and independent judiciary joined with a dedicated professional bar—courageous and faithful to the clients and causes which its members represent. The hallmark of our system is the willingness of our trial bar to stand up to any adversary, even the government itself, and fight vigorously for the cause at hand with the confidence that a fair-minded judge will render an impartial decision without even once looking over his or her shoulder or worrying about the reaction of government leaders.

We must not take this for granted. That would be a grave mistake. For this is a precious heritage which we must treasure and nurture.

Cyrus Vance, November 25, 1981

*   *   *

"Now," said the judge, "I'm going to sentence. Who speaks for the defendant on sentencing?"

[Judah Best, an outstanding American lawyer, who had volunteered to help represent Tiede] stood and strode forward to the lectern. "Your Honor, I will speak for the defendant and present the facts to the Court in order to assist the Court in making an appropriate determination."

"I think I should hear from the government first, since I believe the defendant is entitled to the last word at the time of sentencing."

Adelman stood at his table. "If your Honor please"—his voice was very quiet as he spoke for the last time in the Berlin court—"our recommendation is . . . that the Court impose a four-year sentence. That has been indicated before, I believe . . . earlier in the proceedings, and we indicate that again. We ask your Honor to accept our recommendation."

Moreover, Adelman allowed "that a four-year sentence, coupled with credit for time served, probably would result in release not later than . . . December 15, 1979."

Even still the occupation authorities spoke only in terms of "probable" release date.

"You are asking me to give this man to you for four years, aren't you?"

"Not to me, your Honor," Adelman protested.

"To your client," stated the judge.

"To the government, yes," Adelman acknowledged. "We are not, if I may finish," he quickly added, "we're not personally asking for any action against the defendant."

The judge turned away. "I'll hear from counsel for the defendant," he said to Best waiting at the lectern.

"May it please the Court, your Honor, we stand here at an awesome time in the defendant's life. . . . You know the reasons why Detlef Tiede left, left the East and came to the West. * * *

"The facts of the diversion your Honor knows. There is nothing more that I need repeat with regard to them.

"It seems to me that all of the facts that we have before us, a man who applied twelve times for an opportunity to come to the West, a man whose motivation to come to the West was to see his son, a man who tried non-violent means to come to the West, through the use of false passports, and a man who was involved in a diversion of an aircraft only after all else failed, demonstrates, it seems to me, a man to whom mercy should be shown.

"I respectfully request and recommend to the Court that Detlef Tiede be sentenced to a term which would permit him to be free at the conclusion of today's court proceedings." * * * *

There was nothing left, except the sentence. The judge took a deep breath and plunged in.

"This has been the most unusual proceeding that I have ever participated in. . . . What I'm faced with here is extraordinary, not merely . . . because it involved a balancing of interests as between the safety of civil aviation on the one hand, and the right of an individual to escape an oppressive administration which, in violation of international agreements, forbids people to leave.

"In this case, we have the judgment of the people most close to the situation."

He glanced over at the now vacant jury box, remembering the twelve Berliners who had sat there, just two days before.

"People who have before their eyes constant reminders of the kind of considerations which prompted this defendant to do what he did. . . .

"And it was to their ethical judgment that the question was left as to whether or not, even given the motivations which prompted the defendant in this case, he might properly under German law take the actions which he took."

He wondered if any of the jurors were interested in this stage of the proceedings. He supposed that most of them would follow it.

"And that's why we are here to sentence today, because of the ethical judgment of a cross-section of this community."

His plan was to impose sentence based on that judgment. But that was before the ambassador's letter and Steenland's courtroom performance.

"My task would be in a way more difficult than it is, had those charged with the duty of prosecuting this case adhered to the basic tenets of the American system of government. . . . Had they been content to do what every prosecutor in every United States courtroom does . . . namely, bring the charge, make the accusation, to give the defendant his due, a fair trial before a cross-section of the community in which he resides or is tried, and abide by the result."

But they weren't. They demanded to control the proceedings and the judge.

"Very shortly after I was appointed as a judge of the United States Court for Berlin, the issue arose as to whether or not this defendant was entitled to the benefits of the United States Constitution in this courtroom."

The memories came flooding back. The airplane into Berlin, the confrontation * * * in the courtroom * * *

"The United States, here in this court, filed a brief. . . . And that brief said that there are no rights in the United States Court for Berlin. . . . And I was told in oral argument that that included no right to due process of law."

It's still hard to believe it all happened, he thought.

"The Court was surprised. And, of course, it ruled that such a thing was an impossibility in all courts in which this flag, over my right shoulder, stood."

He pointed behind him, at the American flag in the courtroom.

"And this Court said then and it says now that anybody proclaiming such a doctrine in this court, who purports to speak for the United States of America, had better check his authority: Because"—he leaned forward and looked at the cadre of American lawyers—"if the public, the people, the citizens of the United States of America ever really find out that their representatives say that—in Berlin or anywhere—if the American people ever find out, these representatives will find out that they represent nothing but themselves."

Again he looked at the State and Justice Department lawyers. He wondered what they would say if they ever did account for their actions in Berlin. Just following orders, or just representing their client's position, most likely.

"The Court was prepared to believe that the arguments made by the representatives of the prosecution in this courtroom were excessive in their advocacy and did not reflect the real attitude . . ."

I was too trusting, he thought. But who would think that American lawyers would really implement such a thing?

"And then we heard the evidence concerning . . . the fact that the former defendant Ingrid Ruske and her daughter . . . were held in custody for over two months, without any charge brought against them, or any arraignment. . . .

"It became plain to the Court that not only had an argument been made that the defendants Tiede and Ruske enjoyed no constitutional rights, but that in fact the prosecutorial authorities had been behaving in just that way. . . .

"What other place where the American flag flies could any person be simply housed somewhere for nearly two and a half months under custody, mail censored, no phone calls without permission, and, mind you, without even a case?"

All that, of course, was before there was a court. But once he arrived in Berlin—at their request—they continued to trample Tiede's rights.

"Then, as we've heard, the defendant demanded the right to trial by jury. . . . And, from that point on, based on the stipulated facts on this record, it is apparent to this Court that the prosecutorial authorities in this matter, for reasons which they regarded to be reasons of state or foreign policy considerations, were bound and determined that this defendant should not have a right to trial by jury. And they did everything possible . . . to coerce him in ways totally improper into waiving what this Court found to be his right and what the United States Supreme Court has held to be a fundamental right."

He looked over to Adelman and Surena, and then beyond them to Lee Marks, who, with Feldman, had supervised all this from Washington.

"This Court was turned into a charade. The rules meant nothing. Because the prosecutors here conceived themselves to be free from any constraints of due process or constitutional limitation, they simply passed whatever laws were necessary at any moment it was necessary."

He gestured over toward Tiede. "All to do what? To coerce this man into waiving a trial by jury." He shook his head in disgust.

"We may begin to ask ourselves: What kind of court is this, in which judges are told how to decide cases, not asked; in which rules of court are abrogated on a moment-to-moment basis by secret conversations between the prosecutor and the one accused of crime, or his lawyer; by special legislation passed to get around the judge? And if you can't do it that way, why, send him a letter and tell him what to do."

He caught his breath, doing a mental count of ten.

"Now we ask ourselves why. What has brought this about? Was it a fear of losing a case? Was it simply the fear that if the defendant went to trial, he might be acquitted that caused all this? The Court finds that this was not the reason. . . . It was because it was intolerable to the prosecutors that there should be, in this courtroom, a jury comprised of Germans, or that there should function in this courtroom an authority to which those who viewed themselves as occupiers were accountable. Namely, the judge that they themselves appointed and which our Constitution demands shall act as an independent arbiter of the cases that come before him."

For weeks he had restrained himself, to keep the proceedings together. Now there was nothing to hold together anymore. But no one could end the court before he had his chance to speak his mind—and he intended to do it.

"Why have a court," he told them, "if you are not bound by the rules of court? What is a judge if he is something that you can tell what to do? Is this a charade, all of it, for your convenience, to have a forum so you can satisfy your international treaties on the one hand, but not your Constitution on the other? Here," he demanded to know, "in *this* city, do we have to have *more* judges who follow orders?"

He paused for a final breath.

"Gentlemen, I will not give you this defendant. . . . I have kept him in your custody now for nine months, nearly. . . . You have persuaded me. I believe, now, that you recognize no limitations of due process. . . .

"I don't have to be a great prophet to understand that there is probably not a great future for the United States Court for Berlin here."

One of the spectators barked an involuntary laugh. The judge nodded.

"Under those circumstances, who will be here to protect Tiede if I give him to you for four years? Viewing the Constitution as nonexistent, considering yourselves not restrained in any way, who will stand between you and him? What judge? What independent magistrate do you have here? What independent magistrate will you permit here?

"When a judge sentences, he commits a defendant to the custody— in the United States he says, 'I commit to the custody of the Attorney General of the United States'—et cetera. Here I suppose he says, I commit to the custody of the Commandant, or the Secretary of State, or whatever . . . I will not do it. Not under these circumstances. . . .

"I sentence this defendant to time served. You," he pointed at Detlef Tiede, "are a free man right now."

Tiede rose. *"Danke"* was all the man could say.

The judge nodded.   *   *   *

Questions

1. Why was Judge Stern so angry about the arguments advanced by the American government?

2. Why did the judge fear turning the defendant over to the American authorities? On what theory of judicial responsibility was his decision to release the defendant based?

3. How did Judge Stern's experiences as an American lawyer and a judge in an adversarial court affect his decision?

4. Did Judge Stern appear to act as the neutral and passive paragon idealized by adversarial theory? What was the result of his combative posture?

5. In another section of his book Judge Stern describes how the defendant's counsel risked being held in contempt in order to inform the court about the improper conduct of American officials. It was this information that first led the judge to doubt the government's integrity. In light of these facts what is the lawyer's role in the adversary process and has Judge Stern left sufficient room for it?

SECTION B.   A CLASSIC DESCRIPTION AND DEFENSE OF THE ADVERSARY SYSTEM

LON FULLER—THE ADVERSARY SYSTEM

In H. Berman (ed.), Talks On American Law 34–36, 39–45 (1971).
Reprinted with the permission of the editor.

[Professor Lon Fuller of Harvard Law School was one of the leading American legal theorists of his day. This brief "talk" was originally prepared as the script for a radio program to be broadcast to foreign audiences as a means of informing them about basic American institutions.]

The expression "the adversary system" can be used in a narrow sense. When we speak of "the adversary system" in its narrow sense we are referring to a certain philosophy of adjudication, a conception of the way the trial of cases in courts of law should be conducted, a view of the roles that should be played by advocates and by judge and jury in the decision of a controversy.

The philosophy of adjudication that is expressed in "the adversary system" is, speaking generally, a philosophy that insists on keeping distinct the function of the advocate, on the one hand, from that of the judge, or of the judge from that of jury, on the other. The decision of the case is for the judge, or for the judge and jury. That decision must be as objective and as free from bias as it possibly can. The Constitution of Massachusetts provides—in language that in its idiom calls at once to mind the spirit of a great age, the Age of the Enlightenment and of the American and French Revolutions—that "It is the right of every citizen to be tried by judges as free, impartial and independent as the lot of humanity will admit." If the judge is to perform that high function—a function which the Constitution recognizes may put human nature to a severe test—then the rules of procedure that govern a trial must be such that they do not compel or invite him to depart from the difficult role in which he is cast. It is not his place to take sides. He must withhold judgment until all the evidence has been examined and all the arguments have been heard.

The judge and jury must, then, be excluded from any partisan role. At the same time, a fair trial requires that each side of the controversy be carefully considered and be given its full weight and value. But before a judge can gauge the full force of an argument, it must be presented to him with partisan zeal by one not subject to the restraints of judicial office. The judge cannot know how strong an argument is until he has heard it from the lips of one who has dedicated all the powers of his mind to its formulation.

This is the function of the advocate. His task is not to decide but to persuade. He is not expected to present the case in a colorless and detached manner, but in such a way that it will appear in that aspect most favorable to his client. He is not like a jeweler who slowly turns a diamond in the light so that each of its facets may in turn be fully revealed. Instead the advocate holds the jewel steadily, as it were, so as to throw into bold relief a single aspect of it. It is the task of the advocate to help the judge and jury to see the case as it appears to interested eyes, in the aspect it assumes when viewed from that corner of life into which fate has cast his client. * * *

Why have courts and trials at all? Why bother with judges and juries, with pleas and counterpleas? When disputes arise or accusations are made, why should not the state simply appoint honest and intelligent men to make investigations? Why not let these men, after they have sifted the evidence and resolved apparent contradictions, make their findings without the aid of advocates and without the fanfare and publicity of a trial?

Arrangements tending in this direction are not unknown historically. One of them has at various times and in various forms been familiar on the European continent. This is the institution of the investigating magistrate, *le juge d'instruction, der Untersuchungsrichter.* In important criminal cases this official makes his own investigations and reaches his own conclusions on the basis of the evidence. To be sure, he has never been given the power to make a final determination of guilt. Yet his findings tend to influence the trial that follows; the form he has given to his inquiry tends to shape the proceedings in court and often tips the balance in cases of doubt.

No such office or institution exists in the countries of the common law, including the United States. Why do we reject an arrangement that seems so reasonable in its quiet efficiency? In answer I might simply draw on the European experience and quote a French observer who remarked that in cases where the *juge d'instruction* reaches the conclusion that no prosecution should be brought, it is usually with a tinge of regret that he signs the necessary documents. European experience also suggests that political interests are often involved in charges of crime and that it is desirable in order to prevent abuse that every fact bearing on guilt be tried in courts open to the public.

But publicity is not of itself a guarantee against the abuse of legal procedures. The public trials of alleged traitors that nearly always follow violent revolutions are a sufficient testimonial to this fact. What is essential is that the accused have at his side throughout a skilled lawyer, pledged to see that his rights are protected. When the matter comes for final trial in court, the only participation accorded to the accused in that trial lies in the opportunity to present proofs and reasoned arguments on his behalf. This opportunity cannot be meaningful unless the accused is represented by a professional advocate. If he is denied this representation the processes of public trial become suspect and tainted. It is for this reason that I say that the integrity of society itself demands that the accused be represented by counsel. If he is plainly guilty this representation may become in a sense symbolic.

But the symbolism is of vital importance. It marks society's determination to keep unsoiled and beyond suspicion the procedures by which men are condemned for a violation of its laws.

The lawyer appearing on behalf of an accused person is not present in court merely to represent his client. He represents a vital interest of society itself, he plays an essential role in one of the fundamental processes of an ordered community. The rules that govern his conduct make this clear.

It is a fundamental principle of the lawyer's canons of ethics that he may not state to the judge or jury that he personally believes in the innocence of his client. He may say, for example, "I submit that the evidence fails to establish the guilt of my client." But he may not say, "I personally know my client to be innocent," just as he may not be asked by the judge or jury whether he believes his client to be guilty.

These rules concerning the lawyer's conduct in court are not only important in themselves, but also for the spirit that lies back of them. They make it clear that the lawyer is present, not as an individual with all of his likes and dislikes, beliefs and disbeliefs, but as one who plays an important role in the process of social decision. At no time is the lawyer a mere agent of his client. If he disapproves of his client's conduct during the trial, he may—though this is often a painfully difficult decision—withdraw from the case. Obviously, he may not participate in the fabrication of testimony, just as he may not, to free his client, cast suspicion on innocent persons.

So important is the defense lawyer's role that where the accused cannot find a lawyer who will represent him, or cannot afford to pay for a lawyer, it is the practice for the court to appoint a lawyer to represent him. Under our constitutional system a failure of the court to do this may render a conviction against the accused invalid. Notwithstanding these formal guarantees, our American practice at present leaves much room for improvement. The public service of defending a man, who would otherwise be without a lawyer, is usually poorly paid, and busy and able lawyers are often loath to take on the burdens of such an assignment. There is, however, an active movement now to improve this situation and to provide adequately paid and competent counsel for every person accused of serious crime.

I have so far emphasized chiefly the role of the lawyer in the defense of criminal cases. But the need for an adversary presentation, with both sides vigorously upheld, is also present in civil suits. For one thing, there is an element of social condemnation in almost all adverse legal judgments, so that the considerations that apply to criminal cases are also relevant to civil controversies. To be found guilty of negligent driving or of breaking a contract does not carry the stigma of a criminal conviction, but in these cases, too, society must be concerned that even the qualified condemnation implied in an adverse civil judgment should not be visited on one who has not had a chance to present his case fully.

More important in complicated controversies is the contribution that an adversary presentation makes to a properly grounded decision, a decision that takes account of all the facts and relevant rules. In a statement issued recently by a committee of the American Bar Association, it was pointed out how, in the absence of an adversary presentation, there is a strong tendency by any deciding official to reach a conclusion at an early stage and to adhere to that conclusion in the face of conflicting considerations later developed. In the language of the committee:

"What generally occurs in practice is that at some early point a familiar pattern will seem to emerge from the evidence; an accustomed label is waiting for the case and, without waiting further proofs, this label is promptly assigned to it. It is a mistake to suppose that this premature cataloguing must necessarily result from impatience, prejudice or mental sloth. Often it proceeds from a very understandable desire to bring the hearing into some order and coherence, for without some tentative theory of the case there is no standard of relevance by which testimony may be measured. But what starts as a preliminary diagnosis designed to direct the inquiry tends, quickly and imperceptibly, to become a fixed conclusion, as all that confirms the diagnosis makes a strong imprint on the mind, while all that runs counter to it is received with diverted attention.

"An adversary presentation seems the only effective means for combating this natural human tendency to judge too swiftly in terms of the familiar that which is not yet fully known. The arguments of counsel hold the case, as it were, in suspension between two opposing interpretations of it. While the proper classification of the case is thus kept unresolved, there is time to explore all of its peculiarities and nuances." * * *

I do not have time to explore all the implications of the adversary system, nor to compare the different ways in which that system and its underlying philosophy find expression in the laws of different countries. I should like, however, to record my discontent with the implications sometimes drawn from the adversary system in my own country. One of these lies in the notion that a judge should throughout the trial remain passive; somewhat like a well-behaved child, he speaks only when spoken to. His role is thought of as being that of an umpire who is stirred to action only when he must resolve a dispute that arises between the contending lawyers. This notion is, I believe, based on a profound mistake. The essence of the adversary system is that each side is accorded a participation in the decision that is reached, a participation that takes the form of presenting proofs and arguments. If that participation is to be meaningful it must take place within an orderly frame, and it is the duty of the judge to see to it that the trial does not degenerate into a disorderly contest in which the essential issues are lost from view. Furthermore, when the party is given through his attorney an opportunity to present arguments, this opportunity loses its value if argument has to be directed into a vacuum. To argue his case effectively, the lawyer must have some idea of what is going on inside the judge's mind. A more active participation by the judge—assuming it stops short of a prejudgment of the case itself—can therefore enhance the meaning and effectiveness of an adversary presentation. * * *

Questions

1. Professor Fuller's brilliant talk was first published in 1961. It was one of the few efforts, up until quite recently, to address in any detail the theory underlying the adversary system. Why were the premises of the adversarial model so infrequently discussed before the last 15 or 20 years?

2. How can Professor Fuller justify an active role for the judge while arguing so vigorously for judicial neutrality? Is there a conflict here that Fuller fails to appreciate?

3. If an ongoing dialogue between judge and counsel is appropriate, shouldn't jurors be included in the conversations when they sit as fact finders? How, if at all, can this be accomplished?

4. Do you agree with Professor Fuller's suggestion that the inquisitorial fact finder is likely because of personal bias to "prematurely catalogue" and therefore unfairly judge cases before her? It should be noted that there is empirical evidence that adversarial presentation tends to counteract decision maker bias that might otherwise affect judgment. See Thibaut and Walker, *Procedural Justice* 41–52 (1975).

SECTION C. CRITICISMS OF THE ADVERSARY SYSTEM

ROSCOE POUND—THE CAUSES OF POPULAR DISSATISFACTION WITH THE ADMINISTRATION OF JUSTICE

29 A.B.A. Reports 395, 404–407, 417 (1917).

[In 1906 Dean Roscoe Pound delivered a speech before the American Bar Association that shocked the organized bar. He challenged lawyers' smug and complacent belief in the excellence of the legal system and suggested that there was much with which to be dissatisfied. His speech has served as a manifesto for those championing reform of the adversarial mechanism. What follows is an excerpt from Pound's remarks that focuses on the ills of the adversarial method.]

A * * * potent source of irritation [with the justice system] lies in our American exaggerations of the common law contentious procedure. The sporting theory of justice, the "instinct of giving the game fair play," as Professor Wigmore has put it, is so rooted in the profession in America that most of us take it for a fundamental legal tenet. But it is probably only a survival of the days when a lawsuit was a fight between two clans * * *. So far from being a fundamental fact of jurisprudence, it is peculiar to Anglo–American law; and it has been strongly curbed in modern English practice. With us, it is not merely in full acceptance, it has been developed and its collateral possibilities have been cultivated to the furthest extent. Hence in America we take it as a matter of course that a judge should be a mere umpire, to pass upon objections and hold counsel to the rules of the game, and that the parties should fight out their own game in their own way without judicial interference. We resent such interference as unfair, even when in the interests of justice. The idea that procedure must of necessity be wholly contentious disfigures our judicial administration at every point. It leads the most conscientious judge to feel that he is merely to decide the contest, as counsel present it, according to the rules of the game, not to search independently for truth and justice. It leads counsel to forget that they are officers of the court and to deal with the rules of law and procedure exactly as the professional foot ball coach with the rules of the sport. It leads to exertion to "get error into the record" rather than to dispose of the controversy finally and upon its merits. It turns witnesses, and especially expert witnesses, into partisans pure and simple. It leads to sensational cross-examinations "to affect credit," which have made the witness stand "the slaughter house of reputations." It prevents the trial court from restraining the bullying of witnesses and creates a general dislike, if not fear, of the witness function which impairs the administration of justice. * * * The inquiry is not, What do substantive law and justice require? Instead, the inquiry is, Have the rules of the game been carried out strictly? If any material infraction is discovered, just as the foot ball rules put back the offending team five or ten or fifteen yards, as the case may be, our sporting theory of justice awards new trials, or reverses judgments, or sustains demurrers in the interest of regular play.

The effect of our exaggerated contentious procedure is not only to irritate parties, witnesses and jurors in particular cases, but to give to the whole community a false notion of the purpose and end of law. Hence comes, in large measure, the modern American race to beat the law. If the law is a mere game, neither the players who take part in it nor the public who witness it can be expected to yield to its spirit when their interests are served by evading it. And this is doubly true in a time which requires all institutions to be economically efficient and socially useful. We need not wonder that one part of the community strain their oaths in the jury box and find verdicts against unpopular litigants in the teeth of law and evidence, while another part retain lawyers by the year to advise how to evade what to them are unintelligent and unreasonable restrictions upon necessary modes of doing business. Thus the courts, instituted to administer justice according to law, are made agents or abettors of lawlessness. * * *

With law schools that are rivaling the achievements of Bologna and of Bourges to promote scientific study of the law; with active Bar Associations in every state to revive professional feeling and throw off the yoke of commercialism; with the passing of the doctrine that politics, too, is a mere game to be played for its own sake, we may look forward confidently to deliverance from the sporting theory of justice; we may look forward to a near future when our courts will be swift and certain agents of justice, whose decisions will be acquiesced in and respected by all.

Questions

1. Harry Kalven has said that Pound's speech is "a monument to a certain legal attitude. It has an aura of empiricism but displays literally no interest in finding out whether its topic as defined has any reality, or whether its diagnosis has any validity." Kalven, *The Quest for the Middle Range: Empirical Inquiry and Legal Policy,* in Law in a Changing America 60–61 (Hazard ed. 1968). Do you agree?

2. Should the courts' highest priority be to perform in a "swift and certain" manner? What countervailing concerns are there? How ought the balance between these concerns be struck?

3. From Pound's perspective who ought to be ceded more power in the adjudicatory process? What are the risks inherent in the sort of redistribution of power he urges?

MARVIN FRANKEL—PARTISAN JUSTICE

10–20 (1980).

Copyright © 1980 by Marvin E. Frankel. Reprinted by permission of Hill and Wang, a division of Farrar, Straus and Giroux, Inc.

[One of the most outspoken modern critics of the adversary system is former federal district court judge Marvin Frankel. His views have had a serious impact upon the debate about the adversary system. He was one of those instrumental in introducing a number of anti-adversarial reforms into the recently promulgated American Bar Association Model Rules of Professional Conduct. Judge Frankel's book, *Partisan Justice,* provides an extended critique of adversarial methods.]

* * *

In the United States of America, declaring its independence in the very year of Adam Smith's *Wealth of Nations,* the dominant faith has been in the ultimate miracle of social harmony through the free play of competitive greed and self-interest. We have built a society magnificent in notable ways, while strewing mountains of human and material wreckage along the way, on the doctrine Mr. Smith taught—that loosing the individual's "private interests and passions" would produce results "most agreeable to the interest of the whole society. . . ." Until very recently, there has been a broad consensus favoring individualism, classically rugged in style, over governmental control, remembered and feared as deadening, oppressive, and sterile.

That familiar philosophy has informed our legal system generally, including our specific model for the adjudication of legal disputes. In the law courts as in the marketplace, we have fashioned a regime of individual competitive struggle, freeing the contestants to war against each other, decreeing in large measure that the state or its judicial representative should serve as passive umpire to keep the conflict within broad limits. Thinking *a priori*, perhaps from our habits of child rearing or other family ways, one might imagine arrangements in which the first steps toward dispute settlement would be to stop the fray, quiet the combatants, and then inquire about the rights and wrongs of the matter. Whatever might be imagined, we don't do that in our courts. Instead, we continue the battle, transferring it to the public arena and transmuting its forms. As was said by an engaging lawyer-writer (with much of whose views this writer disagrees), "We set the parties fighting." We expect that they will equip themselves with professional fighters—lawyers—to wield the special weapons, gather the added ammunition, and marshal the forces for what will be, if it goes all the way, an all-or-nothing contest. Not infrequently, the lawyers, knowing the desperate stakes and the uncertainties, are useful as detached voices for peace, able to cool emotions and promote compromise. It is by no means unfamiliar, however, that the lawyers themselves catch the hostile spirit, become personally embroiled, and contribute fuel rather than coolth.

It seems probable on balance that the lawyers, like others actually on the battlefield, know the virtues of peace and seek resolutions short of total victory or defeat. Certainly that is the statistically common outcome * * *. Nevertheless, the central theory is what a great jurist, Judge Jerome Frank, called a "fight theory," what a famous law dean (Roscoe Pound) in 1906, like others before that, called a "sporting theory," and what all recognize, by any name, as a grimly combative proposition.

Our leading religions may teach about loving our neighbors, about the expectancies of the meek, and about forbearance, gentleness, and other fond virtues. In our arena for secular justice, however, we enthrone combat as a paramount good. The "adversary system," as we call it, is not merely borne as a supposedly necessary evil. It is cherished as an ideal of constitutional proportions, not only because it embodies the fundamental right to be heard, but because it is thought (often) to be the best assurance of truth and sound results. Decisions of the Supreme Court give repeated voice to this concept. We are taught to presume as a vital premise the belief that "partisan advocacy on both sides," according to rules often countenancing partial truths and concealment, will best assure the discovery of truth in the end. We are not so much as slightly rocked in this assumption by the fact that other seekers after truth have not emulated us. Ours is, after all, a special world of special cases. Even we who made and run that world would fear for our lives if physicians, disagreeing about the cause of our chest pains, sought to resolve the issue by our forms of interrogation, badgering, and other forensics. But for the defendant whose life is at stake— and for the public concerned whether the defendant is a homicidal menace—this is thought to be the most perfect form of inquiry. We live, at any rate, as if we believe this.

Like any sweeping proposition, the claim that our adversary process is best for truth seeking has qualifications and limits recognized by its staunchest proponents. While it would not be essential, we have again the high authority of Supreme Court pronouncements noting that lawyers in the process are often expected, with all propriety, to help block or conceal rather than pursue the truth. These endeavors are commonly justified in the service of interests that outweigh truth finding—interests in privacy, personal dignity, security, autonomy, and other cherished values. The problem of how to weigh the competing values is, obviously, at the heart of the concerns to be addressed in these chapters. Nobody doubts that there are ends of diverse kinds, at diverse times and places, more worthy than the accurate discovery or statement of facts; that there are even occasions, not easily defined with unanimity, when a lie is to be preferred. One way to state the thesis of this book is to say, recognizing the complex relatives of life, that the American version of the adversary process places too low a value on truth telling; that we have allowed ourselves too often to sacrifice truth to other values that are inferior, or even illusory. But the elaboration of the position is best postponed until after we have described how the process works and how its actors perform.

The quality of private initiative and private control is, in its degree, the hallmark of the American judicial process. While the administration of justice is designated as the public's business and the decision-makers are public people (whether full-time judges or the lay judges who sit in jury boxes), the process is initiated, shaped, and managed by the private contestants in civil matters and by the government and nongovernment lawyer-contestants in criminal matters. The deciders, though commissioned to discover the truth, are passive recipients, not active explorers. They take what they are given. They consider the questions raised by counsel, rarely any others. Issues not joined are not resolved, though they might have led to wiser, fairer dispositions than those reached. The parties, almost always the lawyers or those under their direction, investigate the facts, interview possible witnesses, consult potential experts to find opinions most agreeable to their causes, decide what will be told and what will not be told. The judges and jurors almost never make inquiries on their own, and are not staffed or otherwise equipped to do so. The reconstructions of the past to be given in the courtroom are likely to be the sharply divergent stories told by partisans, divergent from each other and from the actual events supposed to be portrayed. If history can never reproduce the past with total fidelity, one wonders often whether we could not miss by margins much narrower than those marked in courtrooms.

The relative work loads and shares of effective responsibility may be reflected in the comparative numbers of lawyers and judges in the United States as compared with other countries. Our rapidly swelling legal profession contains a much larger proportion of lawyers to judges than almost any other country in the world. To take some available figures, the ratio of practicing lawyers to judges in California is more than ten times that of West Germany or Sweden and eight times the similar figure for France, with similar contrasts probably available for most of the other countries we call civilized. The reason is simply that we leave more of the business of justice to lawyers, less to judges.

* * *

Taking the leading roles * * * American lawyers, with and for their clients, chart the stories their respective sides will tell—which witnesses will say what, what documents and other things will be offered as exhibits, what items that could be offered as evidence will not be. Each side is limited and affected throughout by the strategies and choices of the adversary. But the contest by its very nature is not one in which the objective of either side, or of both together, is to expose "the truth, the whole truth, and nothing but the truth."

That the quoted words, from the witness's oath, are not meant quite literally may be seen from more than one perspective. Consider the lawyer's major work of interviewing and "preparing" witnesses, including the client who plans to take the stand. It might be supposed that if the witness were expected simply to tell the relevant things he knew about the events or things in question, there would be no legitimate occasion for preparing him or her. That supposition would probably oversimplify, at least as any American lawyer sees the matter. In matters of any complexity, memories need to be refreshed, ordered, stimulated, all of which may involve perfectly legitimate forms of preparatory assistance. Papers and diaries may have to be reviewed. The proposed testimony may fairly be organized and tailored to eliminate matters that are irrelevant or inadmissible, and even to arrange that honest recollections are given with sufficient flow and verve to avoid some of the tedium that is at best inevitable in large doses during most trials.

Granting that sort of thing, every lawyer knows that the "preparing" of witnesses may embrace a multitude of other measures, including some ethical lapses believed to be more common than we would wish. The process is labeled archly in lawyer's slang as "horseshedding" the witness, a term that may be traced to utterly respectable origins in circuit-riding and otherwise horsy days but still rings a bit knowingly in today's ear. Whatever word is used to describe it, the process often extends beyond helping organize what the witness knows, and moves in the direction of helping the witness to know new things. At its starkest, the effort is called subornation of perjury, which is a crime, and which we are permitted to hope is rare. Somewhat less stark, short of criminality but still to be condemned, is the device of telling the client "the law" before eliciting the facts—i.e., telling the client what facts would constitute a successful claim or defense, and

only then asking the client what the facts happen perchance to be.
* * *

Moving away from palpably unsavory manifestations, we all know that the preparation of our witnesses is calculated, one way and another, to mock the solemn promise of the whole truth and nothing but. To be sure, reputable lawyers admonish their clients and witnesses to be truthful. At the same time, they often take infinite pains to prepare questions designed to make certain that the controlled flow of truth does not swell to an embarrassing flood. "Don't volunteer anything," the witnesses are cautioned. The concern is not that the volunteered contribution may be false. The concern is to avoid an excess of truth, where the spillover may prove hurtful to the case.

* * * It seems enough to say, with confidence, that our own style of witness preparation and direct examination is a major item of battle planning, not a step toward the revelation of objective truth.

Cross-examination is likewise, if sometimes more dramatically, among the partisan arts of courtroom conquest. It undoubtedly happens, and with some frequency, that an untruthful witness, or one who exaggerates or colors what he knows, is exposed by effective cross-examination. But the skillful cross-examiner, whose assignment is to win, not merely or necessarily to arrive at truth, will undertake much more. He or she will employ ancient and modern tricks to make a truthful witness look like a liar. As on direct examination, the cross-examiner will attempt to stop short of complete narratives, the test of high art being to know the stopping point most likely to discomfit the witness and score points for the cross-examiner's side, not only without regard for the whole truth, but commonly through a triumphant perversion in the form of a partial truth. Lawyers' texts on cross-examination teach the classic wisdom of successful veterans concerning the disaster of asking one question too many on cross; that blundering next question may give the entrapped witness a chance to *explain*, heaven forfend, to tell how it really was, not to be left looking as if it was some other, damaging way. The same texts teach comparable professional skills, like how to make it seem by not cross-examining that the witness should be deemed a liar, beneath scorn, or how to employ histrionic stunts of one sort or another to create illusions that the jury may be mesmerized into accepting as facts. The citizenry has probable reason to give thanks that lawyers, despite the extra endowments of ham leading many of us to law school, are rarely accomplished thespians, and that the stunting is not regularly successful. There is success enough, however, to temper the thanksgiving. And the purposes are in any case manifestly indifferent or hostile to truth telling.

The system rests, we must always remember, on the assumption that we can accurately re-create the facts so that our rules of law, democratically evolved, will work just results. If the rule is that the signer of the note must pay, it works acceptably only if we correctly identify the signer. If we fail to make the identification, or, worse yet, falsely identify one who really did not sign, the result will be an injustice. It is no answer that some of our laws are no good. Nobody who thinks the society good enough to preserve, and improve, argues seriously that the cure for bad laws is feckless decisions about facts.

The simple point to be stressed, here and throughout, is that many of us trained in the learned profession of the law spend much of our time subverting the law by blocking the way to the truth. The subversion is not for the most part viewed as a pathology; rather, if somewhat paradoxically, it follows from the assigned roles of counsel in the very system of law which thus finds its purposes thwarted.

* * * During the last half century or so, much has been done through rules of "discovery" to cut down on concealment and surprises at trial. The idea is to allow demands for information before trial and to require responses from the adverse party. The device has on the whole worked substantial improvements. Predictably, however, it has been turned—and twisted—to adversary uses. Lawyers react characteristically by demanding as much as possible and giving as little as possible. What is not demanded is not given. It remains as true as ever that if a lawyer fails to ask the right question, the adversary will cheerfully refrain from disclosing what might be vital or decisive information. The discovery process itself, with rules that frequently are (or are made to be) intricate and abstruse, becomes the occasion for expensive contests, producing libraries full of opinions. * * *

The key point at every stage, which will bear recalling from time to time, is that the single uniformity is always adversariness. There are other goods, but the greatest is winning. There are other evils, but scarcely any worse than losing. Every step of the process, and any attempt to reform it, must be viewed in this light until or unless the adversary ethic comes to be changed or subordinated. * * *

Because the route of a lawsuit is marked by a running battle all the way, the outcome is nothing like the assuredly right result imagined in our dream that "justice will out." In that dream, neither eloquence nor lawyers' techniques nor cunning has much place. The person who is "right" should win. But that is very far from assured in the kind of contest we've been considering. Where skill and trickery are so much involved, it must inevitably happen that the respective qualities of the professional champions will make a decisive difference. Where sheer power and endurance may count, the relative resources of clients become vital. Describing the tendency of the enterprise as the major forces propel it, two students of the American legal system were led to conclude: "In an ideal adversary system, the less skillful antagonist is expected to lose, which under the laissez-faire notion is the proper outcome."

If that is, fortunately, an exaggeration, it describes a probability high and uncertain enough to be harrowing. One of the nation's greatest judges, Learned Hand, paid grim tribute to the uncertainty in a famous utterance: "I must say that, as a litigant, I should dread a lawsuit beyond almost anything else short of sickness and of death."

* * *

[I]t is worth having a sense of the gravity of the problem beyond the occasional alarms judges may sound. The scale and intensity of adversary legal proceedings, with their attendant risks and uncertainties, have brought us to a pass in which the "American way" in court survives at all by virtue of being used only in truncated and abbreviated forms. While Americans continue to litigate on a grand scale, full-scale lawsuits become increasingly impossible on economic grounds for all but the rich fighting over big stakes. The overwhelming majority of lawsuits are settled long before verdict or contested judgment.

The situation in the criminal courts is more thoroughly appalling. We pride ourselves on enlightened procedures. But the actual operation of the criminal-justice process is far from an occasion for pride. Our metropolitan courts sag under the pressure of enormous dockets. Proponents of law and order chafe against refined protections for defendants. Opposed voices call attention to the thousands of unbailed defendants in foul jails waiting too long, while they are presumed innocent, for their cases to be tried. All in all, the full-scale criminal trial becomes, as a noted scholar said, a species of "obstacle course"—"a struggle from start to finish." The bulk of criminal trial lawyers, on both sides, spend the bulk of their time and energies avoiding trials in the bulk of their cases. The overwhelming majority of prosecutions end with guilty pleas, commonly "bargained" pleas, as a result of which the charge and, most importantly, the potential sentence are reduced.

* * *

Both sides, in a word, have compelling reasons for their propensity to avoid trials in most cases. This is a point to be remembered when we are being immodest, on Law Day and other available times, about the superiority of the American system. The centerpiece of that system, the jury trial, amounts in practice to a carefully husbanded ornament, displayed on only a small fraction of its possible occasions. The effort to use it more would clog the machinery beyond management. * * *

Questions

1. Compare Judge Frankel's views about "truth" with those of Professors Saltzburg and Uviller reproduced below beginning at page 67. Who has the better of the argument?

JOHN LANGBEIN—THE GERMAN ADVANTAGE IN CIVIL PROCEDURE

52 U.Chi.L.Rev. 823, 823–30, 833–49, 853–55 (1985).
Reprinted by permission of the publisher, copyright © 1985.
University of Chicago Law Review.

[Professor John Langbein has utilized the tools of legal history and comparative law to criticize the adversary process. His work has ranged from a study of Britain's Old Bailey criminal court in the seventeenth century to modern German adjudicatory procedure. In the present article he contrasts American and German civil procedure and forcefully argues for the superiority of the latter.]

Our lawyer-dominated system of civil procedure has often been criticized both for its incentives to distort evidence and for the expense and complexity of its modes of discovery and trial. The shortcomings inhere in a system that leaves to partisans the work of gathering and producing the factual material upon which adjudication depends.

We have comforted ourselves with the thought that a lawyerless system would be worse. The excesses of American adversary justice would seem to pale by comparison with a literally nonadversarial system—one in which litigants would be remitted to faceless bureaucratic adjudicators and denied the safeguards that flow from lawyerly intermediation.

The German advantage. The main theme of this article is drawn from Continental civil procedure, exemplified for me by the system that I know reasonably well, the West German. My theme is that, by assigning judges rather than lawyers to investigate the facts, the Germans avoid the most troublesome aspects of our practice. But I shall emphasize that the familiar contrast between our adversarial procedure and the supposedly nonadversarial procedure of the Continental tradition has been grossly overdrawn.

To be sure, since the greater responsibility of the bench for fact-gathering is what distinguishes the Continental tradition, a necessary (and welcome) correlative is that counsel's role in eliciting evidence is greatly restricted. Apart from fact-gathering, however, the lawyers for the parties play major and broadly comparable roles in both the German and American systems. Both are adversary systems of civil procedure. There as here, the lawyers advance partisan positions from first pleadings to final arguments. German litigators suggest legal theories and lines of factual inquiry, they superintend and supplement judicial examination of witnesses, they urge inferences from fact, they discuss and distinguish precedent, they interpret statutes, and they formulate views of the law that further the interests of their clients. I shall urge that German experience shows that we would do better if we were greatly to restrict the adversaries' role in fact-gathering. * * *

WITNESSES

Adversary control of fact-gathering in our procedure entails a high level of conflict between partisan advantage and orderly disclosure of the relevant information. Marvin Frankel put this point crisply when he said that "it is the rare case in which either side yearns to have the witnesses, or anyone, give *the whole truth.*"

If we had deliberately set out to find a means of impairing the reliability of witness testimony, we could not have done much better than the existing system of having partisans prepare witnesses in advance of trial and examine and cross-examine them at trial. Jerome Frank described the problem a generation ago:

> [The witness] often detects what the lawyer hopes to prove at the trial. If the witness desires to have the lawyer's client win the case, he will often, unconsciously, mold his story accordingly. Telling and re-telling it to the lawyer, he will honestly believe that his story, as he narrates it in court, is true, although it importantly deviates from what he originally believed.

Thus, said Frank, "the partisan nature of trials tends to make partisans of the witnesses."

Cross-examination at trial—our only substantial safeguard against this systematic bias in the testimony that reaches our courts—is a frail and fitful palliative. Cross-examination is too often ineffective to undo the consequences of skillful coaching. Further, because cross-examination allows so much latitude for bullying and other truth-defeating stratagems, it is frequently the source of fresh distortion when brought to bear against truthful testimony. As a leading litigator boasted recently in an ABA publication: "By a carefully planned and executed cross-examination, I can raise at least a slight question about the accuracy of [an adverse] witness's story, or question his motives or impartiality." [32] * * *

EXPERTS

 * * * At the American trial bar, those of us who serve as expert witnesses are known as "saxophones." This is a revealing term, as slang often is. The idea is that the lawyer plays the tune, manipulating the expert as though the expert were a musical instrument on which the lawyer sounds the desired notes. I sometimes serve as an expert in trust and pension cases, and I have experienced the subtle pressures to join the team—to shade one's views, to conceal doubt, to overstate nuance, to downplay weak aspects of the case that one has been hired to bolster. Nobody likes to disappoint a patron; and beyond this psychological pressure is the financial inducement. Money changes hands upon the rendering of expertise, but the expert can run his meter only so long as his patron litigator likes the tune. Opposing counsel undertakes a similar exercise, hiring and schooling another expert to parrot the contrary position. The result is our familiar battle of opposing experts. The more measured and impartial an expert is, the less likely he is to be used by either side.

At trial, the battle of experts tends to baffle the trier, especially in jury courts. If the experts do not cancel each other out, the advantage is likely to be with the expert whose forensic skills are the more enticing. The system invites abusive cross-examination. Since each expert is party-selected and party-paid, he is vulnerable to attack on credibility regardless of the merits of his testimony. * * *

32. Hanley, *Working the Witness Puzzle,* Litigation, Winter 1977, at 8, 10.

[T]he systematic incentive in our procedure to distort expertise leads to a systematic distrust and devaluation of expertise. Short of forbidding the use of experts altogether, we probably could not have designed a procedure better suited to minimize the influence of expertise. * * *

SHORTCOMINGS OF ADVERSARY THEORY

The case against adversary domination of fact-gathering is so compelling that we have cause to wonder why our system tolerates it. Because there is nothing to be said in support of coached witnesses, and very little to be said in favor of litigation-biased experts, defenders of the American status quo are left to argue that the advantages of our adversary procedure counterbalance these grievous, truth-defeating distortions. "You have to take the bad with the good; if you want adversary safeguards, you are stuck with adversary excesses."

The false conflict. This all-or-nothing argument overlooks the fundamental distinction between fact-gathering and the rest of civil litigation. Outside the realm of fact-gathering, German civil procedure is about as adversarial as our own. Both systems welcome the lawyerly contribution to identifying legal issues and sharpening legal analysis. German civil procedure is materially less adversarial than our own only in the fact-gathering function, where partisanship has such potential to pollute the sources of truth.

Accordingly, the proper question is not whether to have lawyers, but how to use them; not whether to have an adversarial component to civil procedure, but how to prevent adversarial excesses. If we were to incorporate the essential lesson of the German system in our own procedure, we would still have a strongly adversarial civil procedure. We would not, however, have coached witnesses and litigation-biased experts.

The confusion with criminal procedure. Much of the rhetoric celebrating unrestrained adversary domination of judicial proceedings stems from the criminal process, where quite different policies are at work. It has been argued that partisan fact-gathering is appropriate to the special values of criminal procedure—the presumption of innocence, the beyond-reasonable-doubt standard of proof, and the privilege against self-incrimination.[68] Bestowing upon the criminal accused the right to conduct his own fact-gathering, despite the risk that he may misuse this power in truth-defeating ways, can be understood as one more way of adjusting the scales to protect the accused. "The specter of capital punishment and the often barbaric conditions of our penal institutions in the past and present, as well as the unique stigma of conviction of a crime, have had a profound impact upon the protections accorded the defendant and the freedom of action accorded the defense lawyer in a criminal case." While I happen to disagree that adversary

68. See, e.g., Garner v. United States, 424 U.S. 648, 655, 96 S.Ct. 1178, 1182, 47 L.Ed.2d 370 (1976), asserting that "the preservation of an adversary system of criminal justice" is "the fundamental purpose of the Fifth Amendment."

procedure is a particularly effective way to implement our concern for safeguard in the criminal process, my present point is simply that regardless of right or wrong, that concern is absent in the world of civil procedure. In civil lawsuits we are not trying systematically to err in favor of one class of litigants.

Equality of representation. The German system gives us a good perspective on another great defect of adversary theory, the problem that the Germans call "Waffenungleichheit"—literally, inequality of weapons, or in this instance, inequality of counsel. In a fair fight the pugilists must be well matched. You cannot send me into a ring with Muhammed Ali if you expect a fair fight. The simple truth is that very little in our adversary system is designed to match combatants of comparable prowess, even though adversarial prowess is a main factor affecting the outcome of litigation. Adversary theory thus presupposes a condition that adversary practice achieves only indifferently. It is a rare litigator in the United States who has not witnessed the spectacle of a bumbling adversary whose poor discovery work or inability to present evidence at trial caused his client to lose a case that should have been won. Disparity in the quality of legal representation can make a difference in Germany, too, but the active role of the judge places major limits on the extent of the injury that bad lawyering can work on a litigant. In German procedure both parties get the same fact-gatherer—the judge. ∗ ∗ ∗

Prejudgment. Perhaps the most influential justification for adversary domination of fact-gathering has been an argument put forward by Lon Fuller: Nonadversarial procedure risks prejudgment—that is, prematurity in judgment. Fuller worried that the judge would make up his mind too soon.

> What generally occurs in practice is that at some early point a familiar pattern will seem to emerge from the evidence; an accustomed label is waiting for the case and, without awaiting further proofs, this label is promptly assigned to it. ∗ ∗ ∗

> An adversary presentation seems the only effective means for combatting this natural human tendency to judge too swiftly in terms of the familiar that which is not yet fully known. The arguments of counsel hold the case, as it were, in suspension between two opposing interpretations of it. While the proper classification of the case is thus kept unresolved, there is time to explore all of its peculiarities and nuances.

This passage obtains much of its force from the all-or-nothing contrast that so misdescribes German civil procedure. In a system like the German, which combines judicial fact-gathering with vigorous and continuing adversarial efforts in nominating lines of factual inquiry and analyzing factual and legal issues, the adversaries perform just the role that Fuller lauds, helping hold the decision in suspension while issues are framed and facts explored.

In German procedure counsel oversees and has means to prompt a flagging judicial inquiry; but quite apart from that protection, is it really true that a "familiar pattern" would otherwise beguile the judge into investigating too sparingly? If so, it seems odd that this asserted "natural human tendency" towards premature judgment does not show up in ordinary business and personal decision-making, whose patterns of inquiry resemble the fact-gathering process in German civil procedure. Since the decision-maker does his own investigating in most of life's decisions, it seems odd to despair of prematurity only when that normal mode of decision-making is found to operate in a courtroom. Accordingly, I think that Fuller overstates the danger of prematurity that inheres in allowing the decision-maker to conduct the fact-gathering; but to the extent that the danger is real, German civil procedure applies just the adversarial remedy that Fuller recommends.

Depth. Fuller's concern about prematurity shades into a different issue: how to achieve appropriate levels of depth in fact-gathering. Extra investment in search can almost always turn up further proofs that would be at least tenuously related to the case. Adversary domination of fact-gathering privatizes the decision about what level of resources to invest in the case. The litigants who are directly interested in the outcome decide how much to spend on search. In German procedure, by contrast, these partisan calculations of self-interest are subordinated, for a variety of reasons. The initiative in fact-gathering is shared with the judge; and the German system of reckoning and allocating the costs of litigation is less sensitive to the cost of incremental investigative steps than in our system where each side pays for the proofs that it orders. On the other hand, the German judge cannot refuse to investigate party-nominated proofs without reason, and this measure of party control greatly narrows the difference between the two systems.

Writing in 1958, Kaplan and his co-authors recorded their "impression" that German civil "proceedings do not in practice serve as an engine of discovery comparable in strength to the modern American methods," in part because German courts are hostile to fishing. Further, the authors worried that the technique of recording witness testimony in succinct summaries could bleach out "[f]ine factual differentiations." They found German procedure to be "far less preoccupied than the American with minute investigation of factual detail of reliability of individual witnesses."

· Defenders of the American status quo may take too much comfort from these observations. A main virtue of German civil procedure, we recall, is that the principle of judicial control of sequence works to confine the scope of fact-gathering to those avenues of inquiry deemed most likely to resolve the case. Fact-gathering occurs when the unfolding logic of the case dictates that investigation of particular issues is needed. That practice does indeed contrast markedly with the inclination of American litigators "to leave no stone unturned, provided, of course, they can charge by the stone." [81] The primary reason that German courts do less fact-gathering than American lawyers is that the Germans eliminate the waste. Likewise, when American observers notice that there is less harrying of witnesses with "those elaborate testings of credibility familiar to American courtrooms," I incline to think that the balance of advantage rests with the Germans, since so much of what passes for cross-examination in our procedure is deliberately truth-defeating. * * *

JUDICIAL INCENTIVES

Viewed comparatively from the Anglo–American perspective, the greater authority of the German judge over fact-gathering comes at the expense of the lawyers for the parties. Adversary influence on fact-gathering is deliberately restrained. Furthermore, in routine civil procedure, German judges do not share power with jurors. There is no civil jury.

Because German procedure places upon the judge the responsibility for fact-gathering, the danger arises that the job will not be done well. The American system of partisan fact-gathering has the virtue of its vices: It aligns responsibility with incentive. Each side gathers and presents proofs according to its own calculation of self-interest. This privatization is an undoubted safeguard against official sloth. After all, who among us has not been treated shabbily by some lazy bureaucrat in a government department? And who would want to have that ugly character in charge of one's lawsuit?

The answer to that concern in the German tradition is straightforward: The judicial career must be designed in a fashion that creates incentives for diligence and excellence. The idea is to attract very able people to the bench, and to make their path of career advancement congruent with the legitimate interests of the litigants.

The career judiciary. The distinguishing attribute of the bench in Germany (and virtually everywhere else in Europe) is that the profession of judging is separate from the profession of lawyering. Save in exceptional circumstances, the judge is not an ex-lawyer like his Anglo-American counterpart. Rather, he begins his professional career as a judge. * * *

American contrasts. If I were put to the choice of civil litigation under the German procedure that I have been praising in this article or under the American procedure that I have been criticizing, I might have qualms about choosing the German. The likely venue of a lawsuit of mine would be the state court in Cook County, Illinois, and I must admit that I distrust the bench of that court. The judges are selected by a process in which the criterion of professional competence is at best an incidental value. Further, while decent people do reach the Cook County bench in surprising numbers, events have shown that some of

81. Rhode, *Ethical Perspectives on Legal Practice,* 37 Stan.L.Rev. 589, 635 (1985).

their colleagues are crooks. If my lawsuit may fall into the hands of a dullard or a thug, I become queasy about increasing his authority over the proceedings.

German-style judicial responsibility for fact-gathering cannot be lodged with the Greylord judiciary. Remodeling of civil procedure is intimately connected to improvement in the selection of judges. I do not believe that we would have to institute a German-style career judiciary in order to reform American civil procedure along German lines, although I do think that Judge Frankel was right to "question whether we are wise" to disdain the Continental model, and to "wonder now whether we might benefit from some admixture of such [career judges] to leaven or test our trial benches of elderly lawyers." The difference in quality between the state and federal trial benches in places like Cook County is sufficient to remind us that measures far short of adopting the Continental career judiciary can bring about material improvement.

Americans will long remain uncomfortable at the prospect of a more bureaucratic judiciary. We have not had good experience attracting and controlling an able career bureaucracy in the higher realms of public administration, although we have scarcely tried. Some observers point to that elusive construct, national character. Europeans in general and Germans in particular are thought to be more respectful of authority, hence better disposed toward the more bureaucratic mode of justice that judicialized fact-gathering entails.

Cultural differences surely do explain something of why institutional and procedural differences arise in different legal systems. The important question for present purposes is what weight to attach to this factor, and my answer is, "Not much." It is all too easy to allow the cry of "cultural differences" to become the universal apologetic that permanently sheathes the status quo against criticism based upon comparative example. Cultural differences that help explain the origins of superior procedures need not restrict their spread. If Americans were to resolve to officialize the fact-gathering process while preserving the political prominence of the higher bench, we would probably turn initially to some combination of judges, magistrates, and masters for getting the job done. Over time, we would strike a new balance between bench and bar, and between higher and lower judicial office. * * *

Questions

1. Might it not be said of Professor Langbein, as of Dean Pound, that he "displays literally no interest in finding out whether [his] topic as defined has any reality, or whether [his] diagnosis has any validity?" By what sorts of *empirical* data might his argument be strengthened?

2. Why have Americans throughout their history resisted the establishment of an inquiring judiciary armed with broad investigative powers?

3. Is there anything to be said on behalf of a process that systematically devalues the worth of expert testimony?

4. Is Langbein right sharply to distinguish between civil and criminal procedure? Isn't the goal of each identical, that is to impose liability on the basis of substantive legal principles?

SECTION D. REJOINDERS ON THE QUESTION OF TRUTH

STEPHEN SALTZBURG—LAWYERS, CLIENTS, AND THE ADVERSARY SYSTEM

37 Mercer L.Rev. 647, 650, 654–61 (1986).
Reprinted by permission of the publisher, copyright © 1986.
Mercer Law Review.

[In his recent article in the *Mercer Law Review,* Professor Saltzburg has attempted to answer some of the most frequently voiced criticisms of the adversary system. Here he considers the question of truth.]

THE SEARCH FOR TRUTH

[I]n both civil and criminal cases courts—even the nation's highest court—frequently utter bold statements to the effect that both civil and criminal trials are searches for truth.[12] Such statements, however, are often made in connection with doctrines that have little, if anything, to do with enhancing the quest for the truth,[13] and they misdescribe the purpose of trials. If the rules currently in effect do not require a lawyer to answer confidently "no" to the question whether a lawyer may attack a witness who he knows is telling the truth, then it must be clear that the legal profession does not now see trials as courts like to describe them—that is, as necessarily requiring a search for truth. The legal community prefers to invoke grand doctrines like 'search for truth' rather than to state with greater specificity the goals of the adversary system and rules governing lawyers' behavior. * * *

INEVITABLE IMPERFECTIONS

[T]hose who attack the adversary system as failing in a search for truth attack a straw man, the purple prose of appellate courts notwithstanding. The goal of the adversary system is to apply the substantive legal principles so that those who have rights may claim them and those who have liabilities must face them. This the adversary system endeavors to do, while simultaneously announcing that it is an imperfect process. The imperfection is reflected in the choice of burdens of

---

12. See, e.g., *United States v. Havens,* 446 U.S. 620, 626, 100 S.Ct. 1912, 1916, 64 L.Ed.2d 559 (1980) (analyzing precedents as having "stressed the importance of arriving at the truth in criminal trials").

13. A good example is *United States v. Havens,* 446 U.S. 620, 100 S.Ct. 1912, 64 L.Ed.2d 559 (1980). The Court limited the effect of the exclusionary rule used as a remedy for violations of the fourth amendment. Id. at 627–28. The rule itself has nothing to do with the truth.

persuasion. In all cases, civil and criminal, a chance exists that the wrong facts will be found or the facts will be erroneously evaluated. The system not only recognizes the possibility of error, but it also assigns the risk of error between opposing parties. The preponderance of the evidence burden of persuasion frequently used in civil cases assigns the risk almost evenly. It will favor the party who does not have the burden only when the case is so close that a decisionmaker cannot choose between the opponents. In criminal cases, the risk of error is borne largely by the state. Unless a decisionmaker believes beyond a reasonable doubt that a defendant is guilty, the state must lose.

TESTING THE SYSTEM

To test whether the American adversary system works well and to compare it to alternatives, it is necessary to find whether the system succeeds in vindicating rights and imposing liability in furtherance of substantive principles. The procedural system that is in force at any given time—in this instance, the adversary system—and the kinds of substantive laws that are enacted probably are intertwined. If the procedural system were different, the laws might be drafted to eliminate many factors that are 'subjective' and to emphasize factors that appear to be more 'objective.' If this is correct, reason exists to doubt whether anyone will ever be able to devise an experiment that will convincingly demonstrate whether the American adversary system is as effective in furthering substantive rules as it might be. One problem is that the results of the system cannot be measured against the 'true results' because they are unknown. Thus, evaluations of the current system have been and are likely to continue to be based on intuition and anecdotal reports by participants. Even if one could control the experiment, the interrelationship between substantive law and procedural rules makes it difficult to assess whether imperfections arise as a result of the procedures or the way in which the substantive rules are drafted.

The intuitive reason most often expressed for doubting the results of the adversarial process is that litigants do not desire the truth; they prefer victory to the truth and will systematically seek victory in derogation of the truth. Once the 'search for truth' is understood as a poor description of the system, the attack loses most of its force. Some explanation is required, however, since the point most often missed by those who mount the attack on the adversary system is that the goals of individual litigants and the goals of the system are different. This difference must be understood if the proper role of lawyers in the system is to be understood.

GOALS OF LITIGANTS AND GOALS OF THE SYSTEM

The assumption that litigants want to win has appeal because almost everyone involved in a contest prefers winning to losing. (If not, one can surrender.) The American adversary system not only recognizes the desire of litigants to win, but it actually relies on the desire to motivate litigants to produce evidence and to develop legal theories for consideration by the decisionmaker. At the same time, the system employs a variety of mechanisms to assure that the desire is controlled so that it does not detract from the decisionmaker's ability to apply substantive principles properly.

The American adversary process entrusts the decision whether to bring claims and to make defenses to the litigants who seek to claim substantive rights and defenses or to impose liability. The desire to win is the motivating consideration that prompts litigants to seek out, develop, and offer evidence and to bring relevant and persuasive legal doctrines and precedents to a decisionmaker's attention. In order to win, litigants have the motivation to gather the most persuasive evidence, put forth the best theories available to them, and develop evidence and theories that will enable them to respond to their adversaries. The result is that the decisionmaker hears the strongest argument that each litigant who is trying to win can muster to support a finding of fact or an evaluation of fact and the most devastating response each adversary can make to that argument.

This incentive system is similar, of course, to other free enterprise concepts that govern economic thinking. The notion is that people who stand to gain or lose from a transaction are likely to be motivated to act more effectively than those who are indifferent to the transaction.

ALTERNATIVE SYSTEMS

Americans could easily develop another system that would provide an investigator for every dispute that arose. The legal system could charge the investigator with doing as thorough an investigation as if a litigant were carrying out the investigation. The investigator would have no stake in the case, however. It is possible that such a system would work better than the current one. There is no way to know without trying it. The government could design a more elaborate system and assign two or three investigators to every dispute in an effort to decrease the likelihood that a mistake would be made. At some point, however, the investigators would make a decision concerning whether claims should be brought and whether defenses should be considered. The legal system would have to decide whether to give a litigant a voice in the decision. An affirmative decision that the litigant is to have a voice would mean that the desire to win will influence the litigant's participation. If the new system denies the litigant any voice in the decision, then it is doubtful that many litigants would prefer the new system to the current one. It is submitted that this alternative system would be less attractive than the current system.

Some might make the claim that at least the alternative system would eliminate advantages based on wealth or social position. That this would follow is not clear, however. In any system, those with resources at their command are likely to utilize their resources to place in the investigators' hands any favorable evidence that they can locate. As a general rule, the more articulate and educated a disputant is, the better able he is to communicate information. No procedural system is likely to remove all disadvantages associated with distributions of wealth, resources, or personal qualities and abilities.

INCENTIVES AND LIMITATIONS

Absent evidence demonstrating that the incentive system does not work, one may rely upon the system. Most writers who express concern about the system do not suggest that the incentives are inadequate. Rather, they assert that the incentives are too great—that is, the incentive to win distorts the process. Distortions exist, but the distortions are not endemic in the American adversary system.

A series of rules exists that govern the behavior of any party in a legal dispute. No one may lie under oath; lying is perjury. No one may induce another person to lie; this is subornation of perjury. No one may destroy evidence to keep it from a tribunal; this is obstruction of justice. Further, no one may bribe or threaten the decisionmaker; he is expected to be neutral. A court might require a litigant who discovers evidence to share it with another litigant; this is discovery. Evidence rules will apply evenhandedly to prevent any litigant from offering irrelevant or unduly prejudicial evidence. The list could go on and on.

The procedural rules that govern the way cases are litigated establish how those who are not concerned with any particular case (i.e., the lawmakers, rulemakers, and the public at large) believe a correct and fair result is most likely to be secured in all cases. Observers of the adversary process expect that the limitations imposed on the adversary system will channel the incentive to win so that it produces a just outcome between competing litigants.

An understanding of the adversary system must include a recognition of three things: the difference between the litigants' goals and the system's goals, the importance of the incentive effect of the desire to win, and the devices that are employed to assure that the incentive does not lead to misapplication of the substantive law. Once one abandons the 'search for truth' language in favor of a more accurate statement of the goals of the system, and Americans understand that the desire to win is neither wholly beneficial nor wholly detrimental to a process of proper application of substantive law, the adversary system appears to have much to commend it.

Some concerns about the adversary system are based on doubts of the capacity of juries to apply substantive law. Trial by jury in serious criminal cases is constitutionally required, and is guaranteed by federal and state constitutions in actions at law. Although the Author believes that the jury system in the United States is preferable to a system of trial by judge or a mixed panel of judges and lay persons, the adversary system requires only that there be a neutral and fair decisionmaker.

One who has no faith in juries may assume that the decisionmaker is a judge, a panel of judges, or a mixed panel without changing the premises of the adversary system.

Assuming that the litigants act according to society's highest expectations so that they produce the best evidence and theories for consideration by a competent decisionmaker, it would seem that every chance exists that the substantive law will be applied in an appropriate way. Decisionmakers will make errors, but these errors are inevitable. The adversary process would not appear to exacerbate the problems of dealing with uncertainty in examining and evaluating past events.

The key to understanding the adversary system is recognizing that adversaries, whether they are in court or bargaining together, will want to win. They may want to win in several different circumstances. They may want to win because they sincerely believe that the substantive principles support them. They might want to win even though they realize that both sides have support in facts and law but that their arguments are better on balance than their adversaries' arguments. They may want to win even though they know that they should lose. The last circumstance is most likely to produce improper behavior, since a person who wants to win when he should not may need to cheat to have a chance to win. If the adversary system works well, its rules should make winning difficult for the person who should lose. Making victory difficult for the person who should lose is the purpose of the rules governing the conduct of litigants and counsel. That purpose is the reason that these rules are so important in assuring that the parties who ought to prevail in the adversary contest actually do prevail.

IS THE CRIMINAL CASE UNIQUE?

Many writers who have expressed concern about the adversary system cite the criminal case as unique. Some writers find uniqueness in the role of the defense lawyer and assert that "criminal defense is a very special case in which the zealous advocate serves atypical social goals." Others more boldly state "[t]hat criminal trials are significantly different from civil ones in philosophy, procedure, sanction and role of lawyers."

Any assertion that the goal of the adversary process in a criminal case is different from its goal in civil litigation must be rejected. The goal of criminal trials is to impose liability on those whom the substantive law indicates have committed crimes. The goal of civil cases is to permit liability to be imposed according to substantive principles. To say that the criminal case is unique is to confuse the goals of the process with some of its elements.

It is true that the burden of persuasion is the highest in criminal cases, that prison and sometimes even the death penalty may be used as penalties only in criminal cases, and that certain constitutional provisions have unique applicability in criminal cases. It is also true that some aspects of civil and criminal cases are very similar. The role of counsel * * * is little different in civil and criminal cases. The role of juries is virtually the same in all cases.

That incidents of trial may differ somewhat in civil and criminal cases does not mean that the goals of the process also differ. Because of concern for the individual and realization of the power of the state to stigmatize and punish criminal offenders in special ways, the American legal system gives the benefit of uncertainty to the criminal defendant. This means that the government bears the risk of an erroneous decision in a very special way, but it does not mean that the goal of the criminal trial is different from the goal of a civil trial. The difference is nothing more than an expression of an understanding that courts may assign the risks of error unequally when there is good reason to do so.

The Goal of the Criminal Trial

If asked the question whether a guilty defendant should be convicted, both lay persons and lawyers will give an affirmative response (absent the extremely unusual case of nullification). If asked whether an innocent defendant should be acquitted, the response will again be affirmative. In criminal as in civil trials, the goal is proper application of substantive principles. No societal preference for acquitting the guilty exists. There is only a judgment that the risk of error ought not generally be borne by the accused.

Some writers cite the impact of the privilege against self-incrimination in criminal cases and the search and seizure exclusionary rule as demonstrating that criminal trials are different from civil trials. But, most rules such as evidence rules, jury selection rules, and rules governing opening statements and closing arguments are similar in all cases. There are rules with special importance in criminal cases, but these rules are similar to all of the rules that govern litigation. They are not designed to produce errors in the application of substantive principles, but are intended to define the type of procedure that is deemed acceptable in the processing of cases. The enormous power of the state when compared to the individual gives rise to additional rules in criminal cases. From time to time these rules might produce the acquittal of someone who should be convicted. That, however, is not the purpose of the rules. * * *

H. RICHARD UVILLER—THE ADVOCATE, THE TRUTH AND JUDICIAL HACKLES: A REACTION TO JUDGE FRANKEL'S IDEA

123 U.Pa.L.Rev. 1067, 1077–79 (1975).
Reprinted by permission of the publisher, copyright ©1975. University of Pennsylvania Law Review and Fred B. Rothman and Co.

[Professor Uviller's article was prepared in response to an earlier version of Judge Frankel's work concerning truth and the adversary system.]

[H]ow is defense counsel to know or recognize the truth? Judge Frankel, I think, proceeds from the assumption that the shining Truth is known or knowable by all diligent lawyers acting in good faith. But is it? Does the first "spontaneous" account of the accused stand thereafter as the Truth against which counsel must measure later variations in the story? Why such faith in the naïve rendition? Is it any more likely to be true than, say, the versions of the witnesses against him? And what if the spontaneous descriptions of two defense witnesses vary? Is Judge Frankel suggesting not only that counsel is obliged to ferret facts, but to judge credibility as well? Should a defense be shaped according to counsel's "sense" or "suspicion" of the true state of affairs?

A somewhat more subtle dichotomy might be discovered between what I shall term the ultimate and the instrumental facts. The ultimate truth may be that the defendant had drugs in his possession, but the police witness against him may be lying about how he acquired the contraband from the defendant. Does fidelity to the truth preclude counsel's efforts to discredit the police testimony in order to obtain dismissal of the charge? I doubt whether Judge Frankel would argue the affirmative on this one. For the Constitution itself, at least as currently read by the Supreme Court, directs the release of the guilty defendant if the truth is that the evidence was unlawfully acquired. Or does the ultimate-truth-defeating quality of the exclusionary rule argue against its retention, whatever other benefits it might claim in vitalizing the Bill of Rights? To avoid that scorcher, let's take the same problem in an "ordinary" context. Suppose the lawyer is defending a man he believes committed the robbery charged but also believes that one of the witnesses against him is "improving" the case by false testimony. Attacking that witness serves the instrumental truth but may defeat the ultimate truth. Here Judge Frankel's proposition may encounter some difficulties. He cannot very well disparage counsel's good faith efforts to keep the jury's evidence as truthful as possible. Yet, if he approves defense attacks on the credibility of instrumental proof, he comes dangerously close to accepting the very adversarial tactics he elsewhere rejects. Moreover, to demonstrate falsity, counsel may have to resort to the "clever tricks" of cross-examination: leading questions, innuendo, magnification of conflicts in trivial detail. For, off the TV tube, a well-woven falsehood does not become unravelled by a few open-ended and respectful inquiries.

One writer, praised by Judge Frankel as "a thoughtful and humane scholar," has taken the problem one step further. Monroe Freedman argues that to achieve an ultimate truth, the acquittal of an innocent person, a lawyer may have to undermine the credibility of a witness he believes to be telling an instrumental truth. In Dean Freedman's example, an honest witness may give damning circumstantial evidence. Would Judge Frankel hold that to make the instrumentally true seem false here in order to prevent the ultimate untruth (arguments on the unreliability of circumstantial evidence are not always persuasive) constitutes a service or disservice to the interests of Truth?

Inescapably, the supremacy of Truth is easier to assert than to define. Consider the matter of justice in the result. The "search-for-the-truth" view of a criminal trial is usually employed to mean maximum correspondence between the judgment of guilt and the defendant's prior performance of the culpable conduct alleged. Yet we have developed a process which is designed over the long haul to preclude conviction of an innocent person at the social expense of acquitting some guilty defendants. I am sure Judge Frankel has no quarrel with the design of such a process. There is, then, an interest in the preservation of the process in every case though the result in a given case does not correspond to the extra-legal truth. Does Judge Frankel suggest that a lawyer who believes his client to be clearly guilty perverts Truth by holding the prosecution strictly to the burden of due process: to prove the charge beyond a reasonable doubt by admissible evidence?

When the famed Judge Sirica opened the Watergate trial by announcing that rules of evidence might be relaxed in the interests of finding the "t-r-u-t-h," did his New York brother feel no qualm that important safeguards of general application might be sacrificed to a result the court deemed correct?

In short, while the Truth (at least as to facts) may seem simple, admitting of no "legalistic" quibbles, no shadings or interpretations, law cases are tried only on evidence of the truth. And evidence is rarely unflawed and unambiguous. Since fact-finders must rely largely on human observation, recall, and veracity, on interpretation and implication, the truth is often uncertain and unclear. Indeed, the process, designed primarily to discover Truth, may at times obscure it. It is no fault of lawyers nor of the process that the evidentiary manifestations of Truth do not invariably lead to Truth. ＊ ＊ ＊

SECTION E. REJOINDER ON THE QUESTION OF THE ECONOMICS OF LITIGATION

STEPHEN SALTZBURG—LAWYERS, CLIENTS, AND THE ADVERSARY SYSTEM

37 Mercer L.Rev. 647, 697–700 (1986).
Reprinted by permission of the publisher, copyright © 1986.
Mercer Law Review.

＊ ＊ ＊

Although the system has its problems, the practice of law generally cannot be fairly characterized as 'a confidence game.'[143] Nor is advocacy in an adversary process inherently defective.[144]

143. See Blumberg, *The Practice of Law as Confidence Game: Organizational Cooptation of a Profession,* 1 L. & Soc.Rev. 15 (June 1967).

144. See Simon, *The Ideology of Advocacy: Procedural Justice and Professional Ethics,* 1978 Wis.L.Rev. 30 (1978).

The advantages some litigants have over others is cause for concern. It is doubtful, however, that a reasonable way to handicap the judicial process in order to promote greater equality exists. The greater a person's wealth, the more litigation that person can afford. Money can enable some litigants to hire better investigators, better experts, and better lawyers. This ability can increase the chance that the wrong person will win in litigation.

The American system has endeavored to provide some minimal guarantees for all persons. The criminal defendant, for example, has a right to counsel in all serious cases, and the government will pay for counsel if the defendant cannot afford it.[146] The defendant has a right to receive certain expert help.[147] Civil litigants may not be guaranteed lawyers in most circumstances, but in some cases courts must provide them with counsel.[148] Legal services agencies may provide legal help to the very poor. Statutes may give the prevailing plaintiff in civil rights and other litigation the benefit of recovering attorney's fees while not generally permitting the defendant to recover the same fees.

* * * The adversary system has some attributes that might equalize the litigation more than many people realize. The jury, for instance, generally will not be exceptionally wealthy. Corporations and other entities cannot sit on juries. When an individual litigates against an entity with greater resources, the jury might take the disparity in resources into account when it evaluates the evidence and arguments offered by opposing parties. Thus, the guarantee of trial by jury is one way of assuring that those litigants with political power, social influence, and wealth must argue their case before members of the community who most often lack these advantages.

Other aspects of the adversary system might have an equalizing effect. For example, trial judges may impose time limits on opening statements or closing arguments and may exclude cumulative evidence. The limits on time and production will be similar for both sides of a case. That one may hire many lawyers and gather an incredible amount of evidence does not necessarily mean that he can use the talent and evidence.

There are many fine lawyers throughout the United States. Some practice with large firms and represent affluent and powerful interests. Many lawyers, however, have smaller practices or do public interest work, yet are the equals of any other lawyer. A good lawyer can respond to the problem of inequality of resources. After all, the witnesses to an event might have no testimony to offer that is favorable

---

146. Argersinger v. Hamlin, 407 U.S. 25, 92 S.Ct. 2006, 32 L.Ed.2d 530 (1972) and Gideon v. Wainwright, 372 U.S. 335, 83 S.Ct. 792, 9 L.Ed.2d 799 (1963) guarantee the right to counsel in felony cases and in misdemeanor cases in which the court sentences a defendant to jail. Scott v. Illinois, 440 U.S. 367, 99 S.Ct. 1158, 59 L.Ed.2d 383 (1979) holds that no right to court-appointed counsel exists when no incarceration is imposed for a misdemeanor.

147. Ake v. Oklahoma, 470 U.S. 68, 105 S.Ct. 1087, 84 L.Ed.2d 53 (1985).

148. See, e.g., Lassiter v. Department of Social Servs., 452 U.S. 18, 101 S.Ct. 2153, 68 L.Ed.2d 640 (1981).

to the wealthy litigant and money cannot change that possibility. In the courtroom, each side has an equal chance to examine and cross-examine witnesses and to explain its theories to the jury. A wealthy litigant who hires three lawyers and offers much more evidence than an opponent may find that three lawyers are not necessarily better than one and that the more evidence that is offered, the stronger the cross-examination by the opponent. The adversary system provides cross-examination in response to examination; one opening statement in response to another; one side's argument in response to another's. The process treats all litigants equally and does not permit a wealthy litigant to obtain advantages easily.

Equality is promoted only if the lawyers for less wealthy litigants are capable and if the lawyers for more wealthy litigants do not take unfair advantage. The profession has a duty to its customers to work to improve the quality of all lawyers by improving basic legal education and continuing education, and by telling lawyers when they have failed to meet basic obligations. It is urged that courts should be tougher on lawyers who violate ethical rules. Along these lines, courts should consider imposing sanctions directly on lawyers when the courts find certain abuses of the system, such as deliberate attempts to manipulate discovery to unfairly raise an adversary's costs of litigation. Certain aspects of legal work exist—discovery is a good example—in which courts are well aware that lawyers dominate the decision how to proceed. When lawyers dominate and violate the rules, courts should punish them.

This stricter enforcement of guidelines would help promote, but would not guarantee, equality. While society struggles to make the process work better for all litigants, it should seriously consider developing devices that help to reduce the burdens of litigation. The summary jury trial, for instance, is an attractive idea. Some day the legal system might decide to try cases involving small amounts of money by using this technique not simply as a device for promoting settlement, but as a substitute for full trials. It would afford the advantages of the adversary system at a lower cost.

Americans must continually work to improve the quality of justice that courts dispense by reexamining substantive and procedural rules of the legal system. Whether or not changes are made, as long as the process remains adversarial, nothing will be more important than assuring that lawyers perform competently according to the rules governing permissible behavior. If lawyers will do that, they will do well.

Chapter 3

THE TRIAL JUDGE: THE LIMITS OF NEUTRALITY AND PASSIVITY

It is a fundamental principle of the adversary system that the decision maker remain passive while the parties develop facts upon which a decision may be based. If the fact finder strays too far from passivity adversary theory suggests that neutrality will be jeopardized. This concern notwithstanding, judges today face enormous pressure to abandon the passive approach. It is asserted by many within the judicial establishment that the passive judge wastes time, is vulnerable to manipulation by counsel and is likely to be distracted from uncovering the "truth." A new, far more active, style of judging is being championed. This style, frequently referred to as "managerial judging," calls upon the members of the judiciary to take control of the cases before them, to settle all the cases they possibly can, to compel counsel through the mechanisms of pretrial procedure to prepare and present cases as the courts think best, and to intervene whenever necessary to serve a variety of system-oriented (rather than litigant-oriented) objectives.

The management movement reflects the judiciary's desire to deal with ever-increasing workloads and responsibly discharge the burdens imposed by a vast array of socially significant litigation. At the heart of the debate about managerial judging remains the question whether activist judges can fulfill the expectations created by America's reliance on adversarial procedure.

SECTION A. THE PROBLEMS FACED BY JUDGES IN AMERICAN COURTS

JOHN SIRICA—TO SET THE RECORD STRAIGHT: THE BREAK–IN, THE TAPES, THE CONSPIRATORS, THE PARDON

71–81, 92 (1979).
Reprinted with permission of the publisher, copyright © 1979.
W.W. Norton & Company.

[On the morning of June 17, 1972, five men were arrested while in the process of burglarizing the offices of the Democratic National Committee in the Watergate complex. It quickly became evident that the five were associated with staff members of President Richard Nixon's Re-election Committee (the so-called Committee to Re-elect the President or CRP). Eventually, the five (James McCord, Bernard Barker, Frank Sturgis, Virgilio Gonzalez, and Eugenio Martinez) and their superiors (Howard Hunt and Gordon Liddy) were prosecuted for a number of criminal offenses.

There was widespread suspicion that these seven were not operating independently during the break-in but rather, were acting pursuant to orders from some of the most powerful men in the Nixon administration. For months the seven held their silence despite growing pressure. Unbeknownst to law enforcement officials and the public, during this period the President of the United States and a significant number of his subordinates were pursuing a criminal conspiracy to purchase the silence of the burglars and defeat the interests of justice.

As Chief Judge of the Federal District Court for the District of Columbia John Sirica chose to preside over the criminal proceedings in the Watergate matter. He almost immediately decided that the courts had to get to the bottom of the scandal in order to restore public faith in the integrity of government. Sirica used the powers of his office as presiding and sentencing judge in the cases of the seven burglars to pressure the men into revealing the full story. He sentenced the defendants to exceptionally long jail terms subject to revision if they would break their silence. He also sought to question thoroughly all those who appeared as witnesses in his court. His tenacity eventually led to a series of disclosures beginning with those of James McCord. These revelations helped to expose the conspiracy of silence and eventually led to Richard Nixon's resignation from office.

Judge Sirica was widely praised for his vigorous prosecution of the Watergate case. Beyond any doubt he did a great public service by forcing the disclosure of the Nixon conspiracy to obstruct justice. However, as you read the following passage from the judge's book about the case ask yourself whether he maintained the high standards of neutrality and passivity required of a judge in the adversary system.

The following selection from the judge's book begins at the point in the original burglars' trial when five of the seven defendants pleaded guilty and trial was about to resume for the other two.]

With the number of defendants now reduced to two from the original seven, the attorneys for Liddy and McCord moved for a mistrial, arguing that the jury, which had been absent during the guilty pleas, would assume the missing five defendants had pleaded guilty and would therefore be biased against McCord and Liddy. I denied the motion, since it is quite common when several defendants are on trial for one of them to plead guilty, often even appearing as a prosecution witness against those remaining. Alch pressed the point nonetheless.

"I don't think there is any need to argue the point," I told him. "You have the record protected and if the court of appeals thinks that is error, that is their business, not mine. I am not concerned with what the court of appeals does. I am only concerned with what I do and if I do the right thing. I am not awed by appellate courts. Let's get that straight. All they can do is reverse me but they can't tell me how to try the case. All right, let's proceed."

The trial judge doesn't have the appellate judge's advantage of many days of contemplation before deciding questions of law. He has to more or less shoot from the hip. I like that kind of action, and I was not about to slow up the trial of Liddy and McCord out of fear of a possible reversal in the appellate courts. I followed my instincts, hoping I was right. I have always been fairly outspoken on the bench, and sometimes I do get into a little trouble. A few minutes after the exchange with Alch, I noticed that Liddy was talking with his attorney, Peter Maroulis. As I mentioned earlier, Liddy's attitude annoyed me. I said to Maroulis, sarcastically, "I see you're getting some good advice from your client, Mr. Liddy, a former attorney."

Well, Liddy hadn't been found guilty yet and of course hadn't yet been disbarred. Maroulis objected that Liddy was still an attorney at law: "He is a lawyer and a member of the bar of this court."

"I will admit that," I said. Fortunately, the jury wasn't in the room, so no harm was done.

Through the second week of the trial, the prosecutors gradually developed their case, relying heavily on the testimony of Thomas J. Gregory, a college student on leave for "off-campus study." Liddy and Hunt had recruited him to spy on McGovern's headquarters, where, it turned out, Liddy had intended to put another phone bug. The government also brought Alfred Baldwin to the stand, to describe his role in the bugging operation at the Watergate. We took a half day off on January 19, in observance of a government holiday declared by President Nixon in honor of his second inauguration. The jury was still sequestered, and I offered them a room from which to watch Nixon's inaugural parade.

When we resumed for the third week, Baldwin was back on the stand. One fact that interested me in his testimony was that at one point he had personally delivered transcripts of the bugged phone conversations to the headquarters of the Committee to Re-elect the President. He told the court that he could not remember to whom he had delivered the transcript, and that aroused my suspicions. I asked the jury to leave the courtroom and addressed Baldwin: ". . . You stated that you received a telephone call from Mr. McCord in Miami in which I think the substance of your testimony was that as to one particular log he wanted you to put that in a manila envelope and staple it, and he gave you the name of the party to whom the material was to be delivered, correct?"

"Yes, Your Honor," Baldwin answered.

"You wrote the name of that party, correct?"

"Yes, I did," he said.

"On the envelope. You personally took that envelope to the Committee to Re-elect the President, correct?"

"Yes, I did," Baldwin said.

"What is the name of that party?" I asked.

"I do not know, Your Honor," Baldwin said.

"When did you have a lapse of memory as to the name of that party?"

Baldwin said he simply couldn't remember the name even though the FBI had given him several names to test his recollection. He said he handed the envelope to a guard.

"Here you are, a former FBI agent, you knew this log was very important?" I asked.

"That is correct," Baldwin said.

"You want the jury to believe that you gave it to a guard, is that your testimony?" I asked. Every time the path led to the CRP, something happened to memories. We took a recess.

The government finally brought officials of the CRP to the stand to speak for themselves. First was Robert Odle, head of administration for the committee. Then Herbert Porter, and then Jeb Stuart Magruder, deputy director, the highest official of the committee to testify at the trial. Silbert certainly asked him the right questions:

"Mr. Magruder, did you ever give Mr. Liddy any assignment concerning the Democratic National Committee?"

"No," Magruder said.

"Did you ever receive any report of any kind from Mr. Liddy concerning the Democratic National Committee offices and headquarters at 2600 Virginia Avenue [the Watergate]?"

"No," Magruder said.

Magruder was as smooth as silk. He did not appear flustered or nervous. He is a handsome man, well dressed, well spoken. If you wanted a model of the respectable, responsible, honest, young executive, Magruder would be perfect. But listening to Magruder, Porter, and Odle, I was not impressed with the logic of their testimony. They simply put everything on Liddy. I still couldn't understand how the CRP officials could turn over that kind of money to someone without any accountability. It didn't make sense.

The next witness was Hugh Sloan, assistant treasurer of the Nixon campaign. He was the very picture of innocence—young, clean-cut, dressed conservatively, and speaking softly. He testified that he had handed Liddy the money personally, after first checking with his boss, Maurice Stans. He explained how he had given checks to Liddy to convert to cash and how that money was kept in safes at CRP headquarters. He, too, said he didn't know what the money he gave Liddy was to be used for.

I just didn't believe these people. The whole case looked more and more like a big cover-up. I was feeling pretty much alone in those days. I really had only my law clerk Todd Christofferson to talk to about the case. As yet, no Senate investigation had been authorized. With Sloan still on the stand, I realized that if I didn't step in fast, this whole parade would go by, right out of the courthouse, laughing at us. Perhaps some other federal judges would have limited themselves to ruling on objections. But one of the reasons I had always wanted to be a federal judge was that, damn it, nobody could stop me from asking the right questions. I didn't have to sit quietly by and watch this procession.

I didn't care how important Sloan or Magruder or Porter was. Liddy had been given a lot of money. Someone must have authorized the payment. Someone had to know what the money was for. Liddy had to be reporting to someone. Now here was Sloan, who had handled the money. I made up my mind very quickly, right there, to ask him some questions myself. I thought, "Listen, Sirica, this is your last chance." I sent the jury out.

"Mr. Sloan, I want to ask you a few questions. I am interested in the checks—Mexican checks. Let's go back there a few minutes. One for $15,000, one of $18,000, one for $24,000, one for $32,000. We call them the Mexican checks, correct?"

"Yes, sir," Sloan answered.

"You turned these over to Mr. Liddy, is that your testimony?"

"Yes, sir."

"What was the purpose for turning them over to him?"

"My concern in this case as with the subsequent Dahlberg check was the fact that under the law and our interpretation on the way we normally handle our affairs, there is a gift tax deduction, but it would raise questions for instance if a $15,000 check were deposited in any particular account. The intent of the donor was for us to handle his donation in such a way we would not incur for him any gift tax liability; therefore the conversion to cash was an administrative method of breaking these checks down into the elements that would fall beneath the contribution limit." This was also the committee's way of getting around the campaign-spending limits and reporting requirements, but I was more interested in Liddy's involvement.

"Did he [Liddy] tell you how he was going to convert them to cash?" I asked.

"No, he just indicated he would convert them."

"What made you believe he could convert these checks to cash?"

". . . I asked him what the best way to handle this would be and we mutually agreed to conversion to cash. And he merely offered at that point and indicated he had some friends who would do it."

"Tell me about the $25,000 check, the Dahlberg check."

"This was presented to me by Secretary Stans in his office sometime the week following April 7. He indicated to me at that time it represented a contribution pre-April 7 from a donor whose name he gave me and the conversion to cashier's check was just one method of transporting it from Florida to our offices."

"You said, I think, and correct me if I am in error, that you turned over a total of about $199,000 in cash?"

"That is the best of my recollection."

"Where did you get that money from?"

"Cash contributions to the president's campaign."

"What was the purpose of turning over $199,000 to Liddy?"

"I have no idea."

"You have no idea?"

"No, sir."

"You can't give us any information on that at all?"

"No, sir. I was merely authorized to do so. I was not told the purpose."

"Who authorized you to turn $199,000 over to Liddy in cash?"

"Jeb Magruder."

"For what purpose?"

"I have no idea."

"This is a pretty sizeable piece of money."

"In and of itself, but not in the context of the campaign."

"You didn't question Mr. Magruder about the purpose of the $199,000?"

"No, sir, I verified with Mr. Stans and Mr. Mitchell he was authorized to make those."

"You verified it with who?"

"Secretary Stans, the finance chairman, and I didn't directly but he verified it with John Mitchell, the campaign chairman."

"This $199,000 could be turned over to Mr. Liddy, is what you are saying?"

"Not the specific amount but Mr. Magruder, his authorization was authorization enough to turn over the sums in question."

"Did anybody indicate to you by their action or by words or deed what this money was to be used for?"

"No, sir."

"You are a college graduate, aren't you?"

"Yes, sir."

"I think you majored in history, is that correct?"

"That is correct."

"What did you know about Mr. Liddy before the time all this cash was turned over to you?"

"I just had known him through hearsay, that he had been an employee with the Treasury Department, a former FBI agent, a former consultant at the White House."

"You said you got some receipts, didn't you, for this money you turned over to him?"

"No, sir, I did not say that."

"Did you ever get any part of the $199,000 back?"

"No, sir."

"You didn't know what Mr. Liddy used it for?"

"No, sir."

"No idea?"

"No, sir."

"He was never questioned by you or anybody else what he did with the $199,000?"

"No, sir."

"You said you saw him coming to headquarters, I suppose near you, on the morning that these five men broke in the Democratic headquarters, is that correct?"

"Yes, sir."

"You knew, did you not, Mr. Liddy was a former FBI agent?"

"Yes, sir, I heard that."

"You know, don't you, it is common knowledge at least before you can be appointed as an FBI agent you must be a member of the bar?"

"Yes, sir."

"Still, you tell the court and the lawyers you saw him passing you, went by you—yes or no?"

"Yes, sir, that is correct."

"And he said something like—repeat what you claim he said."

"To the best of my recollection what he indicated was: 'My boys were caught last night. I made a mistake by using somebody from here, which I told them I would never do. I am afraid I am going to lose my job.'"

"What did you say to that?"

"He was in a hurry and just passed on. I don't believe I responded."

"Here is a man, a former FBI agent, makes a remark to you, . . . which was incriminating, which indicated to any person I think with common sense that he had done something wrong, didn't that flash in your mind when he said, 'My boys got caught last night, I used somebody from here, which I shouldn't have done'? Didn't that occur to you it was mighty strange you knew nothing about this matter, that you didn't see anything wrong with that remark?"

"Not at that point in time, no, sir."

"When did it dawn on you there might be something wrong or improper about this remark, Mr. Sloan?"

"When I read the *Evening Star* that evening."

"What did you think when you read the *Evening Star* that evening?"

"I thought a possibility might exist of involvement in this matter."

"Shortly after that you retained a lawyer?"

"No sir, it was in July, approximately a month later."

"Was this before you were called down to the United States attorney's office?"

"Yes sir."

"When did you resign [from the CRP]?"

"July 14."

"For what reason?"

"Essentially my reasons for resigning involved the Watergate matter and personal considerations, the fact that it was obvious to me at that point that the FBI was making an investigation, that there would probably be others. I had undertaken this job because I felt I could make a significant contribution to the president's campaign and it became abundantly clear to me in that months' period it would be impossible to discharge those duties because of the increasing pressure I knew would be forthcoming, the internal situations that existed in the committee at that time; my wife was pregnant and in view of what I assumed would be adverse publicity, and so forth, I did not want to put her through those additional burdens."

"As a matter of fact, Mr. Sloan, be perfectly frank about the matter, you resigned primarily because you were concerned about the Watergate matter, isn't that the truth of the matter?"

"Yes, sir, I believe that is what I said."

"Did you ever testify before the grand jury?"

"Yes sir, I did."

"Were you granted immunity [from prosecution]?"

"No, sir."

I had asked Sloan forty-two questions. He had changed his testimony slightly by remembering that Liddy on the morning after the break-in had said he used "somebody from here which I told them I would never do. . . ." In Sloan's earlier testimony, "told them" had been omitted. It would have been interesting, at that point, to ask Liddy to identify "them." But, of course, Liddy wasn't about to testify. Sloan had also said that Stans and Mitchell had approved the payment to Liddy. I did feel that my questioning of Sloan had raised questions about his credibility. I decided later that I should read the questions and answers to the jury so they could make their own judgments. Silbert objected mildly, offering to recall Sloan to ask some of the questions I had asked. I was afraid, however, that Sloan would have a lapse of memory.

Despite the little bit that Sloan did add to our understanding of the Watergate break-in, and despite my skepticism at the time, he was essentially telling the truth. He had had no knowledge of the break-in, and as soon as he saw the attempt to keep the committee's involvement secret, he quit. It was really Magruder who was, at least among those in the courtroom, the key to the cover-up. His was the testimony that placed responsibility directly on Liddy, and that denied any role for himself or others at the committee in what Liddy planned and did at the Democratic headquarters. I have often wondered what would have happened if I had taken over the questioning of Magruder, instead of Sloan. My instinct, however, was to follow the money.

Liddy's attorney, Peter Maroulis, was naturally unhappy about my plan to read the Sloan testimony to the jury. He felt it would place undue weight behind Sloan's recollection of Liddy's remarks on the morning after the break-in. Maroulis hadn't even cross-examined Sloan, as was his right. He wanted Sloan off the stand as soon as possible. But it was my duty to give as much information to the jury as they needed to understand the case. I told Maroulis: "I exercise my judgment as a federal judge and chief judge of this court and have done it on many occasions and in the presence of the jury examined witnesses where I thought all the facts were not brought out by counsel on either side. As long as I am a federal judge I will continue to do it. As I said, the court of appeals might reverse me in this case, I am not concerned with that. I am concerned with doing what I think is the right thing at the moment and that is the reason I am going to read this testimony to the jury. I couldn't care less what happens to this case on appeal, if there is an appeal. I am not interested in that. I am interested in doing what I think is right."

Of course, I overstated my feelings about the court of appeals. I *was* concerned that the trial be without reversible error. But I had to walk the line between that concern and my duty to get the facts out. I was willing to take the risk.

The exchange with Maroulis seemed to amuse Gordon Liddy.

"Now your client is smiling," I said to Maroulis. "He is not impressed with what I am saying. I don't care what he thinks either. Is that clear to you?" That wasn't an overstatement. I didn't see anything funny about the entire case. It is a most serious matter when an election campaign can't be conducted without bugging and burglary being part of the strategy. Liddy had had all the advantages. He had been to college. He was a lawyer. He had been an FBI agent. He had run for Congress. He wasn't like the poor Miamians who had been sold a bill of goods. Now he was turning himself into the great, silent martyr. I thought, "Let him be the martyr." I have always been amazed that the men around the president tolerated someone like Liddy. I have often thought of Liddy making his bizarre proposals in the meeting with Mitchell. The attorneys general I had known, men like Herbert Brownell, would have locked Liddy up right then and there. * * *

There were people who already thought I had gone too far during the trial in trying to get the truth out. Some believe that a federal judge should sit quietly by, like an umpire at a ball game, and make sure the trial runs smoothly, simply ruling on objections raised by the attorneys. I knew the case would go to the court of appeals in the event of a conviction, because of the way I had handled myself, but I have never believed I should sit through a trial with one eye cocked toward the court of appeals. They can tell you after the fact whether you made a mistake, but they can't tell you how to conduct a fair trial at the moment when you have to make a decision from the bench. I have always wanted trials over which I presided to be above all fair— fair to the defendants, to the government, and to the public. The trial of the original Watergate defendants was fair to the defendants and the government, but it didn't seem to me to have been fair to the public. They were asked to believe a theory about how our election process had been corrupted that made no sense to me whatsoever. * * *

Questions

1. How did Judge Sirica feel about the defendant Gordon Liddy? Could he insure that Liddy got a fair trial? What affect did the judge's feelings about Liddy have on the way the trial was conducted?

2. Why did Judge Sirica question Hugh Sloan? Did he have sufficient information to serve as an effective questioner? Why didn't the prosecutor ask the questions that interested the judge? What should a judge do when the prosecutor (or any other lawyer) fails to ask the questions the judge thinks are important? Is there any alternative to judicial interrogation? See Saltzburg, *The Unnecessarily Expanding Role of the American Trial Judge,* 64 Virginia Law Review 1 (1978).

3. If you had been a juror in the Watergate case what impressions would you have formed based on Judge Sirica's questions and comments?

4. Did the ends sought by Judge Sirica in the Watergate case justify the means he adopted to achieve them? Is your opinion in any way influenced by the fact that the Court of Appeals resoundingly endorsed Judge Sirica's approach when the case came before it on appeal? See *United States v. Liddy,* 509 F.2d 428 (D.C.Cir.1974).

5. If you had been Liddy's lawyer what tactics might you have adopted in response to Judge Sirica's actions?

6. If you were Liddy how would you have felt about the trial?

MARVIN FRANKEL—PARTISAN JUSTICE

39–48 (1980).

[In his book *Partisan Justice,* Judge Marvin Frankel wrote not only about the alleged shortcomings of the adversary system in modern America but about the difficulties faced by American trial judges. In the following passage he provides one trial judge's view of the pressures inherent in the system.]

The judge is in familiar theory the impartial director of the trial as well as the decision-maker. The judicial umpire regulates the contest, then decides who won. The office carries in theory large powers of direction in the courtroom, mitigated and justified by entire neutrality. The practice reflects the theory, but incompletely. In fact, the judge's managerial powers are limited by procedures that give to the lawyers, not to the judge, the functions of initiating, organizing, and conducting the court-room struggle. As for neutrality, the judges are among the species of umpires who are with some frequency drawn into the fray— unwittingly run down in the scrimmage, or actually used (or attempted to be used) in the strategies of the contestants, or choosing on their own to be embroiled. The resulting role is not quite the imperial one some have seen, but more than that of the bland umpire others perceive or desire. An effort to suggest the character of the alloy was made a while ago by describing it as "umpireal." * * *

With exceptions, as always, our trial judges tend to be recruited from the ranks of people with substantial experience as trial lawyers. This sounds like a good idea, especially to those of us who have lived with it all our lives. If the judge is thought of as managing or directing the trial process, it makes sense to have as a qualification some decent record of experience as a participant. The thought does not evaporate upon reflection. It does become somewhat less self-evident, both on analytical grounds and because most countries of the world, equally eager to have judicious deciders in their courts, handle judicial recruitment quite differently.

Trial lawyers are the gladiators, the forensic athletes, of the trial process. In that light, the selection of trial judges from among them has at first blush a familiar and "natural" quality. It is not unlike the progression of former athletes into jobs as managers, coaches, and umpires, especially umpires. * * * If the analogy is plausible, however, it does not erase questions that occur after a while concerning the transfer of elderly, or at least quite mature, legal gladiators from the arena to the bench. It is also plausible to wonder whether years of partisan combat are necessarily ideal training for the qualities of detachment and calm reflection that we suppose ourselves to desire on the bench. Experience with our judges yields a mixed answer. Many of our most successful lawyers who acquire robes become fighting judges—quick on the uptake, speedily seeing where the answers are (without always waiting for all the questions), ready to take up arms against the "wrong" side or to lend a hand to the "right" side as need or occasion is thought to appear. Others, having played all the tricks themselves, become ferociously righteous—the scourge of "crooked" lawyers, vengeful toward convicted defendants, wise to every covert design, including some never formed. There are those, too, more numerous and agreeable, who remember the sights and smells of personal combat with benign affection, and preside now in the still warm glow, chuckling with nostalgia as the truth suffers injury or death now and again at the hands of a clever advocate. * * *

While these are all interesting and not uncommon species, they probably add up to only a minority. The majority of those who become judges manage, for many reasons, to rechannel the adversary habit. The expected stance of neutrality is assumed. The aggressive drives of former times are turned toward the quest for right, accurate—just— outcomes. The years of desiring, if not always experiencing, fairness and reason from the judge create a pressure to follow the ideal.

Still, there is room to speculate whether a substantial career of adversary jousting is clearly the best training for the role of detached judging. * * *

* * * A standard item of trial court business is the careful recording of claimed errors by the trial judge to be invoked if necessary as grounds for reversing an adverse decision on appeal. The process is conducted with vivid awareness on the part of all, not excluding the judge, that each side is "making a record" of this sort. For all its familiarity and regularity, it is an element causing the detachment of the trial judge to be tested, threatened, and sometimes impaired if not entirely lost.

Destined often to be a target * * * the trial judge is led commonly to sense that the preparation for that stage is in progress right here and now, in the trial over which the judge is presiding. Every ruling is a potential weapon on appeal for one side or the other. The appeals, when they happen, will be times for careful study and reflection by a panel of higher-court judges. The rulings destined for that scrutiny are in most cases relatively instantaneous responses to questions that burst upon the trial scene with insistent suddenness. Trial judges may be about as capable as their appellate superiors of study and reflection. But the demands and rhythms of the trial process leave little or no time for that. Sometimes certainly it is feasible and prudent to call a halt for some thought, perhaps some research. But it is not routinely acceptable to send the jury away for days, or even for hours, while subtleties about the law of evidence or other subjects are tracked in the library. The demand for swift rulings is compelling. For the judge to risk error is better than to dissipate attention and destroy continuity. There is loss for interests more important than the judicial ego—but for that as well—if the judge regularly wavers, temporizes, shows insufficient self-confidence to command respect. * * *

[T]he possibility of eventual reversal on appeal is a staple of the trial judge's life. There is a corollary awareness that one side or the other is at any given moment laying a foundation for the realization of that prospect. This aspect of the encounter between lawyer and judge ruffles, very visibly at times, the Olympian serenity the latter is expected both to feel and to display. The lawyer is seen in some measure as a threat—an adversary. It is standard doctrine among trial judges that one is indifferent to, if not utterly oblivious of, the possibility of reversal on appeal. It is also standard learning in all quarters of the profession that the lower court judge worried incessantly about what a higher court may do is likely to be a weak fumbler on the bench. Nevertheless, the trial judge who in fact follows the boastful folklore of lower-court jurists and is really indifferent to what may happen on appeal is probably a lawless menace. Judges of lower courts are *supposed* to obey higher courts and avoid reversals—whether the higher-court directions are about racial discrimination or the rules concerning hearsay evidence. They're also expected as significant professionals to care about their work, including their reputations in doing their work, and about avoiding too many errors. So they should be concerned about being reversed. And they are.

This means inevitably that the judges are attentive to those who work at trying to get them reversed or laying plans for reversals just in case. The attentiveness need not, and usually does not, imply personal hostility or animus. The respective roles are familiar parts of an old and familiar design. The design plainly includes, however, the clash of opposed interests in which a separate and individual stake leads the judge toward qualities and responses that are, in one word, adversarial.

* * *

The judges themselves have been among the writers reporting the sense of judicial embattlement generated by the clash of objections, the swiftly responsive rulings, and the attendant risks of reversible error. The tension heightens in "big cases," where publicity, number of lawyers, and the sheer noise level add strain. In such a case, a question to a witness will be followed at unpredicted times by an explosion of activity as lawyers scramble to their feet and object, not always in dulcet tones, obliged as they are to act with some haste and possible heat to cut off assertedly objectionable answers. The warriors thus unleashed may present, all unintentionally, an aspect experienced from the bench, all unconsciously, as somehow menacing and assaultive. Menace of sorts there actually is, in the sense that the judge is tested and threatened by the call for prompt and fallible judgment. The noisy throng of lawyers may add a sense of being outnumbered, surrounded, a little at bay. * * *

The ideal of neutrality is furthered * * * by the fact that there are at least two sides to the controversy and that at least one is presumably satisfied each time a ruling goes against the other. But the fact that the buffeting comes from more than one direction is not altogether pacifying. It may serve indeed to promote a feeling of beleaguerment. The pervasive air of combat envelops the judge as a combatant with a shifting but seemingly endless series of opponents. There are constant reminders of this condition, usually quite explicit, usually, though not always, put in customarily deferential terms. The lawyer who says he is "making a record" or announces an objection "merely for the record" may be heard by the judge, depending a little on the degree of the judge's self-confidence, to be saying: "Your blunder is now preserved for your betters to see, correct, and denounce you for." Sometimes the challenge is flung without the ceremonial forms, just possibly to nettle the judge and enhance in that way the hope of fatal error. A well-publicized if relatively cheery instance occurred during the Watergate trial of Messrs. Ehrlichman, Haldeman, *et al.*, when a veteran defense lawyer pointed out more than once to Judge John Sirica that he was filing an "error bag" with the judge's misdeeds for later exploitation, if it came to that, in a higher, better court. The judge, an equally seasoned warrior, was described as responding with bantering, good-natured defiance. But it was the response of a confident adversary, not an uninvolved referee. * * *

Implicated somewhat personally in the serious business of winning and losing, the judge is drawn, or is in danger of being drawn, off the high middle ground of neutrality. Normally an old hand, the judge is a live, moving, reactive target. If baiting is thought to be fair, countermeasures are in order. The black-robed figure, for all the physical elevation and detachment, is in the arena being tested for prowess, poise, and forensic skill. Discussion of "strong" and "weak" judges, whatever else it may signify in other contexts, refers in this respect to the capacity for contending with and *against* the lawyers. Thus, so austere a personage as England's Lord Chief Justice echoed the adversary note in 1975, when he said: "No advocate will be tempted to pull a fast one if he knows that the judge is at least his equal in the craft." Similarly, back home in Ohio, a federal district judge spoke this way of the testing time following his appointment: "They [the lawyers] would have run me ragged in court if I hadn't learned the rules and tricks of the trade as a trial lawyer and judge." These are not the sentiments of detached referees. They import a kind of personal engagement that may lead at any moment to direct, spirited confrontations.

This kind of combativeness is perhaps fully consistent with impartiality in the sense that the judge will take adversarial measures indifferently, now against one side, now against the other, depending on when and whence the challenges come. In practice, however, the adversary judge too often gravitates toward a relatively fixed position on one side or the other. Personal chemistry sometimes plays a part. Ideological predispositions may cause a tilt or the sharp appearance of a leaning. All courthouse denizens have observed the judicial thumb, whether purposefully or not, weighing on one side or the other of the adversary contest.

Questions

1. How do Judges Frankel and Sirica react to the pressures of the job of judging? Is theirs the only response one might expect?

2. Who does Judge Frankel think should be given greater power in the adjudicatory process? Why? Is he right?

3. Should we continue to select our judges in the way Frankel describes? Is there a better way? What is it?

4. Doesn't Frankel's description of the "adversarial judge" demonstrate the need for the sort of neutrality and passivity advocated by Professor Fuller in the preceding chapter?

SECTION B.   THE JUDGE AS MANAGER

ALVIN RUBIN—THE MANAGED CALENDAR: SOME PRAGMATIC SUGGESTIONS ABOUT ACHIEVING THE JUST, SPEEDY, AND INEXPENSIVE DETERMINATION OF CIVIL CASES IN FEDERAL COURT

4 Justice System J. 135, 136–37 (1978).
Reprinted with permission of the author, copyright © 1979.
Institute for Court Management.

[Federal appellate court judge Alvin Rubin has been one of the most articulate and influential spokesmen on behalf of "managerial judging." Here he briefly describes the reasons for adopting a managerial approach.]

A host of respectable lawyers, and many able judges, think that any effort by trial judges to manage court calendars will lead to immeasurable injury. If left alone, the lawyers will get the case ready for trial at some convenient time or will settle it. The best thing the judge can do for the administration of justice is to stay out of case management. Judges should merely decide the preliminary matters brought before them, and make trial dates available when the lawyers say they are ready. This group shares the opinion that the good judge also grants continuances amiably when one of the lawyers later decides he is not ready after all. And when the case does come to trial, he lets the lawyers try it in their own way. Let the best lawyer win.

Whether we who are judges meddle with administration or not, however, we are effectively beyond human judgment, even most of those of us who happen to be elected. This is true unless we are short-sighted and irrascible enough to mouth off about some contemporary ideology or repeatedly commit some indiscretion in public. Let no one therefore compare our work habits, or suggest changes in our practices, or compile statistics about what we do.

Still there are some, including the Chief Justice of the United States, representatives of the Federal Judicial Center, the National Center for State Courts, the Institute for Court Management and a growing number of state and federal judges, who, perhaps out of simple madness, think that there must be a better way to conduct litigation than the traditional one of leaving the lawyers to go about their work. These missionaries share a "passion for suggesting reforms" with "even quite simple people." One of the paramount reforms, though by no means the only one, is the judicial assumption of responsibility for docket management.

The judge must be truly neutral in deciding cases. But this does not imply that he must remain aloof from the litigation process. The judicial role is not a passive one. "A purely adversarial system, uncontrolled by the judiciary, is not an automatic guarantee that justice will be done. It is impossible to consider seriously the vital elements of a fair trial without considering that it is the duty of the judge, and the judge alone, as the sole representative of the public interest, to step in at any stage of the litigation where his intervention is necessary in the interests of justice." Judge Learned Hand wrote, "[a] judge is more than a moderator; he is charged to see that the law is properly administered, and it is a duty which he cannot discharge by remaining inert."

The public too has an interest in how and for what purposes the courts are used. If courts are crowded and dockets are long, if demand for judicial services exceeds supply, then it is in the public interest to see that courtrooms are used for proper purposes. A litigant is entitled to a fair trial, but not to a blank check on the time of judges, jurors and the use of public facilities. Litigants who await their day in court have a right to expect that those whose turn comes earlier do not squander the resource for which they wait. Taxpayers and litigants alike have a right to expect effective docket management.

Docket management, however, is not a goal in itself. It ought not be merely busy work, with much shuffling of forms and compilation of statistics. Unless the court's administrative supervision of the cases pending before it can achieve some purpose of value to the litigants, the public, and the judicial process, it is a vexatious preoccupation.

Questions

1. What is "docket management"? Should it include such matters as the content of the parties' claims, the names of their witnesses, the scope of their discovery efforts, and their willingness to settle? If it does encompass all these factors, is there anything that courts should not "manage"?

2. If judges ought firmly to control pretrial procedure shouldn't they, for the same reasons, take charge of trials as well?

3. Is Judge Rubin right about the nature of the "public interest" in adjudication? Are there countervailing concerns that argue for less intrusive judicial conduct? What are they?

HUBERT WILL—CIVIL CASE–FILING TO DISPOSITION

In Seminars for Newly Appointed District Judges 15–16 (1971).
Reprinted with the permission of the author copyright © 1971.
West Publishing Company.

[Federal district court judge Hubert Will is another leading spokesman for the managerial point of view. Here he discusses some of the practical implications of the managerial position.]

GENERAL PRINCIPLES OF JUDICIAL ADMINISTRATION
BASIC ASSUMPTIONS—HYPOTHESES

1. The objective and the responsibility of our legal system is to produce the highest quality of justice in the shortest time and at the lowest cost consistent herewith.

2. Justice, particularly the highest quality, is unique in each case—must be handcrafted by the most skilled artisans available—each case tailored to its own characteristics—the production of justice is essentially a jobshop, as distinguished from a mass production operation.

3. The available work or production force in court cases consists of 1) the judge, 2) the counsel, 3) the judge's law clerk(s), 4) the courtroom deputy or minute clerk, 5) the magistrate, 6) the judge's secretary, 7) the official court reporter, 8) the crier, bailiff or deputy marshal, 9) in jury cases, the jury, and 10) other para-judicial personnel such as probation officers, court experts, interpreters, etc.

4. The judge's time is the least expandable of all the work force—judge's time should be utilized in performing those functions which the constitution and statutes require he perform or those he can do much more effectively than anyone else. All other functions should be

performed by other members of the work force—para-judicial personnel.

5. The responsibility of the judge is to be superintendent of the production of justice—the traditional concept of judge as a skilled referee is incompatible with production of highest quality of justice.

6. So far as humanly possible, a trial should be a rational search for the truth, not an unprepared improvised amateur theatrical played to a captive audience. The latter is likewise incompatible with production of the highest quality of justice. The more effective the trial, the better the quality of justice produced.

7. The expeditious production of the highest quality of justice in court cases cannot be left to counsel—their relative interest in various cases will depend on factors sometimes inconsistent with that objective, e.g., size of case, importance of client, abrasiveness or persistence of client, tactical considerations such as defense by delay or economic attrition, relative importance or personal interest of counsel in issues involved, etc. As a result neither the progress of discovery, the fixing of trial date nor minimum adequate trial preparations can be left solely to the discretion of counsel.

8. In most controversies, most court cases, the highest quality of justice is not the all or nothing, black or white end result of a trial but is in the grey area—in most cases a freely negotiated settlement is a higher quality of justice which is obtainable earlier and at less cost. Approximately 90 per cent of all suits filed in federal courts are disposed of without trial.

PRINCIPLES WHICH FOLLOW FROM FOREGOING HYPOTHESES:

1. Court supervision of case development should be instituted at the earliest feasible point.

2. Court supervision should not be relinquished until final disposition—no case without a set date for next step.

3. Procedures should be adopted to move each case ahead consistent with its own characteristics.

4. Procedures should be adopted to maximize possibilities of settlement.

5. Procedures should be adopted to insure at least minimum adequate preparation for an effective trial by both counsel and court.

6. Procedures should be adopted to minimize judge participation and maximize parajudicial participation.

Questions

1. Is it appropriate to classify all those involved in adjudication as either judicial or "parajudicial" personnel? Doesn't such a scheme mask serious divisions of responsibility and loyalty especially with respect to trial counsel?

2. Why is Judge Will so vigorous in his criticism of the idea of the judge as "skilled referee?"

3. If you were a newly appointed judge would you adopt Judge Will's point of view? If you did, how would you try to run your court? What difficulties might you encounter?

4. Why is settlement better than adjudication? Is this true in all cases, even those touching on fundamental constitutional or other concerns?

5. What is Judge Will's view of the scope of judicial power?

McCARGO v. HEDRICK

United States Court of Appeals, Fourth Circuit, 1976.
545 F.2d 393, 394–401.

[In this case the Fourth Circuit came face to face with managerial judging in an extreme form.]

CRAVEN, CIRCUIT JUDGE:

This is an appeal by Pauline McCargo from the district court's sua sponte dismissal of her consolidated actions for failure to prosecute. For the reasons stated below, we reverse.

I.

McCargo's suits against Hedrick, Buch, and Green were consolidated in the Northern District of West Virginia on January 19, 1973. Both suits claim that plaintiff's horse racing license in West Virginia was wrongfully revoked. After the pleadings were closed, and after the 120–day discovery period had expired, there arose under Local Rule 2.08 a duty for counsel to "confer and . . . meaningfully and effectively express and commit themselves in a written statement on matters and issues involved in and controlling determination of the action." The district court extended the deadline for the meeting of counsel to November 27, 1973, and later extended the time for submitting the proposed pretrial order to February 28, 1974.

Counsel were not prompt but filed it about a month later, on April 4, 1974. It was ten pages long. That is not surprising since it was necessarily cut from the pattern of Rule 2.08, which itself runs 11 and a half single-spaced pages. Even so it was not complete. On September 26, 1974, the United States Magistrate instructed counsel that certain amendments to the proposed pretrial order were needed and required their submission by November 18, 1974. This date was extended, and on April 23, 1975, the second proposed pretrial order was filed. The magistrate measured it against Local Rule 2.08 and found it wanting. He returned it to the lawyers on May 13, 1975, with a four-page-plus letter of transmittal.

The magistrate made suggestions which he characterized as "by no means exhaustive" for the preparation of yet another pretrial order. His suggestions were to "serve as a basis for . . . further work in preparing an amended pretrial order which will more nearly structure this action for placement on a trial calendar." * * *

By October 9, 1975, the third proposed amended order had not been filed, and no extension of time had been sought from the court. On that date the district court notified the parties that the consolidated actions would be dismissed with prejudice pursuant to Local Rule 2.09 unless good cause for retention was shown within 30 days. The reason cited for the proposed dismissal was that there had been "no manifest interest and action shown in [the suit's] prosecution" and that the case had been on the court docket for more than 12 months.

McCargo's attorney responded to this notice on October 21, 1975, stating that counsel for the parties had been trying to amend the pretrial order pursuant to the magistrate's instructions. He explained, however, that preparation of the amended order had been delayed due to defendants' failure to provide him their lists of documentary evidence. He then moved the court to retain the case on the docket.

By order dated December 4, 1975, the district court sua sponte dismissed the consolidated actions with prejudice and removed them from the docket. He attached to the order the second 13–page proposed amended pretrial order that had been tendered by counsel and stated that it failed to comply with the suggestions made by the magistrate at the pretrial conference and in his May 13, 1975, letter. The district court later denied McCargo's motion to reconsider the order of dismissal. * * *

III.

The facts of this case illustrate the burden put upon litigants and their counsel by a pretrial procedure that appears to have become an end in itself. Rule 16 of the Federal Rules of Civil Procedure was and is a great idea. It authorizes the district courts to conduct a *conference* with counsel for the purpose of *aiding* in the disposition of the case, *i.e.,* to make the trial easier. The idea is to help the lawyers and the litigants—not to exhaust them. * * *

A.

Local Rule 2.08 breaks the promise of Rule 16. * * *

Compliance with Local Rule 2.08 and its prescribed format produced in this case a proposed pretrial order 13 pages in length. By way of contrast, we reproduce in the margin a typical form of pretrial order consisting of two pages in its entirety, which we think is sufficient to accomplish the purposes of Rule 16. * * *

Local Rule 2.08 is a distortion of such purposes. Simplicity has been forgotten. The theory seems to be that if two pages are good, four must be better, and ten or 13 or 21 may prevent a trial altogether, as happened here. Rule 16 was never meant to make lawyers try a case on paper instead of in a courtroom. In fact, it contemplates that the district judge himself will dictate the pretrial order. Of course, the court may seek the aid of counsel in preparing the order, but Rule 16 should not be implemented in such a manner that the pretrial procedure itself is more difficult and time consuming than the actual trial.

Ours is an adversary system of justice. Local Rule 2.08 is inquisitorial in tone and purpose. In our system lawyers worry about the whereabouts of witnesses. The court does not. Lawyers worry about proof. The court does not—except in the rare case of collusion. Lawyers get the case ready for trial. The court does not. Local Rule 2.08 subordinates the role of the lawyer to that of the administering magistrate, reducing counsel to the role of clerical assistants who are to anticipate imaginatively what other matters ought to be embraced within an endless pretrial order. * * *

Questions

1. Is the procedure described in *McCargo* consistent with that endorsed by Judge Will? Why does the Court of Appeals object?

2. What role does the magistrate play pursuant to Rule 2.08? Is this the sort of role that ought to be ceded to "parajudicial" rather than judicial personnel?

3. Who drafted and promulgated Rule 2.08? Why was it structured in the way it was?

4. What can a lawyer do when faced with the sort of burden imposed by Rule 2.08? Who should pay the expenses related to any challenge of such rules?

JUDITH RESNIK—MANAGERIAL JUDGES

96 Harv.L.Rev. 374, 376–80, 424–31 (1982).
Reprinted with permission of the publisher, copyright © 1982.
The Harvard Law Review Association.

[Professor Judith Resnik here critically examines the trend toward "managerial judging." She sees it as arising because of a judicial desire to reduce counsel's control of litigation, to increase court authority, and to speed cases to resolution. Its manifestations in the pretrial context include a range of pretrial orders, hearings, and submissions, designed to allow the judge a firmer hand in disposing of cases. All these procedures are marked by extreme informality and the absence of a tangible record for appeal. There is relatively little restraint placed upon judges in this new style of management and the value of passivity is flatly rejected. The risks of such an approach are succinctly described in the following passage.]

Until recently, the American legal establishment embraced a classical view of the judicial role. Under this view, judges are not supposed to have an involvement or interest in the controversies they adjudicate. Disengagement and dispassion supposedly enable judges to decide cases fairly and impartially. The mythic emblems surrounding the goddess Justice illustrate this vision of the proper judicial attitude: Justice carries scales, reflecting the obligation to balance claims fairly; she possesses a sword, giving her great power to enforce decisions; and she wears a blindfold, protecting her from distractions.

Many federal judges have departed from their earlier attitudes; they have dropped the relatively disinterested pose to adopt a more active, "managerial" stance. In growing numbers, judges are not only adjudicating the merits of issues presented to them by litigants, but also are meeting with parties in chambers to encourage settlement of disputes and to supervise case preparation. Both before and after the trial, judges are playing a critical role in shaping litigation and influencing results.

Several commentators have identified one kind of lawsuit—the "public law litigation" or "structural reform" case—in which federal judges have assumed a new role. In these cases, judges actively supervise the implementation of a wide range of remedies designed to desegregate schools and to reform prisons and other institutions. Some commentators have questioned the legitimacy of judges' dominance in what is now generally acknowledged to be a "new model of civil litigation." Few, however, have scrutinized the managerial aspects of such postdecision judicial work. Even less attention has been paid to the role judges now play in the pretrial phases of both complex and routine cases.

I believe that the role of judges before adjudication is undergoing a change as substantial as has been recognized in the posttrial phase of public law cases. Today, federal district judges are assigned a case at the time of its filing and assume responsibility for shepherding the case to completion. Judges have described their new tasks as "case management"—hence my term "managerial judges." As managers, judges learn more about cases much earlier than they did in the past. They negotiate with parties about the course, timing, and scope of both pretrial and posttrial litigation. These managerial responsibilities give judges greater power. Yet the restraints that formerly circumscribed judicial authority are conspicuously absent. Managerial judges frequently work beyond the public view, off the record, with no obligation to provide written, reasoned opinions, and out of reach of appellate review.

This new managerial role has emerged for several reasons. One is the creation of pretrial discovery rights. The 1938 Federal Rules of Civil Procedure embodied contradictory mandates: a discovery system ("give your opponent all information relevant to the litigation") was grafted onto American adversarial norms ("protect your client zealously" and therefore "withhold what you can"). In some cases, parties argued about their obligations under the discovery rules; such disputes generated a need for someone to decide pretrial conflicts. Trial judges accepted the assignment and have become mediators, negotiators, and planners—as well as adjudicators. Moreover, once involved in pretrial discovery, many judges became convinced that their presence at other points in a lawsuit's development would be beneficial; supervision of discovery became a conduit for judicial control over all phases of litigation and thus infused lawsuits with the continual presence of the judge-overseer.

Partly because of their new oversight role and partly because of increasing case loads, many judges have become concerned with the volume of their work. To reduce the pressure, judges have turned to efficiency experts who promise "calendar control." Under the experts' guidance, judges have begun to experiment with schemes for speeding the resolution of cases and for persuading litigants to settle rather than try cases whenever possible. During the past decade, enthusiasm for the "managerial movement" has become widespread; what began as an experiment is likely soon to become obligatory. Unless the Supreme Court and Congress reject proposed amendments to the Federal Rules, pretrial judicial management will be required in virtually all cases.

In the rush to conquer the mountain of work, no one—neither judges, court administrators, nor legal commentators—has assessed whether relying on trial judges for informal dispute resolution and for case management, either before or after trial, is good, bad, or neutral. Little empirical evidence supports the claim that judicial management "works" either to settle cases or to provide cheaper, quicker, or fairer dispositions. Proponents of judicial management have also failed to consider the systemic effects of the shift in judicial role. Management is a new form of "judicial activism," a behavior that usually attracts substantial criticism. Moreover, judicial management may be teaching judges to value their statistics, such as the number of case dispositions, more than they value the quality of their dispositions. Finally, because managerial judging is less visible and usually unreviewable, it gives trial courts more authority and at the same time provides litigants with fewer procedural safeguards to protect them from abuse of that authority. In short, managerial judging may be redefining *sub silentio* our standards of what constitutes rational, fair, and impartial adjudication.

*　*　*

THE BY-PRODUCTS OF JUDICIAL MANAGEMENT: THE EROSION OF TRADITIONAL DUE PROCESS SAFEGUARDS

In the rush to conquer case loads, few proponents of managerial judging have examined its side effects. Judicial management has its own techniques, goals, and values, which appear to elevate speed over deliberation, impartiality, and fairness. Ironically, the growth of federal judges' interest in management has coincided with their articulation of due process values, their emphasis on the relationship between procedure and just decisionmaking.

1. *Vast New Powers.*—Judges are very powerful: they decide contested issues, and they alone can compel obedience by the threat of contempt. As a result, those subject to judges' authority may challenge it only at great risk. Under the individual calendar system, a single judge retains control over all phases of a case. Thus, litigants who

incur a judge's displeasure may suffer judicial hostility or even ven-geance with little hope of relief.

Transforming the judge from adjudicator to manager substantially expands the opportunities for judges to use—or abuse—their power. * * *

In addition to enhancing the power of judges, management tends to undermine traditional constraints on the use of that power. * * *

Further, no explicit norms or standards guide judges in their decisions about what to demand of litigants. What does "good," "skilled," or "judicious" management entail? * * *

Given the lack of established standards, judges are forced to draw on their own experience. Judges certainly are familiar with the problems of the courts; they were among the first to identify the need for reform. But awareness of the problems does not necessarily qualify judges to design the solutions, especially on an individual, ad hoc basis. As familiar adages discouraging self-medication by doctors and self-representation by lawyers suggest, self-interest often makes profession-als less objective, dispassionate, and adept at their work. Moreover, judges may well overestimate the extent of their wisdom. Many have been trial lawyers; they have some appreciation for which litigant tactics are well founded and which are dilatory. But because few have practiced in all of the diverse areas of federal court jurisdiction, they may reach ill-founded conclusions in cases about which they really know very little.

2. *The Threat to Impartiality.*—Privacy and informality have some genuine advantages; attorneys and judges can discuss discovery schedules and explore settlement proposals without the constraints of the formal courtroom environment. But substantial dangers also in-here in such activities. The extensive information that judges receive during pretrial conferences has not been filtered by the rules of evi-dence. Some of this information is received ex parte, a process that deprives the opposing party of the opportunity to contest the validity of information received. Moreover, judges are in close contact with attor-neys during the course of management. Such interactions may become occasions for the development of intense feelings—admiration, friend-ship, or antipathy. Therefore, management becomes a fertile field for the growth of personal bias.

Further, judges with supervisory obligations may gain stakes in the cases they manage. Their prestige may ride on "efficient" manage-ment, as calculated by the speed and number of dispositions. Competi-tion and peer pressure may tempt judges to rush litigants because of reasons unrelated to the merits of disputes. * * *

In the past, such exposure to parties and issues and such a comparable interest in the proceedings might have resulted in recusal or disqualification. Despite a flexible approach to the procedural safeguards required to ensure due process, the Supreme Court has consistently required an "impartial" judge—an individual with no prior involvement or interest in the dispute. Interest is broadly defined; indirect as well as direct benefits suffice to require disqualification. Statutory disqualification rules, recently amended and made more stringent, impose similar limits that disqualify judges with only a minute financial interest in the controversies before them. Nevertheless, neither the Supreme Court, the lower federal courts, nor Congress has considered the effect of judicial management on impartiality.

* * *

Having supervised case preparation and pressed for settlement, judges can hardly be considered untainted if they are ultimately asked to find the facts and adjudicate the merits of a dispute.

Unreviewable power, casual contact, and interest in outcome (or in aggregate outcomes) have not traditionally been associated with the "due process" decisionmaking model. These features do not evoke images of reasoned adjudication, images that form the very basis of both our faith in the judicial process and our enormous grant of power to federal judges. The literature of managerial judging refers only occasionally to the values of due process: the accuracy of decisionmaking, the adequacy of reasoning, and the quality of adjudication. Instead, commentators and the training sessions for district judges emphasize speed, control, and quantity. District court chief judges boast of vast statistics on the number of cases terminated, the number and type of discrete events (such as trial days and oral arguments) supervised, and the number of motions decided. The accumulation of such data may cause—or reflect—a subtle shift in the values that shape the judiciary's comprehension of its own mission. Case processing is no longer viewed as a means to an end; instead, it appears to have become the desired goal. Quantity has become all important; quality is occasionally mentioned and then ignored. Indeed, some commentators regard deliberation as an obstacle to efficiency.

Proponents of management may be forgetting the quintessential judicial obligations of conducting a reasoned inquiry, articulating the reasons for decision, and subjecting those reasons to appellate review—characteristics that have long defined judging and distinguished it from other tasks. Although the sword remains in place, the blindfold and scales have all but disappeared. * * *

Questions

1. How would Judges Rubin and Will respond to Professor Resnik's concerns? Who would have the better of the discussion?

2. Is the case against judicial management overstated, especially in light of increasing judicial workloads and responsibilities?

3. Is there some middle-ground between the extremes of absolute passivity and uncontrolled judicial managerialism? How might this middle-ground be found?

SECTION C. THE JUDGE AS SETTLEMENT NEGOTIATOR

HUBERT WILL, ROBERT MERHIGE, JR., AND ALVIN RUBIN—THE ROLE OF THE JUDGE IN THE SETTLEMENT PROCESS

75 F.R.D. 203, 203–05, 211–12, 214–18, 220–22 (1977).
Reprinted with permission of the authors.

[One specific means of managing cases is to secure a settlement without trial. Here several exponents of managerial techniques discuss appropriate methods of facilitating settlement.]

JUDGE WILL: One of the fundamental principles of judicial administration is that, in most cases, the absolute result of a trial is not as high a quality of justice as is the freely negotiated, give a little, take a little settlement. About 90% of all civil cases are disposed of without trial, and have to be or we would all be out of business. That means that a substantial number of them are disposed of by settlement. Some of those which are not tried are disposed of on other grounds, but the largest single category of non-trial dispositions is, of course, the cases that are settled. Therefore, it is essential as part of your procedures to provide some techniques that will maximize the possibility of freely negotiated settlements in cases for which you are responsible.

There is probably no aspect of the art of judging which is more personal, more subjective in the sense both that each judge does it his or her own way, and also with respect to the extent that a judge participates in settlement negotiations. I know judges who will not participate at all, and all settlements are achieved without the judge's assistance or prodding. I know other judges who enjoy participating in the process of negotiating settlements because they rightly feel that they are making a significant contribution to the just disposition of the particular case. * * *

My preliminary pretrial is held normally between 60 and 90 days after the case is filed in those cases in which I hold a preliminary pretrial. There are a number of routine cases in which I do not. In those that I do, however, after we talk about jurisdiction and issues, the scope of discovery, the probable length of discovery and any other questions that may be involved, the last thing we discuss is the possibility of settlement at that time. * * *

I always say, "Do you want me to participate in the discussions, or do you want to go off and have them by yourselves?" This is because, as far as I'm concerned, the use of judge time in settlement negotiations is valuable only if desired. Moreover, psychologically you're in a much better position to be useful in settlement discussions if the lawyers want you to participate. I don't think you can shoot yourself into settlement negotiations effectively unless you're prepared to shoot all the way, which I strongly oppose.

If you coerce a settlement at some figure that you suggest, or come close to coercing it, that is a terrible mistake. I don't think it's a judge's role to decide the case without a trial. In my practice days, I've been the beneficiary, if you like, or the victim of judges who have told me what to pay or what to take in a case at a settlement conference. I think that's outrageous, and not a judicial function at all.

We are catalysts in settlement. Our role is not that of a traditional judge. Our role at that stage is that of a mediator. The settlement has to be, as far as I'm concerned, a voluntary one on the part of the parties. * * *

One final word on the difference between jury and non-jury cases. I have no hesitation in rolling up my sleeves and going the whole way in an analysis of a jury case. I have some reservations about non-jury cases, but, if asked by counsel to participate, I will do so. You have to be a little more careful, and you have to indicate the possibility that you'll transfer the case to another judge for trial if it becomes apparent that, as a result of the negotiations, you are now prejudiced, or believe one side thinks you're now prejudiced, to the point where you couldn't fairly try the case. * * *

JUDGE MERHIGE:

* * *

[M]y practice is to make the lawyers talk about settlement. As I say, I rarely speak of numbers because I don't want to know the numbers. If a jury comes in and goes wild or something, I may have to consider a post-verdict motion, and it might prejudice me if I know that somebody was perfectly willing to pay $50,000.00. If the evidence indicates that that's an excessive demand, I ought not to be influenced.

But I do ask them, "How far apart are you?" Now, everybody has to use their own way of doing it, and—I remember a lesson I learned many years ago when I hadn't been on the bench very long. I was asked to come down to Lynchburg, Virginia, to try a case, by a Judge Dalton, a really loveable guy. I had not been on the bench very long, and the lawyers involved in the case were men of some substance and much older than I. Before the case started, I brought them into chambers and asked them how close they were; whether there was any chance of getting it settled. They assured me there was not.

Then I said, "Well, just how far apart are you?" The lawyers said, "We are $1200.00 apart." And I just really flipped my lid. I had gotten up at 5:00 in the morning to drive down to Lynchburg. About 40 jurors had been summoned. I just really fussed. I said, "Well, that's just disgraceful, gentlemen, to have me come down here, and the court reporter, and staff, and all these jurors. That's just inexcusable."

They responded, "Judge, the clients just won't move, but, in the light of your statements we'll go back and speak to our clients." Well, they went through the usual charade every lawyer's gone through. One came back and said, "Well, I guess I've lost a client because he didn't really want to take that offer but I forced it on him."

And the other guy said, "Yes, I've lost mine too." And I said, "Well, that's unfortunate." But the case was settled.

Then I thought, well, maybe I'd been a little too rough, because I hadn't been very gentle in my statements and they were older men. So I thought I ought to apologize. And I did. I said, "Gentlemen, I'm sorry if I sounded too rough. I made up my mind that, except for the natural arrogance that Congress gives you when you get the robe, I was going to try to restrain myself from exhibiting any that I was born with. And I hope you don't think I pushed you too hard."

They both started to smile, and finally one of them said, "Judge, don't you worry about that." He said, "Let me tell you of an experience I had here with Judge Dalton about a month ago.

"We came in to try a case, and he did exactly as you did. He called the lawyers in and asked, 'How far apart are you?' We told him we were $2,200.00 apart. Judge Dalton got up, took his hat off the coat tree, put his hat on, never said another word to the lawyers, said to his secretary, 'Tell the clerk this case is settled, I'll be at the farm'."

And Hale Collins said, "The lawyers just looked at each other, and they jumped up and looked out the window, and sure enough, there was Judge Dalton going down to the car." And so he said, "Don't apologize. You didn't put quite as much muscle on us as you may have thought."

*   *   *

I think it's our responsibility to push settlements. A lot of judges think it isn't. I think it is because I don't think we could run the courts if we didn't get it, and you know most cases are going to get settled. Most cases should be settled.   *   *   *

Questions

1. Do you agree that the quality of justice achieved is likely to be lower if a case is tried rather than settled? What factors of cost or interpersonal friction might make it so? Are there any sorts of cases in which a trial is more advantageous? See Owen Fiss' article *Against Settlement* excerpted infra, beginning at page 106.

2. What risks do the judges see in excessive judicial involvement in settlement negotiations? Why do they stress their concern about forced settlements? How does a judge know when to stop applying settlement pressure? Can counsel effectively control judicial pressures of this sort?

3. Why are the judges so reluctant to get involved in the settlement of non-jury cases? What are the risks of involvement? Do they underestimate the risks in jury matters?

4. In light of Judge Merhige's story, how far apart must opposing counsel be before compelling settlement becomes improper? Is money likely to be the only issue in such circumstances?

STEPHAN LANDSMAN—THE DECLINE OF THE ADVERSARY SYSTEM: HOW THE RHETORIC OF SWIFT AND CERTAIN JUSTICE HAS AFFECTED ADJUDICATION IN AMERICAN COURTS

29 Buffalo L.Rev. 487, 503–07 (1980).
Reprinted with permission of the publisher, copyright © 1981.
The Buffalo Law Review.

[Professor Landsman explores the system-wide impact of the judiciary's growing desire to settle, rather than try, lawsuits.]

* * *

[R]eformers have sought to curtail the use of adversary process. To accomplish this end, critics have urged that settlement rather than adjudication be used to resolve most disputes.

Settlement is not necessarily antithetical to the adversary process. A high percentage of settlements may even be intrinsic to an adversarial system. Today, over ninety percent of all cases are settled, and the proportion of settlements is growing. If this trend continues, the percentage of settlements may become so great and the pressure for settlement so intense, adversarial reliance on contested trials will be compromised.[76]

[T]he idea that routine cases should not be tried has been frequently endorsed. This is perhaps most apparent in the criminal context, where plea bargaining has received official judicial sanction. Almost without exception, judicial decisions approving the components of the plea system have been justified in terms of the need for speedy adjudication as well as conservation of judicial resources.

A typical holding is the Supreme Court's opinion in *Santobello v. New York.*[78] Chief Justice Burger writing for the Court stated:

> The disposition of criminal charges by agreement between the prosecutor and the accused, sometimes loosely called "plea bargaining," is an essential component of the administration of justice. Properly administered, it is to be encouraged. If every criminal charge were subjected

---

76. See [H. Zeisel, H. Kalven, Jr. & B. Buchholz, *Delay in the Court* 43 (1959)] ("As a matter of policy, it is very doubtful whether the 2 or 3 percent of all claims that are tried to verdict should be reduced any further. It is quite possible they constitute the core of cases which *ought* to be litigated.") (emphasis in the original); Watkins, *Remedies for Court Congestion*, in *Justice on Trial* 179 (D. Douglas & P. Noble eds. 1971); Greene, *Court Reform: What Purpose?*, 58 A.B.A.J. 247, 250 (1972) ("pleas of guilty would be presumed to be the result of undue influence whenever their rate exceeded 90 or 95 percent of all convictions in a particular court").

Some commentators feel that the percentage of settlements has already compromised adversarial reliance on contested trials. See Bazelon, *New Gods for Old: 'Efficient' Courts in a Democratic Society*, 46 N.Y.U.L.Rev. 653, 663–64 (1971) (criminal plea bargaining seeks to persuade "defendants to forego the very rights that government is established to secure" and has substituted the values of "the marketplace" for those appropriate to the criminal justice system); Blumberg, *The Practice of Law as Confidence Game: Organizational Cooption of a Profession*, 1 L. & Soc'y Rev. 15, 18–24 (1967) (the plea system has "coopted" the defense bar) * * *

78. 404 U.S. 257, 92 S.Ct. 495, 30 L.Ed. 2d 427 (1971).

to a full-scale trial, the States and the Federal Government would need to multiply by many times the number of judges and court facilities.

The Supreme Court has not, in *Santobello,* or any other plea bargaining case, considered the potentially adverse effect of bargaining on the adversary process. It has apparently assumed that savings in judicial time and resources justify arrangements in which defendants are strongly encouraged to trade their right to trial for consideration in sentencing.

The reformers have not only sought to reduce the number of cases tried by adversarial methods, they have attempted to alter the nature of the process itself. Basic components of the adversary system, such as judicial passivity, advocate responsibility for the development of cases, jury primacy, traditional rules of procedure and evidence, and thoroughgoing appellate review, have all been sharply criticized. Passivity has been challenged in a number of contexts. In the name of efficiency, judges have been admonished to take charge of settlement negotiations at the earliest moment, to supervise the bargaining process, to render opinions concerning issues not yet litigated, and to settle as many lawsuits as possible. A large number of judges have adopted these and similar practices. The chief justification for change has been the claimed need for greater speed and efficiency. Neither critics nor settlement oriented judges have paid much attention to apparent conflicts created between their approach and the principle of passivity, which has traditionally been viewed as limiting a judge's involvement in the compromise of a case. * * *

OWEN FISS—AGAINST SETTLEMENT

93 Yale L.J. 1073, 1075–78, 1082–83, 1085–90 (1984).
Reprinted with permission of the publisher, copyright © 1984.
The Yale Law Journal Company and Fred B. Rothman and Co.

[Professor Owen Fiss of Yale Law School here analyzes the problems caused by the modern tendency to encourage negotiated settlements to the virtual exclusion of formal adjudication.]

The advocates of [negotiated resolution] are led * * * to exalt the idea of settlement * * * because they view adjudication as a process to resolve disputes. They act as though courts arose to resolve quarrels between neighbors who had reached an impasse and turned to a stranger for help. Courts are seen as an institutionalization of the stranger and adjudication is viewed as the process by which the stranger exercises power. The very fact that the neighbors have turned to someone else to resolve their dispute signifies a breakdown in their social relations; the [supporters of settlement] acknowledge this, but nonetheless hope that the neighbors will be able to reach agreement before the stranger renders judgment. Settlement is that agreement. It is a truce more than a true reconciliation, but it seems preferable to judgment because it rests on the consent of both parties and avoids the cost of a lengthy trial.

In my view, however, this account of adjudication and the case for settlement rest on questionable premises. I do not believe that settlement as a generic practice is preferable to judgment or should be institutionalized on a wholesale and indiscriminate basis. It should be treated instead as a highly problematic technique for streamlining dockets. Settlement is for me the civil analogue of plea bargaining: Consent is often coerced; the bargain may be struck by someone without authority; the absence of a trial and judgment renders subsequent judicial involvement troublesome; and although dockets are trimmed, justice may not be done. Like plea bargaining, settlement is a capitulation to the conditions of mass society and should be neither encouraged nor praised.

By viewing the lawsuit as a quarrel between two neighbors, the [proponent of settlement] implicitly asks us to assume a rough equality between the contending parties. It treats settlement as the anticipation of the outcome of trial and assumes that the terms of settlement are simply a product of the parties' predictions of that outcome. In truth, however, settlement is also a function of the resources available to each party to finance the litigation, and those resources are frequently distributed unequally. Many lawsuits do not involve a property dispute between two neighbors, or between AT & T and the government (to update the story), but rather concern a struggle between a member of a racial minority and a municipal police department over alleged brutality, or a claim by a worker against a large corporation over work-related injuries. In these cases, the distribution of financial resources, or the ability of one party to pass along its costs, will invariably infect the bargaining process, and the settlement will be at odds with a conception of justice that seeks to make the wealth of the parties irrelevant.

The disparities in resources between the parties can influence the settlement in three ways. First, the poorer party may be less able to amass and analyze the information needed to predict the outcome of the litigation, and thus be disadvantaged in the bargaining process. Second, he may need the damages he seeks immediately and thus be induced to settle as a way of accelerating payment, even though he realizes he would get less now than he might if he awaited judgment. All plaintiffs want their damages immediately, but an indigent plaintiff may be exploited by a rich defendant because his need is so great that the defendant can force him to accept a sum that is less than the ordinary present value of the judgment. Third, the poorer party might be forced to settle because he does not have the resources to finance the litigation, to cover either his own projected expenses, such as his lawyer's time, or the expenses his opponent can impose through the manipulation of procedural mechanisms such as discovery. It might seem that settlement benefits the plaintiff by allowing him to avoid the costs of litigation, but this is not so. The defendant can anticipate the plaintiff's costs if the case were to be tried fully and decrease his offer by that amount. The indigent plaintiff is a victim of the costs of litigation even if he settles.

There are exceptions. Seemingly rich defendants may sometimes be subject to financial pressures that make them as anxious to settle as indigent plaintiffs. But I doubt that these circumstances occur with any great frequency. I also doubt that institutional arrangements such as contingent fees or the provision of legal services to the poor will in fact equalize resources between contending parties: The contingent fee does not equalize resources; it only makes an indigent plaintiff vulnerable to the willingness of the private bar to invest in his case. In effect, the ability to exploit the plaintiff's lack of resources has been transferred from rich defendants to lawyers who insist upon a hefty slice of the plaintiff's recovery as their fee. These lawyers, moreover, will only work for contingent fees in certain kinds of cases, such as personal-injury suits. And the contingent fee is of no avail when the defendant is the disadvantaged party. Governmental subsidies for legal services have a broader potential, but in the civil domain the battle for these subsidies was hard-fought, and they are in fact extremely limited, especially when it comes to cases that seek systemic reform of government practices.

Of course, imbalances of power can distort judgment as well: Resources influence the quality of presentation, which in turn has an important bearing on who wins and the terms of victory. We count, however, on the guiding presence of the judge, who can employ a number of measures to lessen the impact of distributional inequalities. He can, for example, supplement the parties' presentations by asking questions, calling his own witnesses, and inviting other persons and institutions to participate as amici. These measures are likely to make only a small contribution toward moderating the influence of distributional inequalities, but should not be ignored for that reason. Not even these small steps are possible with settlement. There is, moreover, a critical difference between a process like settlement, which is based on bargaining and accepts inequalities of wealth as an integral and legitimate component of the process, and a process like judgment, which knowingly struggles against those inequalities. Judgment aspires to an autonomy from distributional inequalities, and it gathers much of its appeal from this aspiration. * * *

The [insistence on settlement] trivializes the remedial dimensions of lawsuits and mistakenly assumes judgment to be the end of the process. It supposes that the judge's duty is to declare which neighbor is right and which wrong, and that this declaration will end the judge's involvement (save in that most exceptional situation where it is also necessary for him to issue a writ directing the sheriff to execute the declaration). Under these assumptions, settlement appears as an almost perfect substitute for judgment, for it too can declare the parties' rights. Often, however, judgment is not the end of a lawsuit but only the beginning. The involvement of the court may continue almost indefinitely. In these cases, settlement cannot provide an adequate basis for that necessary continuing involvement, and thus is no substitute for judgment.

The parties may sometimes be locked in combat with one another and view the lawsuit as only one phase in a long continuing struggle. The entry of judgment will then not end the struggle, but rather change its terms and the balance of power. One of the parties will invariably return to the court and again ask for its assistance, not so much because conditions have changed, but because the conditions that preceded the lawsuit have unfortunately not changed. This often occurs in domestic-relations cases, where the divorce decree represents only the opening salvo in an endless series of skirmishes over custody and support.

The structural reform cases that play such a prominent role on the federal docket provide another occasion for continuing judicial involvement. In these cases, courts seek to safeguard public values by restructuring large-scale bureaucratic organizations. The task is enormous, and our knowledge of how to restructure on-going bureaucratic organizations is limited. As a consequence, courts must oversee and manage the remedial process for a long time—maybe forever. This, I fear, is true of most school desegregation cases, some of which have been pending for twenty or thirty years. It is also true of antitrust cases that seek divestiture or reorganization of an industry. * * *

[Those who champion settlement make it] appear as a perfect substitute for judgment, as we just saw, by trivializing the remedial dimensions of a lawsuit, and also by reducing the social function of the lawsuit to one of resolving private disputes: [S]ettlement appears to achieve exactly the same purpose as judgment—peace between the parties—but at considerably less expense to society. The two quarreling neighbors turn to a court in order to resolve their dispute, and society makes courts available because it wants to aid in the achievement of their private ends or to secure the peace.

In my view, however, the purpose of adjudication should be understood in broader terms. Adjudication uses public resources, and employs not strangers chosen by the parties but public officials chosen by a process in which the public participates. These officials, like members of the legislative and executive branches, possess a power that has been defined and conferred by public law, not by private agreement. Their job is not to maximize the ends of private parties, nor simply to secure the peace, but to explicate and give force to the values embodied in authoritative texts such as the Constitution and statutes: to interpret those values and to bring reality into accord with them. This duty is not discharged when the parties settle.

In our political system, courts are reactive institutions. They do not search out interpretive occasions, but instead wait for others to bring matters to their attention. They also rely for the most part on others to investigate and present the law and facts. A settlement will thereby deprive a court of the occasion, and perhaps even the ability, to render an interpretation. A court cannot proceed (or not proceed very far) in the face of a settlement. To be against settlement is not to urge that parties be "forced" to litigate, since that would interfere with their autonomy and distort the adjudicative process; the parties will be inclined to make the court believe that their bargain is justice. To be against settlement is only to suggest that when the parties settle, society gets less than what appears, and for a price it does not know it is paying. Parties might settle while leaving justice undone. The settlement of a school suit might secure the peace, but not racial equality. Although the parties are prepared to live under the terms they bargained for, and although such peaceful coexistence may be a necessary precondition of justice, and itself a state of affairs to be valued, it is not justice itself. To settle for something means to accept less than some ideal. ＊   ＊   ＊

Questions

1.   Is Professor Fiss correct that settlement is usually "truce not true reconciliation"? What proof does he offer?

2.   Is Professor Fiss accurate in his description of the possible sources of coercion that can lead to unfair settlements?

3.   Aren't wealth and power factors that will have a serious impact on trials as well as settlements?

4.   How many lawsuits raise the sorts of constitutional or statutory issues Professor Fiss is concerned about?

5.   Is Professor Fiss right when he argues that settlement imposes hidden costs on society by depriving courts of the opportunity to address the issues raised?

SECTION D. THE JUDGE AS ACTIVE PARTICIPANT IN LITIGATION—PURSUING THE "PUBLIC INTEREST"

RESERVE MINING CO. v. LORD
United States Court of Appeals, Eighth Circuit, 1976.
529 F.2d 181, 182, 184–88.

[The United States government and the State of Minnesota along with a number of others sued to stop the discharge of taconite tailings (the waste produced as part of the refining process that turns low grade iron ore, taconite, into a product that can be used to make iron and steel) into the air above Silver Lake, Minnesota, and into the water of Lake Superior. After lengthy and acrimonious proceedings including a nine month trial with more than 100 witnesses and 1600 exhibits, Federal District Court Judge Miles Lord found that the discharge was a threat to public health because the tailings were essentially identical to a form of asbestos known to cause cancer in humans. The district judge issued an order that all refining operations cease at once and sought by the exercise of judicial authority to impose a series of orders upon all the parties to the case.

The Court of Appeals for the Eighth Circuit agreed that there was a need to arrange for the eventual abatement of the taconite tailing pollution. It held, however, that the Reserve Mining Company should be given time to alter its method of refining taconite and that the risk to public health was not so grave as to warrant immediate cessation of operations. In the opinion reproduced below the Eighth Circuit turned its attention to the complaint of Reserve Mining about the extremely active involvement of Judge Lord in proceedings subsequent to the court of appeals' order in the litigation.]

Opinion of the Court by CIRCUIT JUDGE LAY, CIRCUIT JUDGE BRIGHT, CIRCUIT JUDGE ROSS, CIRCUIT JUDGE STEPHENSON, CIRCUIT JUDGE WEBSTER AND CIRCUIT JUDGE HENLEY.

* * *

II. RECUSAL.

A. Denial of Due Process and Judicial Bias.

The request for recusal which was made at oral argument in this court arose out of a series of hearings in November, 1975. A hearing on the state's motion to order the Corps of Engineers to continue filtration commenced on November 10 in the district court before Judge Lord. At that time it was the state's position that although the City of Duluth might be able to undertake adequate supervision of water filtration, the smaller communities could not. The district court orally ruled that he would deny the state's motion, but would entertain and sustain a motion to have the City of Duluth filter the water at Reserve's expense.[3] The court then continued the matter until November 14, and as we later discuss, requested officials of the Minnesota Pollution Control Agency to attend that hearing.

After the proceedings on November 14, the matter was continued to the following day. On Saturday morning, November 15, after a short proceeding, the court ordered:

> Reserve Mining Company, as of Monday morning at 10:00 o'clock, shall hand to the City Treasurer of the City of Duluth, a check in the amount of $100,000.00. And there will be no stay on that. That is a firm and final order. That may be appealed, but I do not certify it for appeal because I am not at all in doubt about its propriety.

Transcript of November 15, 1975 hearing at 137.

---

3. The court said:

I would like to see the Mayor of Duluth, the Duluth City Attorney and the members of the city council, because if they don't move for clean water, Duluth will have no clean water. * * * I will re-

quire that they pay it themselves out of their city treasury unless they move to collect it from Reserve.

Transcript of November 10, 1975 hearing at 23.

Reserve alleged lack of notice and opportunity to be heard, sought a writ of mandamus to enjoin interference with the state proceedings and filed its notice of appeal from the order requiring deposit of $100,000.00.

The record reveals that Reserve had no notice of any motion to assess damages against it at the proceedings held on November 10, 14, 15 and 19. Reserve was afforded no opportunity to be heard or to cross-examine any witnesses. For the most part the proceedings constituted a review of the evidence relating to air pollution. The court called witnesses and testified himself. Early in these proceedings the court announced:

> I have dispensed with the usual adversary proceeding here, because I simply do not have time to spend, as I did, nine months in hearing, six months of which was wasted by what I find now, and did find in my opinions, to be misrepresentations by Reserve Mining Company. Six out of nine months.

Transcript of November 14, 1975 hearing at 26.

Ordinarily, when unfair judicial procedures result in a denial of due process, this court could simply find error, reverse and remand the matter. Recusal would be altogether inappropriate. However, the record in this case demonstrates more serious problems. The denial of fair procedures here was due not to good faith mistakes of judgment or misapplication of the proper rules of law by the district court. The record demonstrates overt acts by the district judge reflecting great bias against Reserve Mining Company and substantial disregard for the mandate of this court.

It is urged that the district court's actions were nothing more than a judge acting upon his deep convictions formed after nine and one-half months of trial. No one can doubt that Judge Lord does have deep convictions in this matter or that such convictions largely influenced his actions. However, the record reveals more than a trial judge merely acting in accord with his prior judgment. In the November proceeding Judge Lord called and examined the witnesses and interspersed testimony of his own; the trial judge announced on the record that witnesses called by Reserve could not be believed, "that in every instance Reserve Mining Company hid the evidence, misrepresented, delayed and frustrated the ultimate conclusions;" and that he did not have "any faith" in witnesses to be called by Reserve. Transcript of November 14, 1975 hearing at 2–5, 56, 109. He further announced that the court would have to take depositions since the lawyers opposing Reserve "did not know anything about it." Transcript of November 19, 1975 hearing at 25.

Judge Lord seems to have shed the robe of the judge and to have assumed the mantle of the advocate. The court thus becomes lawyer, witness and judge in the same proceeding, and abandons the greatest virtue of a fair and conscientious judge—impartiality. * * *

Questions

1. Why did Judge Lord act the way he did? Why did he feel the need to act on his own despite the presence of a host of plaintiffs inlcuding the United States government and the State of Minnesota?

2. What was the effect of Judge Lord's behavior upon the quality and integrity of the proceedings in the *Reserve Mining* case? Can a judge be both extremely active and impartial?

3. Are there ever circumstances when courts must take charge of remedial activities? What are they?

ABRAM CHAYES—THE ROLE OF THE JUDGE IN PUBLIC LAW LITIGATION

89 Harv.L.Rev. 1281, 1282–84, 1296–98 (1976).
Reprinted with permission of the publisher, copyright © 1976.
Harvard Law Review Association.

[Professor Chayes was one of the first to identify and describe the trend toward "public law" adjudication. His affirmative view of this development and careful analysis have served as a focal point for much of the modern debate about judicial activism.]

* * * We are witnessing the emergence of a new model of civil litigation and, I believe, our traditional conception of adjudication and the assumptions upon which it is based provide an increasingly unhelpful, indeed misleading framework for assessing either the workability or the legitimacy of the roles of judge and court within this model.

In our received tradition, the lawsuit is a vehicle for settling disputes between private parties about private rights. The defining features of this conception of civil adjudication are:

(1) The lawsuit is *bipolar*. Litigation is organized as a contest between two individuals or at least two unitary interests, diametrically opposed, to be decided on a winner-takes-all basis.

(2) Litigation is *retrospective*. The controversy is about an identified set of completed events: whether they occurred, and if so, with what consequences for the legal relations of the parties.

(3) *Right and remedy are interdependent*. The scope of the relief is derived more or less logically from the substantive violation under the general theory that the plaintiff will get compensation measured by the harm caused by the defendant's breach of duty—in contract by giving plaintiff the money he would have had absent the breach; in tort by paying the value of the damage caused.

(4) The lawsuit is a *self-contained* episode. The impact of the judgment is confined to the parties. If plaintiff prevails there is a simple compensatory transfer, usually of money, but occasionally the return of a thing or the performance of a definite act. If defendant prevails, a loss lies where it has fallen. In either case, entry of judgment ends the court's involvement.

(5) The process is *party-initiated and party-controlled*. The case is organized and the issues defined by exchanges between the parties. Responsibility for fact development is theirs. The trial judge is a neutral arbiter of their interactions who decides questions of law only if they are put in issue by an appropriate move of a party.

This capsule description of what I have called the traditional conception of adjudication is no doubt overdrawn. It was not often, if ever, expressed so severely; indeed, because it was so thoroughly taken for granted, there was little occasion to do so. Although I do not contend that the traditional conception ever conformed fully to what judges were doing in fact, I believe it has been central to our understanding and our analysis of the legal system.

Whatever its historical validity, the traditional model is clearly invalid as a description of much current civil litigation in the federal district courts. Perhaps the dominating characteristic of modern federal litigation is that lawsuits do not arise out of disputes between private parties about private rights. Instead, the object of litigation is the vindication of constitutional or statutory policies. The shift in the legal basis of the lawsuit explains many, but not all, facets of what is going on "in fact" in federal trial courts. For this reason, although the label is not wholly satisfactory, I shall call the emerging model "public law litigation."

The characteristic features of the public law model are very different from those of the traditional model. The party structure is sprawling and amorphous, subject to change over the course of the litigation. The traditional adversary relationship is suffused and intermixed with negotiating and mediating processes at every point. The judge is the dominant figure in organizing and guiding the case, and he draws for support not only on the parties and their counsel, but on a wide range of outsiders—masters, experts, and oversight personnel. Most important, the trial judge has increasingly become the creator and manager of complex forms of ongoing relief, which have widespread effects on persons not before the court and require the judge's continuing involvement in administration and implementation. School desegregation, employment discrimination, and prisoners' or inmates' rights cases come readily to mind as avatars of this new form of litigation. But it would be mistaken to suppose that it is confined to these areas. Antitrust, securities fraud and other aspects of the conduct of corporate business, bankruptcy and reorganizations, union governance, consumer fraud, housing discrimination, electoral reapportionment, environmental management—cases in all these fields display in varying degrees the features of public law litigation.

THE CHANGING CHARACTER OF FACTFINDING

The traditional model of adjudication was primarily concerned with assessing the consequences for the parties of specific past instances of conduct. This retrospective orientation is often inapposite in public law litigation, where the lawsuit generally seeks to enjoin future or threatened action, or to modify a course of conduct presently in train or a condition presently existing. In the former situation, the question whether threatened action will materialize, in what circumstances, and with what consequences can, in the nature of things, be answered only by an educated guess. In the latter case, the inquiry is only secondarily concerned with how the condition came about, and even less with the subjective attitudes of the actors, since positive regulatory goals are ordinarily defined without reference to such matters. Indeed, in dealing with the actions of large political or corporate aggregates, notions of will, intention, or fault increasingly become only metaphors.

In the remedial phases of public law litigation, factfinding is even more clearly prospective. [T]he contours of relief are not derived logically from the substantive wrong adjudged, as in the traditional model. The elaboration of a decree is largely a discretionary process within which the trial judge is called upon to assess and appraise the consequences of alternative programs that might correct the substantive fault. In both the liability and remedial phases, the relevant inquiry is largely the same: How can the policies of a public law best be served in a concrete case?

In public law litigation, * * * factfinding is principally concerned with "legislative" rather than "adjudicative" fact. And "fact evaluation" is perhaps a more accurate term than "factfinding." The whole process begins to look like the traditional description of legislation: Attention is drawn to a "mischief," existing or threatened, and the activity of the parties and court is directed to the development of ongoing measures designed to cure that mischief. Indeed, if, as is often the case, the decree sets up an affirmative regime governing the activities in controversy for the indefinite future and having binding force for persons within its ambit, then it is not very much of a stretch to see it as, *pro tanto,* a legislative act.

Given these consequences, the casual attitude of the traditional model toward factfinding is no longer tolerable. The extended impact of the judgment demands a more visibly reliable and credible procedure for establishing and evaluating the fact elements in the litigation, and one that more explicitly recognizes the complex and continuous interplay between fact evaluation and legal consequence. The major response to the new requirements has been to place the responsibility for factfinding increasingly on the trial judge. The shift was in large part accomplished as a function of the growth of equitable business in the federal courts, for historically the chancellor was trier of fact in suits in equity. But on the "law side" also, despite the Supreme Court's expansion of the federal right to jury trial, there has been a pronounced decline in the exercise of the right, apart, perhaps, from personal injury cases.

The courts, it seems, continue to rely primarily on the litigants to produce and develop factual materials, but a number of factors make it impossible to leave the organization of the trial exclusively in their hands. With the diffusion of the party structure, fact issues are no longer sharply drawn in a confrontation between two adversaries, one asserting the affirmative and the other the negative. The litigation is often extraordinarily complex and extended in time, with a continuous and intricate interplay between factual and legal elements. It is hardly feasible and, absent a jury, unnecessary to set aside a contiguous block of time for a "trial stage" at which all significant factual issues will be presented. The scope of the fact investigation and the sheer volume of factual material that can be exhumed by the discovery process pose enormous problems of organization and assimilation. All these factors thrust the trial judge into an active role in shaping, organizing and facilitating the litigation. We may not yet have reached the investigative judge of the continental systems, but we have left the passive arbiter of the traditional model a long way behind. * * *

Questions

1. Would Professor Chayes approve of Judge Lord's conduct in the *Reserve Mining* case?

2. Where ought the line between proper and improper judicial behavior be drawn in "public law" litigation? Who has the authority to draw such a line?

3. What, if any, adversarial constraints on judicial activity would Professor Chayes recognize as valid?

4. In an article entitled, *The Judiciary: Umpire or Empire*, 6 Law and Human Behavior 129 (1983), Professor Donald Horowitz has argued that one of the least effective ways to develop new policies or reform institutions is to use the judicial process because "(1) access is voluntary; (2) participation is narrow; (3) decision is mandatory; (4) the decision maker is isolated from the environment in which the decision must operate; [and] (5) enforcement is largely private." How do you think Professor Chayes would respond to this observation? Who has the better of the argument?

5. If "public law" litigation is so much like legislative activity why not leave such matters to the legislatures? What should courts do when legislatures refuse to act?

SECTION E. THE JUDGE AS PARTICIPANT—COMMENTARY, EXAMINATION, AND DECORUM

STEPHEN SALTZBURG—THE UNNECESSARILY EXPANDING ROLE OF THE AMERICAN TRIAL JUDGE

64 Va.L.Rev. 1, 7–10, 35, 43–45, 52–53, 55–56, 71–72, 80–81 (1978).
Reprinted with permission of the publisher, copyright © 1978.
Virginia Law Review Association and Fred. B. Rothman and Co.

[Professor Saltzburg summarizes the restraints that use of an adversarial system and a jury trial mechanism ought to be seen as imposing on trial judges.]

* * *

JUDICIAL INSTINCTS, PERCEPTIONS, AND PRESSURES

Against the background of criticism of the capabilities of trial lawyers, and in light of increasing complaints of incompetence formally filed with courts, it is understandable that the trial judge is emerging as a more active participant at trial, rather than as a neutral observer. First, because an adversary system assumes that competing litigants are capable of protecting their respective interests by presenting their cases to the trier of fact in an effective way, trial judges sometimes may believe that lawyer error or incompetence detracts from the "search for truth" and unfairly threatens a litigant's interest. Second, in an era of burgeoning caseloads, complex litigation, and overworked judges, it is readily apparent why some judges believe they must intervene at trial to maintain a reasonable pace and to protect their dockets from unnecessary overcrowding.

The more important of these factors seems to be judicial dedication to the view that a trial is a search for truth, not merely a battle of wits between adversaries. Proponents of this view often believe that the judge not only shares "the role of all lawyers . . . to see that justice is done," but also has a special responsibility, because, unlike most lawyers, he is present during a trial, is capable of taking action, and, as an "unbiased" observer, is in a good position to do so. Moreover, it is natural for a trial judge to believe that his selection as a judge from the ranks of the practicing bar was a recognition of his special litigation skills. As an ex-trial lawyer, the courtroom judge instinctively may desire to participate as much as possible in the making of a case. To the extent that a judge can rationalize his intervention as an ameliorative device to cushion the ill effects attributable to lawyer incompetence or as a mechanism for efficient caseload management, he is apt to follow his natural instinct to intervene.

At times, this natural instinct is characterized as a judicial duty. Judge Learned Hand, for example, wrote that "[a] judge is more than a moderator; he is charged to see that the law is properly administered, and it is a duty which he cannot discharge by remaining inert." A more recent appellate opinion declares that "the trial judge may, and indeed should, take an active part in the trial where necessary to clarify evidence and assist the jury." Suggestions are made that, unless the judge assumes an active role, the adversary system will not always yield a just result.

An Alternative Thesis

This article contends that there has been, still is, and probably always will be merit to the notion that the good trial judge—who is a careful and impartial listener, who believes that the parties to litigation should be able to expect that an accurate and fair result will be reached if reasonably possible, and who recognizes that defective presentations by counsel are not a necessary part of most trials—should be permitted to act in an effort to improve the quality of courtroom justice. But this action almost always should be channeled through the attorneys for the parties, even in nonjury cases. This procedure insures that the trial judge will appear as neutral as possible, that he will carry out the supervisory function at trial intended by our adversary procedure, and that there will be no judicial skewing of the cases presented by the parties. When contrasted with the competing model of judicial intervention, the approach advocated herein is more consistent with the philosophy and goals of the adversary system and the right to jury trial provided by federal and state constitutions. Hence, this article opposes the authority of trial judges to sum up and to comment upon evidence and urges that trial judges be granted only the most limited authority to call and to interrogate witnesses. Adoption of this position should not damage the judge's capacity to monitor an efficient "search for truth" in an adversary setting. * * *

The Threat to the Adversary System

The judicial powers of summation and comment interfere * * * with the adversary system [and] the right to jury trial. A fundamental element of the adversary system is the opportunity during trial for counsel of the opposing parties to analyze the bias of trial participants and to meet the contentions raised by opposing counsel. This opportunity ensures that all evidence presented to the jury has been challenged from the perspective of each party.

No such opportunity, however, exists at any point during litigation to expose to the jury the potential biases of the trial judge. The lawyers cannot question the judge to probe his experience, attitudes, and prejudices. They cannot argue that the judge's view of the issues or the facts is incorrect. Because the judge's summation and comment often conclude the case except for his jury instructions, the lawyers typically have no opportunity at all to reargue the case. Even if such an opportunity existed, an attempt to impeach the judge's integrity or to contradict his statements could antagonize the jurors. Thus, the lawyers are unable to challenge sufficiently the views of the trial judge.

Because the judge's views cannot be challenged directly by the parties, his opinions are likely to have an undue impact on the jury's deliberations. His statements are the only part of the trial that is nonadversarial and thus may convey an unwarranted sense of impartiality. Whereas the attorneys are identified with the parties they represent and their biases are obvious when they argue, the quirks or peculiarities of the judge are not so obvious. The jurors are apt to assume that the judge is completely neutral and infinitely wise. * * * The presumption of neutrality, combined with the timing of the judge's comments and the inability of the parties to rebut his opinions, render the judge's summation or comment a powerful influence on the jury. This influence runs counter to the principle of the adversary system that the parties, acting in their own interest, are supposed to present and to argue the evidence to their own advantage. * * *

JUDICIAL INTERROGATION OF WITNESSES

In most jurisdictions, trial judges are empowered to interrogate witnesses. As Wigmore has noted, "[o]ne of the natural parts of the judicial function, in its orthodox and sound recognition, is the judge's power and duty to *put to the witnesses* such *additional questions* as seem to him desirable to elicit the truth more fully." McCormick has written that "[t]he judge in his discretion may examine any witness to bring out needed facts which have not been elicited by the parties."

But the source of a trial judge's power to question witnesses and the restraints upon his power "rest on the same considerations as qualify his right to comment and sum up . . . ." The general rule is that the trial judge is not permitted to do by questioning what he is not permitted to do directly by summation or comment. Thus, if the judge is restricted from offering opinions on the credibility of particular witnesses, on the ultimate issues in the case, or on other specific subjects, he may not express the court's opinion on these subjects by invoking the power to interrogate witnesses.

Active judicial interrogation runs afoul of basic principles underlying the adversary system. One such principle, as important as any other and arguably the most important, is that the adversary system permits opposing parties, unencumbered by outside intervention, to present their strongest arguments to the trier of fact. By disrupting an attorney's preferred order of presentation, a judge's active interrogation may minimize the impact of some witnesses' testimony, while maximizing the impact of others'. Therefore, the judge's questioning may confer an unintended advantage upon one party that the lawyer could not have obtained otherwise and that the opposing party cannot counteract during trial.

[T]he judge who actively interrogates a witness is interfering with the opportunity of the adversaries to make their cases as strong as possible and with their opportunity to give the trier of fact, whether judge or jury, the chance to see the full strength of each competing position.

Active interrogation also interferes with the independence of the jury. Such questioning is apt to suggest to a jury that the attorney's interrogation is misguided, inept, or incomplete. In addition, the judge may prejudice the jury against a party by conveying the inference that counsel is deliberately concealing information. As with summation and comment, the judge's questioning introduces his opinions to the jury and suggests that he has discerned the "truth." Judge Frankel has observed that trial judges "should be candid . . . in recognizing that juries are probably correct most of the time if they glean a point of view from the judge's interpolations." Judicial interrogation, however, poses even greater dangers than summation and comment. In questioning witnesses, the judge, rather than merely expressing an opinion on the evidence, creates new evidence for the jury's consideration. The jury may accept this evidence rather than that of the parties and may use the evidence to reach the result it believes the judge prefers.
* * *

JUDICIAL CALLING OF LAY WITNESSES SUA SPONTE

With the possible exception of calling expert witnesses, the trial judge should not interfere with the adversary process by calling a witness that neither party wishes to call. This position is consistent with the parties' obligation to prepare a case as well as to present it at trial. Because the judge does not assist in pretrial preparation, he often does not know what witnesses exist. Even a pretrial conference may not inform the judge of all the potential witnesses. If the judge learns of such witnesses, he may not know what relevant information they have to provide. Lacking independent knowledge of both the case and the witnesses' testimony, the judge is not in a position to determine whether the witnesses' testimony would advance or retard the proceedings. "Without an investigative file, the American trial judge is a blind and blundering intruder, acting in spasms as sudden flashes of seeming light may lead or mislead him at odd times."

Moreover, the court's intervention may introduce an element of unfair surprise into the trial. Having made the decision not to call a witness, the parties may not be able to deal with the court's witness in the same manner as they deal with other witnesses. This would be most unfortunate, because the jury is apt to give the court's witness special treatment. Once again, the judge who wishes to ease the factfinding burden of the jury must be careful not to distort the proceedings. * * *

CONCLUSION

Beginning with the premise that the adversary system and the right to a jury trial are recognized as fundamental parts of the American trial system, this article has attempted to outline permissible and impermissible techniques of judicial intervention in trials. It must be noted that criticism of the contemporary role of the judge in federal courts and in some state courts runs against the grain of current comment. The trend seems to be to let the judge become more active, to let the judge search for truth, to let the judge do what he believes must be done in order to provide a "fair trial" for the litigants. The position asserted here is that the trial judge can act in many ways to assist the litigants in trying their cases fully and fairly, but that the trial judge who attempts to usurp control from the parties compromises the integrity of the bench and often threatens the independence of the jury.

Thus, there is no current need for judges to exercise the power to sum up or comment upon evidence adduced at trial. Nor is there a need, at least in progressive jurisdictions, for trial judges to call witnesses either sua sponte or at the request of a party. Although there may be a need for judges to call witnesses in some less progressive jurisdictions, the practice still should be avoided in favor of an alternative procedure outlined above. Moreover, although the trial judge should ask a witness questions necessary to clarify his testimony, it is dangerous for the trial judge to explore new territory with any witness, even one called by the court in an exceptional case.

In suggesting alternatives to the exercise of powers that some have regarded as desirable, this article has attempted to establish a regime in which the trial judge can work with counsel for a more effective trial system. One wise judge made the following remark to his colleagues:

> Although you may be the smartest and wisest judge anywhere, when you are trying a case that you have to decide you are dependent on the lawyers. It's very hard to be better than the lawyers. So the whole thrust of your pre-trial and trial actions in a case to be submitted to you is to help the lawyers to do their thing so that your brilliance and wisdom will be permitted to do justice.[330]

Questions

1. Do you agree with Professor Saltzburg's arguments about judicial restraint?

2. What are the dangers of such an approach?

3. Is the final quotation used by Professor Saltzburg, concerning cooperation between court and counsel, correct? Can cooperation be fostered by judicial "management" and active participation in the case?

---

330. Joiner, *Non–Jury Trials,* in *Seminars for Newly Appointed United States District Judges,* 1973–75, at 305, 309 (Federal Judicial Center ed. 1976).

Chapter 4

THE PLACE OF THE JURY IN ADVERSARIAL ADJUDICATION

One of the ways the American adversary system has traditionally ensured the passivity and neutrality of the fact finder is by use of the jury trial. The laymen who serve as jurors are not permitted any part in the prosecution of the cases they hear. Their passivity is complete until they are called upon to render a verdict. While every decision maker brings biases to the adjudicatory process the jury mechanism offers a number of methods of curtailing prejudice including a pre-selection questioning procedure to identify and remove the partial (generally referred to as voir dire), a collegial decision making process designed to neutralize idiosyncratic views, and an evidentiary screening mechanism intended to restrict disclosure of provocative or misleading information.

The jury consists of men and women drawn from virtually every walk of life. Our law requires that those summoned represent a cross-section of the populace with respect to race, sex, religion, national origin and economic status. Once summoned the potential jurors form a pool, or venire, from which those who will actually sit on each case are picked. Jury trials get under way with the voir dire, or question-ing, of potential jurors drawn at random from the venire. Those whose answers reveal prejudice or fixity of attitude will be excused for cause. Additionally, the lawyers representing each litigant will be allowed to strike a limited number of potential jurors without cause. Such strikes are generally referred to as peremptory challenges.

Once impanelled the jury is presented with all the admissible evidence and then charged to render a verdict. Its verdict may be either general in form ("we find for the plaintiff/defendant") or, if the court requires, may be fashioned in response to a set of specific questions submitted by the judge. Traditionally, the law required that each case be decided by twelve jurors in unanimous accord about their verdict. The jury of twelve and unanimity requirements have, howev-er, been seriously eroded over the past 20 years.

122

The jury has long been a part of the American legal system. Since the time of the ratification of the Constitution, the Sixth and Seventh Amendments have required the use of juries in most criminal and civil matters heard in federal courts. Virtually every state also insists upon jury trials in serious cases. Despite all this the jury is under serious attack today. Critics claim that juries are slow and unreliable. They urge that jury trial be curtailed whenever possible. At the heart of the debate about the worth of the jury is a set of empirical questions concerning the quality of jury deliberations and the operation of different size juries. The materials that follow are devoted to an exploration of these issues as well as a more general examination of the functioning of the jury.

SECTION A. THE JURY IN ACTION

MELVYN ZERMAN—CALL THE FINAL WITNESS

122–42 (1977).
Reprinted by permission of the publisher, copyright © 1977.
Harper and Row Publishers, Inc.

[Melvyn Zerman served as juror number 11 in the murder trial of Darrell Mathes.[a] Social science research suggests that the *Mathes* jury proceeded in fairly typical fashion. The length of its deliberations was approximately one hour per day of courtroom proceedings as would have been predicted in light of the work of Harry Kalven and Hans Zeisel in their classic study, *The American Jury* (see page 152, infra.). The jury's method of debate (primarily focused on the critical factual questions presented at trial) and pattern of decision-making (beginning with a majority in the eventual direction of decision and ultimately wearing down a lone dissenter) are also consistent with research findings.[b]

The murder under review in the *Mathes* case occurred on October 14, 1974, when Edward Fendt, a delivery man for the Wise Potato Chip Company, was accosted and shot to death during an attempted holdup. A reward of $1000 was offered for the arrest and conviction of the murderer. Three youngsters, Jennifer, Clarissa, and Jimmy, eventually came forward and claimed they had witnessed the crime. They identified Darrell Mathes, nicknamed Ricky, as the murderer. Their accusation was riddled with inconsistencies and did not square with the testimony of a number of adult witnesses. The State, however, on the strength of the youngsters' statements chose to go forward. The case was prosecuted by Assistant District Attorney Bernard Mendelow and defended by attorneys Leroy Kellam and Stephen Singer. The presiding judge was Thomas Agresta. The following passage describes the deliberations of the jury.]

a. Mr. Zerman fictionalized the names of all those involved in the case.

b. See Hastie, Penrod & Pennington, *Inside the Jury* (1983).

THE JOURNAL OF A JUROR

Thursday, October 23, 1975

The Final Day

* * * Kellam delivered his summation first. He was absolutely masterful. At least as much an actor or, more precisely, a thundering evangelist as an attorney, he gave a performance that lasted over an hour and kept me riveted for its entire length. His voice would drop to just above a whisper and then soar to what was almost a bellow. He gestured lavishly, pointing an accusing finger toward heaven itself and pounding his fist on the rail of the jury box as if he wanted to splinter it.

Throughout he focused on the weakness of the state's case; rarely did he proclaim Ricky's innocence. Every inconsistency, contradiction, and improbability in the testimony of the three kids was exposed to his ridicule and contempt. At one point he shouted that if he thought Ricky had invited Jennifer to join him in the robbery and then later had stopped in his flight to show the kids his gun, then Kellam would have pleaded insanity as a defense. All the stunning conflicts in testimony about time and place and which of the three were present, including some that I had not thought of before, were reviewed, as was the police's failure to follow up on their many leads. * * * He emphasized the pressure on the police to solve this crime, to get someone accused. He suggested that the kids may have borne ill will toward Ricky, reminding us of the broken-chair incident and the fact that Jimmy's mother had had the defendant's brother arrested. He came up with a striking new theory: that the kids had arrived at the scene of the crime sometime after the murder had been committed. This would explain why Jimmy had thought he heard broken glass (which he later decided was gunshots)—the police had to break the right front window of the van to get inside. It would explain why Clarissa said (on the tape and I had not caught it) that she was looking for a policeman to report her mother's accident and there were a lot of police around but she couldn't find one. It would explain why in their earliest statements to the police all the kids had insisted that they got to Murdock Avenue at five-thirty.

Kellam concluded with a poem entitled "Dream of Freedom," which he attributed to Langston Hughes. There were tears in his eyes as he spoke the last words. The judge recessed the court immediately after and as we filed out I noticed that Juror 9 was crying. With the gift of hindsight I would say now that Kellam's was an astonishingly effective performance for anyone already nurturing the seeds of doubt, but too emotional to persuade someone who was then strongly leaning toward a guilty verdict.

* * * We were back in court around eleven-thirty, to hear Mendelow's summation. He showed far more passion than he ever had before, and indeed, given the crippled condition of his case, he thrust as much force and reason into his arguments as anyone reasonably could. His most telling points, for me, centered on Ricky's testimony: Where were the boys he had shot baskets with, where was this supposed girlfriend, how could Ricky not know the Murdock Avenue stores when for ten years he had lived only three blocks away. (Wasn't it about six blocks?) Mendelow said he could not produce a movie film of the crime being committed, but he had offered us the next best thing: *three* eyewitnesses. And their testimony, he vehemently repeated over and over and over, was overwhelming. Since he could not totally ignore the kids' inconsistencies, he whipped out the law-school experiment that proved how different people can see and remember the same sequence of events in entirely different ways. * * * He cried out that it would be "an insult to the intelligence of a sophisticated group" like us to suggest that the three kids would frame Ricky just for the money. Breaking down the sum into three hundred dollars per person * * * he said these kids would have to be the lowest of the low to do something so vile. Did we really think that of them?

He began his summation by saying we all like poetry and Kellam's poem about dreams was very nice, but he reminded us that there was one person who would never dream again—Edward Fendt, the victim of this brutal murder. To Fendt he returned just before he concluded, emphasizing once again the utter horror of the crime. His last words reminded us of the promises we had made during the *voir dire:* not to be biased in the defendant's favor because of his age (to that he added the fact of Ricky's mother's death, which prompted a loud but futile objection from Kellam), not to demand more than proof beyond a reasonable doubt, not to be swayed by unsavory incidents in the past of his witnesses, and to use our common sense. If we remembered all those promises, he was sure we would find the defendant guilty as charged.

Both attorneys had prefaced their summations with expressions of gratitude for our attentiveness, but I noticed Juror 8 nodding off again—for just a few seconds—while Mendelow spoke.

His summation took about an hour and the judge's charge to the jury, which followed immediately, was almost as long. Agresta began by explaining that our purpose was to determine the facts of the case—to decide, by weighing and comparing the credibility of the various witnesses, whether the defendant had broken a law. It was not our function to question or interpret the law. Laws are made by our legislators and it is our job only to help enforce them. He continued with a thorough review of all the evidence that had been presented, witness by witness. He was remarkably fair and complete. He then went into a long and rather complicated explanation of the two counts of murder in the second degree: The first count, felony murder, referred to homicide committed during the course of an attempted robbery; the second, common law murder, was homicide with intent to kill. We could find the defendant guilty of either or both or neither. He said far more than I include here and I am giving short shrift to an outstanding, wholly admirable man (whatever else we may disagree about, we the jurors are unanimous in our praise for Agresta), but in view of the outcome of the jury's deliberations it seems superfluous to try to recall all his remarks. However enlightening they may have been as regards the law and however useful in recalling the substance of the trial testimony, in our deliberations there was scarcely any reference to Agresta's charge to the jury. Our verdict was determined by what we thought we heard from the witness box, not from the bench.

Our lunch was waiting for us when we returned to the jury room. It was immediately clear that we were all reluctant to begin deliberations and, in the easiest decision of the day, we chose not to until we had finished eating. Sandwiches were distributed about one-thirty. We ate in relative silence; then, rather elaborately and fastidiously, we gathered up the debris and cleared the table. At last, shortly before two o'clock, discussions began.

We asked first to see all the evidence that had been so frustratingly denied to us throughout the trial. It was brought into the jury room without delay, but strangely, it now seemed to me anticlimatic, a matter of curiosity rather than of pertinent interest. * * *

We read the police reports and the kids' statements. In black and white, the inconsistencies seemed no more or less glaring than when spoken on the witness stand. The many exhibits were passed around, conscientiously examined, commented upon, but it was all a holding action: much movement and exclamation and theorizing that served only to delay what we all sensed was inevitable conflict.

From just about the first significant words spoken, however, I knew, with a great rush of relief, that I would not be the lone holdout and that we would never declare Ricky guilty. Hung jury, perhaps. Guilty, no.

We did not start with a vote, but if we had I'm reasonably certain the outcome would have been as follows:

Juror 1 — Not guilty
Juror 2 — Undecided
Juror 3 — Not guilty
Juror 4 — Undecided
Juror 5 — Guilty
Juror 6 — Guilty
Juror 7 — Undecided
Juror 8 — Not guilty
Juror 9 — Not guilty
Juror 10 — Not guilty
Juror 11 (me)—Not guilty
Juror 12 — Undecided

Those first significant words prompted not only relief but surprise, and the surprise stemmed not only from their content but from their source. They were spoken by, of all people, Juror 8—the former first alternate, the occasional snoozer * * * What he said—tersely, flatly, and with that somewhat choked quality fat men's voices sometimes have—was: "The state ain't got no case." Then there was silence in the room.

It was broken by Juror 1, our forewoman, and she proved the biggest surprise of all. She, who over eight days had smiled a lot and said very little, took command immediately and she was nothing short of remarkable. As we began deliberating, with the exhibits gathered up and put aside, she exchanged seats with Juror 5 and moved to the end of the table opposite me. From then on, where she sat became the head of the table.

She opened the discussion by asking Juror 8 if he wanted to elaborate on his statement. When he was unwilling or unable to do so, she turned to the rest of us: Would anyone volunteer his or her reconstruction of the case? Getting no immediate response, she proceeded to do it herself, and she stated my views almost exactly: she discounted all the police testimony as failing to implicate Ricky in any way; she reviewed the descriptions given by the adult eyewitnesses, particularly Clare Anderson, and reminded us that they did not resemble Ricky at all; therefore, she said, the state's case had to rest solely on the testimony of the three kids—and she for one could not believe it. She suggested that they were motivated by the promise of a reward—or perhaps for some other reason—but no matter what, to her their stories were transparent, and she went on to enumerate an inescapable series of flaws. She went further than I had in my mind by speculating that after the kids had spoken to the police, they realized they had embarked on a very dangerous course and now they were afraid. Perhaps they even regretted what they had done. Fear or regret or both would explain why they were reluctant witnesses. In any case, their testimony was so incredible that she would have to find Ricky not guilty.

She suggested then that we go around the table and each of us talk in turn. Juror 4, sitting to Juror 1's right, said he was undecided, Juror 8 in a minimum of words agreed with Juror 1, Juror 12 said he was bothered by things Ricky had said on the stand. There was silence again, and though I was not next around the table, I finally spoke up. I said I agreed with Juror 1 entirely, though I hadn't thought about the reasons the three kids were reluctant witnesses. I admitted right off that I was not at all certain that Ricky was innocent, but I was certain I couldn't convict him on the evidence offered. I listed the inconsistencies that bothered me the most in the kids' testimony (where they were when they observed the crime, what time it was, how many of them were there). I suggested that at some point they had decided Jimmy was too unreliable a witness and thus had to be separated from the two girls, though Clarissa's first police interview, one of the documents offered in evidence, revealed that she originally had Jimmy standing with her and Jennifer when they saw Ricky running from the truck.

Juror 3 spoke up and said that "deep in her gut" she suspected Ricky was "guilty as hell," but she was also sure that the kids were lying and therefore she had to vote not guilty. Juror 7 agreed and, soon, so did Juror 12. At this point there was a kind of informal voice vote: eight not guilty, two undecided (Jurors 4 and 2), and two guilty (Jurors 5 and 6). We had been deliberating for about an hour and a half.

* * * The "not guilty" faction was strongly on the offensive at this point. Encouraged by the fact that we had already swayed two of the "undecideds," we hammered at two key arguments: Ricky's dissimilarity to the sketch of the suspect drawn from Clare Anderson's description and the unmistakable discrepancies between Clarissa's original police interview, her later interview (taped) with an assistant D.A., and her aborted testimony on the stand. I'm sure Jurors 4 and 2 were already leaning heavily toward the majority when they asked if we could hear Clarissa's tape again. This was quickly arranged. Our door was unlocked, from the outside, and we were brought back into the courtroom to have the tape replayed for us. The two "undecideds" had probably reached their verdict by the time we returned to the jury room. In any case, when we finally took our first paper ballot—it was now about 6 P.M.—the vote was ten to two. We had been deliberating for about four hours.

I have put off consideration of the arguments of the two holdouts, Jurors 5 and 6, because I know it will be a Herculean task to treat their views sympathetically, or at least dispassionately. It will be almost as difficult to communicate the mounting impatience and, ultimately, the rage that these men gave rise to. But it will be most difficult of all to dig into and expose the roots of the opposition with which they tried to "hang" us. Juror 5, probably the oldest person in the room, was convinced to the end that Ricky was guilty, but in objective terms he never really explained why. He kept alluding to "bad vibes" and to the "feeling in his gut"—he rarely went beyond the viscera to the brain. Thus, for as long as he was a holdout, he was mostly content to allow Juror 6 to do battle for them both. His occasional contributions were usually incorrect, irrelevant, or incredible. He forgot testimony, seemed incapable of understanding some of the arguments we offered, was mired in that "gut" certainty that Ricky was "guilty as hell" (how many times was that phrase used tonight—ten, fifteen, fifty?). * * *

Juror 6. Came to the U.S. from Czechoslovakia twenty-five years ago, a CPA with one of New York's largest accounting firms, a command of English—though he, like Juror 4, speaks with an accent—probably greater than that of anyone else in the jury room. Loquacious. Stentorian. Ready with an anecdote on any subject. A self-proclaimed expert on gourmet cooking, the stock market, and—so unfortunately for the rest of us—guns and human nature. * * *

On human nature, or more precisely black human nature, he knew more than the rest of us because he sees blacks socially. His first memorable statement once deliberations began: "I am sorry there are no blacks on this jury." Because blacks know how other blacks think. Said Juror 1, then, and repeatedly over the next nine hours, "Phillip, we shouldn't, we mustn't, talk about color." Juror 6 smiled condescendingly. At one point I mentioned one of Jennifer's most astonishing statements: that she and Clarissa and Jimmy had *never* discussed among themselves seeing Ricky commit the crime, not even after their mother gathered them into her car and drove them to the precinct house to talk to the police. "What wheels turning in her head could make her think that we would believe something like that?" I asked, rhetorically. Juror 6 announced, "Black wheels."

He had quickly conceded that the kids' testimony was full of contradictions. But that didn't trouble him. He had a theory: the four of them were in it together. They had all attempted to rob—and succeeded in murdering—the potato chip man. But a month later something happened—perhaps the offer of a reward, perhaps something else—to cause Jennifer, Clarissa, and Jimmy to decide to make Ricky their scapegoat. In effect, then, all the blacks were guilty, but since only one was on trial, he could convict only one.

For every * * * inconsistency, contradiction, or improbability he attempted to offer an answer. Failure of memory over so long a period, failure of perception in the excitement of the moment, or—when he was truly desparate—"That's not important"; "That doesn't bother me. I can live with it." What he could not live with would be his conscience if he allowed this killer to go free.

What about the eyewitness descriptions given by the adults on the day of the crime? Particularly Clare Anderson's description and the sketch that was drawn from it. Juror 6: "They all said the murderer was black, didn't they?" But in hardly any other way did their descriptions correspond to Ricky, and Clare Anderson, who claimed to have actually faced the man for a second or two, could not identify Ricky in the line-up. Juror 6: "She was frozen with fear and shock and in such a state perceptions are meaningless." It seemed he could not be moved.

But he could be caught. At one point, after a long, aimless pause in the deliberations, Juror 6 said with a sly smile, "You all keep asking me to explain to you why I think Ricky is guilty. Well, now I ask you: How can you prove to me that he is innocent?" Without a breath of hesitation—almost as if she had been waiting for this question—Juror 1 met the challenge: "Phillip, we don't have to prove he is innocent. He is *presumed* innocent. That's our system here. The prosecution has to prove him guilty." Juror 6's smile faded but did not disappear. Was he embarrassed by his unthinking lapse? He conceded nothing. The smile became a look of condescension, as if to say, "And that, my dear, is what is wrong with your system."

It was close to 7 P.M. when Juror 1 reminded us of the theory Kellam had introduced in his summation: that the kids arrived at the crime scene *after* the murder was committed. This would explain why Jimmy said he heard glass breaking, why Clarissa said there were a lot of cops around but she couldn't find one to whom to report her mother's accident, why all three *originally* told the police they saw Ricky commit the crime about five-thirty. On the second point, said Juror 5, "I never heard her say that"; said Juror 6, "That isn't exactly what she said." Juror 1: "Yes, it is. We heard it again on the tape this afternoon— 'There were a lot of cops around but I couldn't find one.' Would you like to have the tape played for us again?" We agreed to ask for the transcript (actually, the court reporter's record) of the tape.

Juror 1: "What about their insistence in their early testimony that it all happened at five-thirty?" Juror 6: "They didn't have watches." Juror 1: "But Detective McKinley testified that when he interviewed Clarissa she at first insisted that she saw Ricky at *five-thirty,* even after he reminded her that the murder was committed at five." (Now how did she remember that? She's brilliant.) Juror 6: "I don't remember that." Juror 5: "I don't either."

We agreed to ask to have that bit of testimony read back to us also. We summoned Jack, who took our request and then told us we would soon be going out to dinner. "You're eating Italian tonight." Italian in that neighborhood probably meant Luigi's, where I hadn't been in years.

The prospect of soon leaving this smoky, supercharged room served to reduce the tension. Juror 5 admitted that he would have to be influenced by Clarissa's reference to "a lot of cops around" if that proved to be what she said on the tape.   *   *   *

Dinner conversation was relaxed; jovial, in fact. The two holdouts were at opposite ends of the table, Juror 6 at my end, indeed directly opposite me. But there was no mention of the disagreement that had raged between us and would again. Instead four of us talked, surprisingly, of politics (Juror 6 abhors Hubert Humphrey; Juror 4 remarked that though he votes Republican 75 percent of the time, he just can't tolerate Ford), of book publishing (Juror 12, to my left, could not believe how low is the average first printing of a book), of travel (Juror 12 has been to Scandinavia, Juror 4 to Italy). The food was mediocre, the coffee no better, but we lingered over it, reluctant to return to battle. *   *   *

The jury room was no more inviting on our return than it had been when we left, but we were not in it very long before we were recalled to the courtroom, to rehear the testimony we had requested. As we crossed to the jury box and I passed Ricky sitting at the defense table, I noticed that, for the first time, he appeared to be crying. At least he was holding a white handkerchief to his eyes and there it remained for as long as the jury sat in the courtroom.

The court reporter read Clarissa's taped testimony as he had recorded it. Loudly, distinctly, his voice a monotone, he recited: "There were lots of cops around but I couldn't find one." The words were indeed Clarissa's, and though they were now spoken without expression or stress, they seemed far more dramatic and telling than when we had heard them before, in her own small, breathy, barely audible tape-recorded voice. I looked at Juror 5 but could see only his profile, which stared ahead impassively.

After reading the taped testimony in its entirety, the court reporter found that isolated passage from Kellam's cross-examination of Detective McKinley. There could be no doubt now. McKinley had flatly admitted that when Clarissa was first questioned she stuck to five-thirty as the time she saw Ricky running away, even after she was told that the potato chip man had been murdered much closer to five o'clock. Kellam was right. He had to be right. All three kids had initially given five-thirty as the crucial time simply because that was the time of Mrs. Custis's car accident and the accident was the anchor of reality to which their story was tied. We would never know who, or what, later caused them to move the time of their arrival on Murdock Avenue to five o'clock. But originally all three had clung to that one shred of truth—five-thirty in the afternoon.

Back in the jury room, I knew it was merely a matter of time before Juror 5 abandoned his ally. The immediate response was from Juror 6: Hearing the testimony again had not swayed him at all. He knew even before this last excursion to the courtroom *exactly* what had been said, and it made no difference to him. Was it at this point or earlier that, dropping his voice to just above a whisper, he confessed that the "vibes" from Ricky were what had persuaded him that the boy was a killer? With the kids' stories crumbling around him, he moved to a clearer spot: the testimony, and, more important, the demeanor of Ricky on the stand. The kid was arrogant, he was hostile, he was evasive. Couldn't we all tell he was guilty?

Juror 5 could tell. Of course Ricky was guilty. He had that feeling in his gut. But he had to admit now there *was* a doubt. The state's case was weak. Yes, Ricky was guilty, guilty as hell—but he was changing his vote. Sadly but with a kind of flourish. He wanted the respect that age commands. He got a few smiles at least. For now it was eleven to one. We had been deliberating for over eight hours.

Instead of bringing relief, the capitulation of Juror 5 recharged the atmosphere. The pressure on Juror 6 should have been insupportable. But without any evident rancor toward the sudden renegade, he made it immediately clear that *he* was not planning to change *his* vote, now or in the future. Anger burst around him. He was being totally unreasonable. How could he still insist on "guilty" when the state's case had been exposed to him, over and over again, as a fraud? What more could any of us say? He repeated, with that exasperated but not yet spent patience that teachers show to mischievous children, "I don't care about the kids' stories. Sure, they may be lying. But not about the important thing. Ricky is on trial, not the kids."

There seemed to be no more avenues of attack open to us. We had tried to wear him down by confronting him with all the flaws in the kids' testimony, but he had made it inescapably clear that this strategy was futile. I sat silently for a moment, trying to come up with a new argument, yet certain that it would prove as useless as all the others.

I thought to myself: He believes all four were conspirators in the crime. Can we build on that? Of course! Trying to keep my voice down and free of hostility, I asked Juror 6 how he could be sure, if they were all in it together, that it was Ricky rather than one of the other three who had pulled the trigger. Someone else answered, "It couldn't have been one of the girls." Had I believed the shared-guilt theory, I would not have conceded even that, but for the moment it didn't matter. "Just Jimmy, then. How do you know Jimmy didn't do it?" "Because," replied Juror 6, "the description of the killer given by the four adults sounded much more like Ricky." "But you've already said we should discount their statements. They were in shock or too frightened to be reliable witnesses. You can't have it both ways— dismissing what they said when it favors Ricky and accepting it when it doesn't!" Silence again and then a barely audible remark from Juror 6: "Let me sleep on it."

For me this was the first hopeful note of the evening, but to my surprise, I was virtually alone in my reaction. The others seemed more irate at the implied suggestion that we be sequestered overnight than they were by the possibility of our never reaching a verdict. Indeed, the sense of outrage now was almost palpable. "That's so unfair. That's so selfish!" shouted Juror 3, sitting to my right—she who had, for the past week, talked about little except her home and family. She whispered to me that the time had come for us to report to the judge that we were at an impasse. "Let it be a hung jury and let's go home," she said. I answered that it was very likely that the judge would insist that we continue to deliberate. "But how can he do that?" she whined. Around us indignation was boiling. The surrender of Juror 5 had proved to be like the dropping of a single shoe. Everyone had waited for the second to fall and now frustration was more intense than it had ever been, for it appeared that the shoe would not fall tonight.

Somehow, by offering the faint suggestion that he might *eventually* change his mind, Juror 6 seemed more stubborn, quixotic, and self-indulgent than he had when he was proclaiming that he would never vote for acquittal. Shouts of abuse and personal hostility were coming from jurors who for hours had said almost nothing. At some point, much earlier, Juror 7 had observed that Juror 6 and I were the most diametrically opposed. I questioned that at the time (and still do) because it seemed to me that the forewoman was at least as firm in her verdict of not guilty as I was. Now, however, there was no doubt that both Juror 6 and I were together in misjudging the mood of the others. His offer to "sleep on it," intended no doubt to reduce the pressure on him and welcomed by me as cause for optimism, had only served to isolate him further from the group. The barrage of arguments and supplications—the same arguments and the same supplications that had been voiced for hours—was now impelled by a renewed rush of anger.

Which only served to stiffen his resistance. Did he immediately regret his vague concession? Perhaps. For when the forewoman, with her own blend of exasperation and studied calm, asked if there was any real possibility that he would ever change his mind, he replied, almost smugly, that it was very remote. And then he added, in a thundering voice, "Only I have to live with my conscience!" The massive egotism here—as if everyone else's conscience were some muddy mess and his were granite—produced another uproar. It was interrupted by a knock on the door and the arrival of the judge's assistant.

He immediately made it clear that Agresta would not accept a "no verdict" decision tonight. If we couldn't come to unanimous agreement soon, we would have to be put up at a hotel to resume deliberations in the morning. What had been the effect, he wanted to know, of the reading of the testimony after dinner? Juror 1 explained that it had changed one vote and we now stood eleven to one. "Well, keep trying," he said as he walked to the door. We had been deliberating for almost nine hours.

Alone again, our mood seemed to change from anger to resignation and disgust. To many, I'm sure, every road seemed blocked and every weapon spent. But the forewoman was determined to try again, and I tried to help her. Between us we reviewed once more all the reasons for our own doubts: the adult descriptions that in no significant way resembled Ricky, Clarissa's remark about the police, the conflicts in time and place, the wild improbabilities, the general sense of untruth that had settled crushingly on the testimony of the three kids. I added a new note, in desperation and regret, for I wanted to persuade Juror 6 by rational arguments and not by group pressure: We were eleven fairly intelligent, fairly perceptive people. Didn't the fact that we all agreed on not guilty—that we all thought there were grounds for a reasonable doubt—didn't that mean anything to him? I could not hear his reply, for other voices were drowning out mine even before I finished my question. And most powerful among those voices was that of Juror 5. "There is a reasonable doubt!" he cried. The next-to-last holdout had joined the pack and at that moment the pack was immeasurably strengthened.

Was what followed the most sustained barrage of the evening? Had some sort of climax been reached? Yes, the voices were rising again, but were they actually louder and sharper than ever before? Perhaps Juror 6 only thought they were. How much pressure can one man take? Suddenly, he broke.

"All right," he said, almost softly. "I've come to respect all of you too much. I can't do this to you and I won't continue any longer. I change my vote."

Landsman—Adversarial Justice ACB—6

Juror 1 started to cry. I felt limp and choked. "Christ almighty, we did it. We did it," I said to myself. But within seconds Juror 6 had leaped to his feet, his eyes blazing, and like a titan of vengeance, tottering and about to collapse, he screamed at us all: "*And how many of you believe with me that we are turning an animal loose on the streets again?*" It seems almost comical now to remember that two or three hands shot up immediately—such a puny gesture in response to such Jehovic wrath. Said Juror 2, "If you add the word 'possibly' . . ." But Juror 6 was not adding anything. He was stumbling away from the table and toward the bathroom, his eyes flooded with tears.

Juror 1 rang the bell and Jack opened the door at once. He smiled when he heard that we had reached a verdict. As he went to report this to the court, we got to our feet. We were exhausted, in every way. Conversation was desultory. In the back of my mind there was a sense of triumph but not of elation, and I felt no comfort at all. Jack returned and had us line up in the hall. We left the jury room at ten forty-five. We had been in there for almost ten hours.

Cleaning men were sweeping the corridors as we waited to file into the courtroom for the last time. While in the past when we crossed to the jury box, I tended to avoid looking at Ricky, his lawyers, and the assistant D.A., now I gazed at them all, and saw nothing.

We stood at our places in the box and enacted the familiar last rite of all the stage, movie, and TV trials I've ever seen. Judge Agresta: "Ladies and gentlemen of the jury, have you reached a verdict?"

Juror 1: "We have, Your Honor."

Clerk of the court: "The defendant will rise and face the jury." (Ricky did, but the defense table was set at an angle to the jury box, and standing in front of his chair he may have faced Jurors 1 and 7, but he didn't face me.) "What is your verdict?"

Juror 1: "We find the defendant not guilty . . . on both counts."

As if he had just been shot, Ricky seemed to crumple and his body toppled over to his right. His arms went out to Kellam, for support and embrace. As he fell on his lawyer, he buried his face in Kellam's shoulder and he sobbed.

Said Judge Agresta, "Young man, every day of your life you should thank your attorney. That was one of the most brilliant defenses I've seen in my career."

Said Kellam, "Thank you, Judge." He smiled broadly, Ricky's head still on his shoulder.

   *   *   * In the jury room, as we picked up our belongings, Juror 7 said, "If we should ever get into trouble we should all remember that name. Kellam." Again there was something we all agreed about.

Down the hall to the elevator, down the elevator to the lobby, across the lobby to the main doors of the courthouse, and there Kellam was waiting. He shook our hands and thanked us all. Some of the jurors continued down the steps, but others hung back. There were two questions I had to ask Kellam: Had Ricky been in jail since last November? "Oh, sure; how could he raise that kind of money? Bail was set at fifty thousand bucks." Was Kellam a court-appointed lawyer? He nodded. Another juror asked, "Legal Aid?" No, he was in private practice.   *   *   *

I didn't hear the question and I don't know who asked it, but it must have been something like "Was Ricky really innocent?" And I heard Kellam's answer: "I was appointed late to this case * * * And when I walked into that cell—he'd been in jail for about eight months— and I looked at Ricky and he looked at me and he said, 'Mr. Kellam, I didn't do it'—then I knew *in my gut* that he was innocent."

It was close to midnight when I got a cab and went home.

Questions

1. How effective were the closing remarks of each attorney in swaying the jurors? What appear to be the limits of this form of advocacy?

2. How effective was the judge's charge concerning the law to be applied in the case? Did the jurors focus more attention on the law or the facts? Is this sound?

3. Was the jury procedure in this case rational and reliable? What about the napping by juror number 8?

4. What role did race prejudice play in these deliberations? How did jury procedure affect the introduction of racial attitudes into the process?

5. How did the jurors treat the presumption of innocence?

6. Why did juror number 1 start to cry when unanimity was achieved?

SECTION B. TRADITIONAL PERCEPTIONS ABOUT THE VALUE OF JURY TRIAL

DUNCAN v. LOUISIANA

391 U.S. 145, 151–56, 88 S.Ct. 1444, 1448–51, 20 L.Ed.2d 491, 497–500 (1968).

[Justice White's decision in the *Duncan* case extended the availability of jury adjudication to defendants in virtually all serious criminal trials, state or federal. The *Duncan* case has been viewed by many as the highwater mark of Supreme Court receptivity to trial by jury.]

MR. JUSTICE WHITE delivered the opinion of the Court.

* * *

Jury trial came to America with English colonists, and received strong support from them. Royal interference with the jury trial was deeply resented. Among the resolutions adopted by the First Congress of the American Colonies (the Stamp Act Congress) on October 19, 1765—resolutions deemed by their authors to state "the most essential rights and liberties of the colonists"—was the declaration:

"That trial by jury is the inherent and invaluable right of every British subject in these colonies."

The First Continental Congress, in the resolve of October 14, 1774, objected to trials before judges dependent upon the Crown alone for their salaries and to trials in England for alleged crimes committed in the colonies; the Congress therefore declared:

"That the respective colonies are entitled to the common law of England, and more especially to the great and inestimable privilege of being tried by their peers of the vicinage, according to the course of that law."

The Declaration of Independence stated solemn objections to the King's making "Judges dependent on his Will alone, for the tenure of their offices, and the amount and payment of their salaries," to his "depriving us in many cases, of the benefits of Trial by Jury," and to his "transporting us beyond Seas to be tried for pretended offenses." The Constitution itself, in Art. III, § 2, commanded:

"The Trial of all Crimes, except in Cases of Impeachment, shall be by Jury; and such Trial shall be held in the State where the said Crimes shall have been committed."

Objections to the Constitution because of the absence of a bill of rights were met by the immediate submission and adoption of the Bill of Rights. Included was the Sixth Amendment which, among other things, provided:

"In all criminal prosecutions, the accused shall enjoy the right to a speedy and public trial, by an impartial jury of the State and district wherein the crime shall have been committed."

The constitutions adopted by the original States guaranteed jury trial. Also, the constitution of every State entering the Union thereafter in one form or another protected the right to jury trial in criminal cases.

Even such skeletal history is impressive support for considering the right to jury trial in criminal cases to be fundamental to our system of justice, an importance frequently recognized in the opinions of this Court. For example, the Court has said:

"Those who emigrated to this country from England brought with them this great privilege 'as their birthright and inheritance, as a part of that admirable common law which had fenced around and interposed barriers on every side against the approaches of arbitrary power.' " [21]

Jury trial continues to receive strong support. The laws of every State guarantee a right to jury trial in serious criminal cases; no State

---

21. *Thompson v. Utah,* 170 U.S. 343, 349–350 (1898), quoting 2 J. Story, Commentaries on the Constitution of the United States § 1779. See also *Irvin v. Dowd,* 366 U.S. 717, 721–722 (1961); *United States ex rel. Toth v. Quarles,* 350 U.S. 11, 16 (1955); *Ex parte Milligan,* 4 Wall. 2, 122–123 (1866); *People v. Garbutt,* 17 Mich. 9, 27 (1868).

has dispensed with it; nor are there significant movements underway to do so. * * *

Those who wrote our constitutions knew from history and experience that it was necessary to protect against unfounded criminal charges brought to eliminate enemies and against judges too responsive to the voice of higher authority. The framers of the constitutions strove to create an independent judiciary but insisted upon further protection against arbitrary action. Providing an accused with the right to be tried by a jury of his peers gave him an inestimable safeguard against the corrupt or overzealous prosecutor and against the compliant, biased, or eccentric judge. If the defendant preferred the common-sense judgment of a jury to the more tutored but perhaps less sympathetic reaction of the single judge, he was to have it. Beyond this, the jury trial provisions in the Federal and State Constitutions reflect a fundamental decision about the exercise of official power—a reluctance to entrust plenary powers over the life and liberty of the citizen to one judge or to a group of judges. Fear of unchecked power, so typical of our State and Federal Governments in other respects, found expression in the criminal law in this insistence upon community participation in the determination of guilt or innocence. The deep commitment of the Nation to the right of jury trial in serious criminal cases as a defense against arbitrary law enforcement qualifies for protection under the Due Process Clause of the Fourteenth Amendment, and must therefore be respected by the States. * * *

Questions

1. Does the history of jury trial in America have any relevance to our deliberations about its worth today?

2. What role does the *Duncan* court see the jury playing vis-a-vis the judge? Vis-a-vis the prosecutor?

3. Is the court's view of the jury's function realistic?

SECTION C. CONTEMPORARY VIEWS ABOUT THE JURY

1. THE CRITICS' VIEWS

JEROME FRANK—COURTS ON TRIAL
109–23 (1949).
Reprinted by permission of the publisher, copyright © 1976.
Princeton University Press.

[JUDGE JEROME FRANK was one of the most astute critics of traditional legal procedure writing during the 1930s and 1940s. He constantly worked to strip away the myth and rhetoric that hamper a clear understanding of the way courts really operate. He vigorously challenged traditional institutions including both the adversary system as a whole and its jury trial component in particular. In this excerpt Frank launches one of the strongest attacks ever aimed at the jury.]

[AMERICA'S SINGULAR ALLEGIANCE TO THE JURY]

* * *

In the United States, the jury still retains much of its glamour. True, there has been something of an increase in the number of civil (i.e., non-criminal) suits in which jury trials have been waived. But in criminal cases the jury still largely keeps its hold. Except in this country, however, trial by jury fell into disfavor in the 20th century. In some Swiss cantons it was abolished. In pre-Hitler Germany and France, its use was more and more limited. This unpopularity cannot be explained as a symptom of decreased interest in liberty and democracy. For Scotland, surely a land of liberty-loving individuals, having virtually rejected the non-criminal jury in the 16th century, readopted it in 1815, and subsequently all but gave it up. In England, even before World War II, it was seldom employed in civil suits, was abandoned in criminal prosecutions except for major crimes, and even there was, and is, used decreasingly. Surely that attitude in England, the birthplace of the modern jury, should give us pause. Especially should it do so, when it is recalled that American defenders of the jury have often asserted that the major ills of our jury system would vanish if only we adopted the English way of using it. If, as Judge Knox says, the jury system "is one of the really great achievements of English and American jurisprudence," why has it all but gone into the discard in England, except in a decreasing percentage of major criminal prosecutions? And why has Congress never granted the privilege of trial by jury in a suit against the United States?

It will not do then to make Fourth–of–July speeches about the glorious jury system, to conceal its grave defects, or merely to palliate them with superficial, cosmetic-like, remedies. We need to have our public comprehend what the jury actually is like in order to arouse public interest to the point where steps will be taken to eradicate its most glaring deficiencies.

2

[THE PROCESS OF DECISION]

I have said that, supposedly, the task of our courts is this: To make reasoned applications of legal rules to the carefully ascertained facts of particular law-suits. You will recall my crude schematization of the alleged nature of the process—$R \times F = D$—i.e., the Rules times the Facts equals the Decision. Where, in that scheme, does the jury fit in?

In most jury trials, the jury renders what is called a "general verdict." Suppose that Williams sues Allen claiming (1) that Allen falsely told him there was oil on some land Williams bought from Allen, but (2) that in fact there was no oil there, so that Williams was defrauded. The jury listens to the witnesses. Then the judge tells the jurors, "If you find Allen lied, and Williams relied on that lie, a legal rule requires that you hold for the plaintiff Williams, and you must compute the damages according to another rule," which the judge explains. "But if you find that Allen did not lie, then the legal rule requires you to hold for the defendant Allen." The jury deliberately deliberates in the jury-room and reports either, "We find for the plaintiff in the sum of $5,000," or "We find for the defendant." In other words, the jury does not report what facts it found. Such an undetailed, unexplained, jury report is called a "general verdict."

* * *

4

[HOW JURIES REALLY BEHAVE]

Now what does bring about verdicts? Longenecker, in a book written by a practical trial lawyer for practical trial lawyers, says: "In talking to a man who had recently served for two weeks on juries, he stated that in one case after they had retired to consider the verdict, the foreman made a speech to them somewhat like this: 'Now boys, you know there was lying on both sides. Which one did the most lying? The plaintiff is a poor man and the defendant is rich and can afford to pay the plaintiff something. Of course the dog did not hurt the plaintiff much, but I think we ought to give him something, don't you?' There were several 'sures'; we thought the plaintiff might have to split with his lawyers, so we gave him a big verdict." A case is reported in which the jurors explained their verdict thus: "We couldn't make head or tail of the case, or follow all the messing around the lawyers did. None of us believed the witnesses on either side, anyway, so we made up our minds to disregard the evidence on both sides and decide the case on its merits." "Competent observers," says Judge Rossman, "who have interviewed the jurors in scores of jury trials, declare that in many cases . . . principal issues received no consideration from the jury." Bear that in mind, when considering these remarks by Ram: "And to what a fearful extent may a verdict affect a person! It may pronounce a man sane or insane; it may establish character, or take it away; it may give liberty to the captive, or turn liberty into slavery: it may continue life to a prisoner, or consign him to death."

Again and again, it has been disclosed that juries have arrived at their verdicts by one of the following methods: (1) Each juror, in a civil case, writes down the amount he wants to award; the total is added and the average taken as the verdict. (2) The jurors, by agreement decide for one side or the other according to the flip of a coin. * * *

How do the courts react to such a disclosure? When it is made known before the jury is discharged, a court will usually reject the verdict. But, frequently, the revelation occurs after the jury's discharge. In most states, and in the federal system, the courts then refuse to disturb the verdict. They say that any other result would mean that jurors would be subjected to pressures, after a case is over, to induce them to falsify what had occurred in the jury-room, so that all verdicts would be imperilled.

One may doubt whether there is much danger of such falsifications. I surmise that the underlying reason for that judicial attitude is this: The judges feel that, were they obliged to learn the methods used by jurors, the actual workings of the jury-system would be shown up, devastatingly. From my point of view, such a consequence would be desirable: The public would soon discover this skeleton in the judicial closet. * * *

5

[THE DIFFICULTIES JURORS HAVE IN COMPREHENDING LEGAL
INSTRUCTIONS]

Are jurors to blame when they decide cases in the ways I've described? I think not. In the first place, often they cannot understand what the judge tells them about the legal rules. To comprehend the meaning of many a legal rule requires special training. It is inconceivable that a body of twelve ordinary men, casually gathered together for a few days, could, merely from listening to the instructions of the judge, gain the knowledge necessary to grasp the true import of the judge's words. For these words have often acquired their meaning as the result of hundreds of years of professional disputation in the courts. The jurors usually are as unlikely to get the meaning of those words as if they were spoken in Chinese, Sanskrit, or Choctaw. "Can anything be more fatuous," queries Sunderland, "than the expectation that the law which the judge so carefully, learnedly and laboriously expounds to the laymen in the jury box becomes operative in their minds in true form?" Judge Rossman pointedly asks whether it "is right to demand that a juror swear that he will obey the instructions (which the lawyers frequently say they are not sure of until they have been transcribed) and return a general verdict in obedience thereto." Judge Bok says that "juries have the disadvantage . . . of being treated like children while the testimony is going on, but then being doused with a kettleful of law, during the charge, that would make a third-year law student blanch."

Under our system, however, the courts are obligated to make the unrealistic assumption that the often incomprehensible words, uttered in the physical presence of the jurors, have some real effect on their thought processes. As a logical deduction from that unfounded assumption, the trial judge is required to state the applicable rule to the jury with such nicety that some lawyers do not thoroughly comprehend it. If the judge omits any of those niceties, the upper court will reverse a judgment based on the jury's verdict. For, theoretically, the jury actually worked in accordance with the $R \times F = D$ formula, applying the R they received from the judge, so that, if he gave them the wrong R, then, in theory, the D—their verdict—must logically be wrong. Lawyers thus set traps for trial judges. Decisions, in cases which have taken weeks to try, are reversed on appeal because a phrase, or a sentence, meaningless to the jury, has been included in or omitted from the charge.

When a decision is reversed on such a ground, it results, at best, in a new trial at which the trial judge will intone a more meticulously worded R to another uncomprehending jury. This leads to an enormous waste of time and money. And note that the prospect of a prolonged expensive new trial often induces a litigant who won in the first trial, and who has only modest means, to accept an unfair settlement.

Many of the precise legal rules on which, according to the conventional theory, men in their daily affairs have a right to and supposedly do rely, are found solely in upper-court opinions admonishing trial judges to use, in charges to juries, words and phrases stating those rules. But if jurors do not understand those words and phrases, and consequently do not apply those rules, then reliance on the rules is unreliable: Men who act in reliance on that purported right to rely are deceived. * * *

6

[THE DIFFICULTY JURORS HAVE IN COMPREHENDING THE EVIDENCE]

Suppose, however, that the jurors always did understand the R's. Nevertheless, often they would face amazing obstacles to ascertaining the F's. For the evidence is not presented all at once or in an orderly fashion. The very mode of its presentation is confusing. The jurors are supposed to keep their minds in suspense until all of the evidence is in.

Can a jury perform such a task? Has it the means and capacity? Are the conditions of a jury trial such as to make for the required calm deliberation by the jurors? Wigmore, who defends the jury system, himself tells us that the court-room is "a place of surging emotions, distracting episodes, and sensational surprises. The parties are keyed up to the contest; and the topics are often calculated to stir up the sympathy, or prejudice, or ridicule of the tribunal." Dean Green remarks: "The longer the trial lasts, the larger the scanning crowds, the more intensely counsel draw the lines of conflict, the more solemn the judge, the harder it becomes for the jury to restrain their reason from somersault."

We may, therefore, seriously question the statement of Professors Michael and Adler that, unlike the witnesses, the jury "observes the things and events exhibited to its senses under conditions designed to make the observation reliable and accurate. In the case of what (the jury) observes directly the factor of memory is negligible." As shown by Wigmore, Green, and Burrill, the first of those comments surely does not square with observable courtroom realities. As to the second—that the factor of the jurors' memory is negligible—consider the following: Theoretically, as we saw, the jury, in its process of fact-finding, applies to the evidence the legal rules it learns from the judge. If the jury actually did conduct itself according to this theory, it would be unable to comprehend the evidence intelligently until it received those instructions about the rules. But those instructions are given, not before the jury hears the evidence, but only after all the witnesses have left the stand. Then, for the first time, are the jurors asked to consider the testimony in the light of the rules. In other words, if jurors are to do their duty, they must now recollect and assemble the separate fragments of the evidence (including the demeanor of the several witnesses) and fit them into the rules. If the trial has lasted for many days or weeks, the required feat of memory is prodigious. As Burrill says: "The theory of judicial investigation requires that the juror keep his mind wholly free from impressions until all facts are before him in evidence, and that he should then frame his conclusion. The difficulty attending this mode of dealing with the elements of evidence (especially in important cases requiring protracted investigation) is that the facts thus surveyed in a mass, and at one view, are apt to confuse, distract, and oppress the mind by their very number and variety. . . . They are, moreover, necessarily mixed up with remembrance of the mere machinery of their introduction, and the contests (often close and obstinate) attending their proof; in the course of which attempts are sometimes made to suppress or distort the truth, in the very act of presentation."

In a discussion I recently had with Professor Michael, he maintained that, since jurymen, in their daily out-of-court living, conduct most of their affairs on the basis of conclusions reached after listening to other men, they are adequately equipped as fact-finders in the court-room. One answer to this argument is that often the issues in trials are of a complicated kind with which most jurymen are unfamiliar. But let us ignore that answer. A more telling criticism of Michael's assertion is this: The surroundings of inquiry during a jury trial differ extraordinarily from those in which the juryman conducts his ordinary affairs. At a trial, the jurors hear the evidence in a public place, under conditions of a kind to which they are unaccustomed: No juror is able to withdraw to his own room, or office, for private individual reflection. And, at the close of the trial, the jurors are pressed for time in reaching their joint decision. Even twelve experienced judges, deliberating together, would probably not function well under the conditions we impose on the twelve inexperienced laymen.

7

[THE ROLE OF PREJUDICE AND SYMPATHY]

* * *

Do the lawyers strive to pick impartial jurors? Do they want jurymen whose training will best enable them to understand the facts of the case? Of course not. If you think they usually do, watch the trial lawyers at work in a court-room. Or read the books written for trial lawyers by seasoned trial lawyers.

Here are a few excerpts from such a book, Goldstein's *Trial Techniques,* a book commended for its accuracy by Professor Morgan of Harvard. Always demand a jury, says Goldstein, if you represent a plaintiff who is a "woman, child, an old man or an old woman, or an ignorant, illiterate or foreign-born person unable to read or write or speak English who would naturally excite the jury's sympathies," especially if the defendant is a large corporation, a prominent or wealthy person, an insurance company, railroad or bank. Then, he advises, seek the type of juror who "will most naturally respond to an emotional appeal." Make every effort, this author counsels, to exclude from the jury anyone "who is particularly experienced in the field of endeavor which is the basis of the law suit." As such a person is likely, says Goldstein, to have too much influence with the other jurors, it is always better to submit the issues "to a jury who have no knowledge of the particular subject."

In that book much is made of the fact that "the jury tries the lawyers rather than the clients," that, "without realizing it, the jurors allow their opinions of the evidence to be swayed in favor of the side represented by the lawyer they like." That notion is repeated in some of the pamphlets, written by eminent trial lawyers, published in 1946 under the auspices of the American Bar Association. They advise the lawyer to "ingratiate himself" with the jury. One of these pamphlets says that the jurors' reaction to the trial lawyer "may be more important than the reaction to the client, for the client appears on the stand only during a relatively brief period, while the lawyer is before the jury all the time." Harris, in his well-known book on "advocacy," says, "It may be that judgment is more easily deceived when the passions are aroused, but if so, you [the lawyers] are not responsible. Human nature was, I presume, intended to be what it is, and when it gets into the jury-box, it is the duty of the advocate to make the best use of it he fairly can in the interests of his client." The Supreme Court of Tennessee has solemnly decided that "tears have always been considered legitimate arguments before a jury," that such use of tears is "one of the natural rights of counsel which no court or constitution could take away," and that "indeed, if counsel has them at command, it may be seriously questioned whether it is not his professional duty to shed them whenever proper occasion arises. . . ."

This is no laughing matter. For prejudice has been called the thirteenth juror, and it has been said that "Mr. Prejudice and Miss Sympathy are the names of witnesses whose testimony is never recorded, but must nevertheless be reckoned with in trials by jury." The foregoing tends to justify Balzac's definition of a jury as "twelve men chosen to decide who has the better lawyer."

In any law-suit, success or defeat for one of the parties may turn on his lawyer's abilities. But, in the light of the fact that juries "try the lawyers," it is peculiarly true, in many a jury trial, that a man's life, livelihood or property often depends on his lawyer's skill or lack of it in ingratiating himself with the jury rather than on the evidence. Not that lawyers, trying to protect their clients, should be censured for exploiting jurors' weaknesses—as long as we retain the general-verdict jury system.

Since, as every handbook on trial practice discloses, and as visits to a few jury trials will teach anyone, the lawyers are allowed—more, are expected—to appeal to the crudest emotions and prejudices of the jurors, and jurors are known often to respond to such appeals, I confess that it disturbs me not a little that we require trial judges to perform the futile ritual of saying to each jury something like this: "The law will not permit jurors to be governed by mere sentiment, sympathy, passion or prejudice, and you will reach a verdict that will be just to both sides, regardless of what the consequences may be." We tell jurors to do—have them take an oath to do—what we do not at all expect them to do.

8

[THE RULES OF EVIDENCE AS A FURTHER IMPEDIMENT]

As I said in a previous chapter, the search for the facts in a courtroom must necessarily be limited by lack of time; also, for important reasons of public policy, some ways of obtaining evidence are precluded—by the rule against self-incrimination, for instance, or by the rule against any unreasonable search and seizure.

But there are other rules of exclusion which, no matter what their origin, have been perpetuated primarily because of the admitted incompetence of jurors. Notable is the rule excluding hearsay evidence. Hearsay may be roughly (and somewhat inaccurately) described as the report in court by a witness of a statement made by another person, out of court, who is not subject to cross-examination at the trial, when the report of that statement is offered as evidence to prove the truth of a fact asserted in that statement. It is, so to speak, second-hand evidence. Now doubtless hearsay should often be accepted with caution. But 90% of the evidence on which men act out of court, most of the data on which business and industry daily rely, consists of the equivalent of hearsay. Yet, because of distrust of juries—a belief that jurors lack the competence to make allowance for the second-hand character of hearsay—such evidence, although accepted by administrative agencies, juvenile courts and legislative committees, is (subject, to be sure, to numerous exceptions) barred in jury trials. As a consequence, frequently the jury cannot learn of matters which would lead an intelligent person to a more correct knowledge of the facts.

So, too, of many other exclusionary rules. They limit, absurdly, the court-room quest for the truth. The result, often, is a gravely false picture of the actual facts. Thus trial by jury seriously interferes with correct—and, therefore, just—decisions. Even if the juries could understand what the trial judges tell them of the R's, the juries would often be unable to apply these rules to anything like the real F's, because of the exclusion of relevant evidence.

But, even apart from that difficulty, since jurors frequently cannot understand the R's, the general-verdict jury trial renders absurd the conventional description of the decisional process—the $R \times F = D$. To my mind a better instrument than the usual jury trial could scarcely be imagined for achieving uncertainty, capriciousness, lack of uniformity, disregard of the R's, and unpredictability of decisions. * * *

Questions

1. What do you make of the declining use of jury procedure in other countries?

2. What do you think of the quality of Judge Frank's proof concerning the way juries actually decide cases?

3. Can legal instructions be made comprehensible to laymen, or is the law simply beyond their ken? For some affirmative suggestions about making the law understandable see Charrow and Charrow, *Making Legal Language Understandable: A Psycholinguistic Study of Jury Instructions,* 79 Columbia Law Review 1306 (1979).

4. Is there any proof that judges are better able to recall evidence and suspend their sympathies than are jurors? If not, is it reasonable to criticize the jury on this basis?

5. Does the law provide any counterbalance to the efforts of a litigant to select favorably disposed jurors?

6. Does Judge Frank offer any empirical evidence to support the thesis that juries try the lawyers rather than the cases or that juries decide primarily on the basis of sympathy or prejudice? For a strong empirically based rejection of these arguments see Kalven and Zeisel, *The American Jury,* infra.

EDWARD DEVITT—FEDERAL CIVIL JURY TRIALS SHOULD BE ABOLISHED

60 A.B.A.J. 570, 571–74 (1974).
Reprinted with permission from the *ABA Journal,* The Lawyer's Magazine, copyright © 1974. American Bar Association Journal.

[JUDGE DEVITT is one of the most vocal modern critics of the jury. Here he couples his analysis with a number of procedural proposals.]

THE CAUSE OF DELAY IS THE JURY SYSTEM

Several commentators have advocated elimination of juries in civil cases.

When he was presiding justice of an appellate court in New York State, David W. Peck wrote (18 F.R.D. 455): "The cause of delay *is* the jury system. It is the inherent slowness of trial by jury, a pace which cannot keep up with the flood of cases coming into court, which creates a bottleneck and prevents timely disposition."

Sen. Robert A. Taft, Jr., told the Cincinnati Bar Association on April 15, 1971:

> I think the time has come to seriously question the institution of the civil jury. Thirty-six years ago the British abolished jury trial for civil cases except for a few types of cases such as libel and slander. The Federal Tort Claims Act of 1947 provides for a trial without a jury. At a time when dockets are overcrowded, litigation is expensive, and delays are costly to the litigants, we should ask ourselves whether civil juries are really a necessary ingredient in our judicial process. Quite aside from the expense of civil juries, I have long been troubled by our myth of reversing a judgment because of an erroneous instruction that the jury members possibly could not understand, and probably did not remember. The abolition of civil juries would do much to take the theatrical element out of our civil courts. It is a reform which might be long overdue.

As far back as 1936 Prof. Fleming James, Jr., declared in 45 *Yale Law Journal* 1022 that "Jury trial as a method of settling disputes is expensive and dilatory—perhaps anachronistic." In 1963, when he was chief judge of New York State, Charles S. Desmond strongly urged the abolition of jury trials in civil cases (36 *New York State Bar Journal* 104). Judge Desmond did not challenge the jury as a fact-finding and law-deciding body but reasoned that trials by jury consume more time than trials by judges alone and consequently are a cause of court congestion as well as a waste of time for citizens called to jury duty. Judge Learned Hand said in 1921 that he was "by no means enamored of jury trials, at least in civil cases." And Justice Cardozo observed in *Palko v. Connecticut,* 302 U.S. 319, 58 S.Ct. 149, 82 L.Ed. 288 (1937): "Few would be so narrow or provincial as to maintain that a fair and enlightened system of justice would be impossible without them [jury trials and indictments]."

In addition to saving actual trial court time and jury expense, the amount of time and expense saved in not having to discuss, argue, and decide such issues as proper jury instructions, claimed misconduct of counsel, right to jury trial, and other similar issues, both at the trial and appellate level, would be very substantial. * * *

Those in favor of jury trials often praise them as the "palladium of our liberties." In criminal cases, yes; in civil cases, no. Alexander Hamilton said in *The Federalist* (No. 81): "I must acknowledge that I cannot readily discern the inseparable connection between the existence of liberty and the trial by jury in civil cases."

When the Declaration of Independence was adopted and the Constitution drafted, we had every reason to be concerned about citizen-juror protection from King George's judges. But King George is long gone, and so are his judges. We have our own now, and they are competent, experienced, fair, and well qualified to decide law and fact issues in civil cases.

I believe that a federal judge, who is recommended by a senator, nominated by the president, passed on as to character and competency by the Federal Judiciary Committee of the American Bar Association, and confirmed by the Senate, in effect, for life, is likely to be well qualified professionally and morally and at least as competent to determine issues of liability and damages in a negligence case as a jury of lay persons.

JUDGES MUST AFFORD LEADERSHIP

* * *

Of course, it is all very good to say what should be done, but it is another to say how it can be done. Unlike the British, we have a written Constitution, and firmly a part of this Constitution is the Seventh Amendment, which guarantees a jury trial "in suits at common law where the value in controversy shall exceed twenty dollars."

It would take many years to satisfy two thirds of the membership of each body of Congress and three fourths of the state legislatures of the wisdom of repealing or substantially modifying the compulsory jury trial provision of the Seventh Amendment. But this does not mean that we shouldn't advocate the constitutional change and work for general public understanding of the need for it. It is the bench and bar, and especially the judges, who must afford leadership in the movement for change. They are best qualified to judge the merits of and the need for civil juries.

But while working for that change, what steps can be taken short of constitutional amendment to achieve the desired objectives, at least in part? I suggest three.

ENCOURAGE LITIGANTS AND COUNSEL TO WAIVE JURY TRIALS

1. Litigants and counsel should be encouraged to waive jury trials in civil cases. With assurances that their case would be tried, not by one who had a reputation as a "plaintiff's judge" or a "defendant's judge" but by a fair judge, parties would be willing to waive their rights to jury trial. Most competent lawyers would be agreeable to waiving civil jury trial if our disqualification statute, 28 U.S.C. § 144, were amended to provide a peremptory challenge when counsel questioned the fairness of the assigned judge. * * *

CHARGE REASONABLE FEES TO DEFRAY COSTS

2. A reasonable fee, taxable as costs, might be charged the party demanding a jury trial to defray in part the expense of the jury. Twenty-eight states have these provisions, most of which provide for waiver of the fee on the filing of an indigency affidavit, the same as is done now as to filing fees and other fees and costs in civil cases (28 U.S.C. § 1915). This would ensure that an indigent is not deprived of his Seventh Amendment rights. * * *

ARBITRATION AND MEDIATION PROVIDE ALTERNATIVES

3. Arbitration and mediation provide the most potentially fruitful alternatives to civil jury trials. Careful consideration should be given to each of these alternatives, particularly now that we have the assistance of United States magistrates. Arbitration as a method of settling disputes has grown tremendously in recent years. The American Arbitration Association is encouraging judges and lawyers to channel disputes cognizable by the courts to arbitration. Several states have provided for compulsory arbitration in some contract and tort cases: New York, California, and Pennsylvania have led the way. Medical malpractice litigation is being channeled to arbitration. Many informal committees operate locally to keep these cases out of the courts. The Department of Health, Education, and Welfare has sponsored research on the subject with the end of recommending model arbitration procedures. Masters now may be appointed to arbitrate disputes under the Equal Employment Opportunity Act. * * *

Questions

1. What proof does Judge Devitt offer that jury adjudication is the cause of delay? Is this a convincing empirical demonstration?

2. How important is speed in the disposition of lawsuits? At what point should other values override the desire for celerity?

3. Can lawyers effectively exercise a right to peremptorily challenge judges without any sort of voir dire mechanism?

4. What is the cost of a jury trial? Is this cost a significant factor in the total cost of litigation?

5. Should we repeal the Seventh Amendment?

2. THE QUALITY OF DELIBERATIONS AS SEEN FROM THE SOCIAL SCIENTIST'S POINT OF VIEW

HARRY KALVEN AND HANS ZEISEL—THE AMERICAN JURY

149–59 (1966).
Reprinted by permission of the authors, copyright © 1966.
Harry Kalven and Hans Zeisel.

[Harry Kalven and Hans Zeisel have been leaders in the movement to link legal scholarship and social science. In the late 1950s they embarked on a massive study of the way American juries actually decide cases. Their painstaking and sophisticated analysis of thousands of American jury trials yielded data that have permanently altered our understanding of the jury mechanism. After more than 20 years, their work, *The American Jury,* stands as the undisputed masterpiece in the social science literature about the law. In the following excerpt they examine the quality of jury deliberations in criminal cases.]

[THE QUESTION OF JURY UNDERSTANDING]

We begin our inquiry into what the jury makes of the evidence by establishing two basic propositions. The first is simply that, contrary to an often voiced suspicion, the jury does by and large understand the facts and get the case straight. The second proposition is that the jury's decision by and large moves with the weight and direction of the evidence. * * *

The hypothesis that the jury does *not* understand the case has loomed large in the debate over the jury. It has not infrequently been charged that the modern jury is asked to perform heroic feats of attention and recall well beyond the capacities of ordinary men. A trial, it has been argued, presents to the jury a mass of material which it cannot possibly absorb, and presents it in an artificial sequence which aggravates the jury's intellectual problem. The upshot is said to be that the jury often does not get the case straight and, therefore, is deciding a case different from the one actually before it.

Perhaps the most vivid spokesman in recent years for this challenge to the jury system was the late Judge Jerome Frank. In the course of a long criticism of the jury system, centered primarily on the jury's freedom to disregard the law totally and to do what it pleases, Judge Frank offers serious criticism of the jury's capacity to follow the facts. * * *

In the counterpoint of the debate over the jury, its defenders have suggested several offsetting considerations. First, although the trial is not a perfectly logical enterprise, it nevertheless is based upon a highly structured argument. Again, it is not necessary that every member of the jury recall every fact of the trial record. In many instances it will suffice if only some members are able to do so and then make these facts available to the other jurors. The collective recall of the jury, it is argued, is certain to be superior to the average recall of the individual juror.

When the challenge of not understanding is put most strongly, it becomes apparent that it goes to the heart of the jury system. If the jury with any great degree of frequency does not understand the facts, it is difficult to defend it. Further, even when the challenge is put somewhat less strongly, it becomes, at the least, a plea for blue ribbon juries, that is, for recruiting the jury, not from a representative sample of the people at large, but from an educated elite, who would be intelligent enough to handle the difficult, intellectual job.

Our concern is not to debate these points a priori, but rather to look to the data to see what we can learn about whether the jury does in fact understand.

[DISAGREEMENT BETWEEN JUDGE AND JURY AS A MEASURE OF JURY UNDERSTANDING]

It may come as something of a surprise that a survey of judge-jury disagreements can throw light on this particular issue. One might have thought that the jury's understanding could be ascertained only by directly interviewing the jurors and conceivably by giving them some sort of test to measure their recall. Actually, however, the data yield powerful inferences concerning the jury's understanding. There are several converging lines of analysis.

The first runs as follows. If the jury misunderstands the facts of a case, it will then, of necessity, be deciding a different case from the judge, who presumably does understand the facts. And, if the jury is deciding a different case, whether or not it agrees with the judge will be a matter of chance. To the extent that, in actual fact, jury and judge agree considerably more often than chance would dictate, the hypothesis of substantial jury misunderstanding would seem defeated. The basic table of disagreements provides critical evidence on this issue in two respects. The amount of agreement, 75 per cent of all cases, is so substantial as to make it highly improbable that much of it was caused by chance. Equally important, the disagreement * * * is highly directional [strongly favoring the defendant in criminal cases], thus compelling the conclusion that misunderstanding cannot in and of itself be a major factor in causing judge-jury disagreement and, hence, cannot be a major determinant of the jury's behavior.

[THE REASONS FOR JUDGE/JURY DISAGREEMENT]

A second line of analysis is based on * * * materials [concerning the jury's reasons for its decisions.] * * * Two important points emerged. First, in 90 per cent of the disagreements [between judge and jury] it is possible to find a reason or reasons for the disagreement without recourse to misunderstanding of the case; hence, in the great majority of disagreements there is a plausible explanation which, by its nature, precludes the notion that the jury did not understand the case. More significant, the judge almost never advances the inability of the jury to understand as a reason for disagreement. Actually there is only one clear instance out of all of the disagreements where the judge states outright that the reason the jury disagreed with him was because of its inability to understand. In this case the charge was embezzlement by a city bookkeeper who had worked out an involved system to cover withdrawals. The trial lasted some ten days, and at the end the jury, after three hours of deliberation, acquits. While the judge notes that the jurors "all were poorly educated and an expert witness had to carry them through many steps of bookkeeping," he explicitly tells us:

> The jury simply was not able to understand the case which was perfectly presented.

The uniqueness of this case among the thousand instances of disagreement argues impellingly against any general hypothesis that the jury does not understand the case.[7]

7. Even in this case, the misunderstanding appears not to have been the sole explanation; there were other reasons for the jury's disagreement, such as several sentiments about the defendant who was "an attractive woman" with a "loyal husband who was well liked," the "mother of a fine 12–year old boy," and "provided for

[THE SMALL NUMBER OF CASES THAT ARE DIFFICULT TO
COMPREHEND]

The matter need not rest on inferences, good as these are. The Sample II questionaire furnishes data permitting a more direct approach to the problem. The judge was asked the following questions:

Compared to the average criminal case, was the evidence as a whole—

> easy to comprehend?
>
> somewhat difficult?
>
> very difficult to comprehend?

Table 46 provides an important map of how difficult the criminal case that goes to the jury actually is.

TABLE 46

Difficulty of Case as Graded by the Judge

	Per Cent
Easy to comprehend	86
Somewhat difficult	12
Very difficult	2
Total	100%
Number of cases *	*1191*

* Sample II only.

Despite its simplicity the table makes an important contribution to the solution of the problem: it shows that the great bulk of cases are routine as to comprehension and hence unlikely to be misunderstood.

[JURY PERFORMANCE IN CASES THAT ARE DIFFICULT TO
COMPREHEND]

We now make a critical analytic use of this distinction between difficult and easy cases. The analysis involves two steps: First, it will appear that the jury in several ways sufficiently acknowledges the difference between easy and difficult cases, so that we can be sure that the jury perceives the difficult cases as difficult. Second, if the jury has a propensity not to understand, it must be assumed that the propensity is greater for difficult cases than for easy cases. We thus reach a prediction that, *if the jury does not understand the case,* it will disagree with the judge more often in difficult cases than it does in easy cases.

There are at least two ways to test the jury's sensitivity to the difficulty of the case. There are the data on how often the jury comes back to the court during its deliberations with an inquiry or a question. In the majority of cases the jury does not come back at all, once the deliberation starts. But there are enough cases in which it does, to provide a helpful reading on whether the jury perceives the difference

her mother." Further, the judge notes that the defendant's expert witness offered testimony which "bordered on perjury," and that he was at the time of the trial up for disciplinary action.

between easy and difficult cases. Table 47 shows that in difficult cases the jury comes back with questions about twice as often as in easy cases.

TABLE 47

Frequency of Jury's Coming Back with Questions by Difficulty of Case

	Easy Cases	Difficult Cases *
Jury comes back	14%	27%
Number of cases	*1024*	*167*

* Somewhat Difficult and Very Difficult combined.

[THE TIME THE JURY TAKES TO DELIBERATE IN DIFFICULT AND EASY CASES]

A second line of proof is a bit more complicated; it comes from data on jury deliberation time. One test of the jury's perception of the difference between difficult and easy cases is whether the jury deliberates longer in the difficult cases.

[Generally, the data show that] the jury deliberates a little more than one hour for every trial day, except for the very brief trials, for which the deliberation lasts relatively longer, and for very long trials, which require a relatively shorter deliberation than one hour per trial day. * * *

Table 49 brings this segment of the analysis into sharper focus by showing the average length of deliberation time for cases of different degrees of difficulty when the trial length is held constant. For the purposes of this table we distinguish three degrees of difficulty: clear and easy, close and easy, and difficult, irrespective of whether clear or close on the evidence.

For any given length of trial, the jury deliberates longer in the difficult case than it does in the easy case. The conclusion is therefore justified that the jury does indeed perceive sensitively the different degrees of difficulty in the cases presented to it.

TABLE 49

Average Length of Deliberation by Difficulty of Case

Length of Trial	Clear and Easy Hours	Close and Easy Hours	Difficult Hours
Under 2 complete days	1.5	1.9	2.2
2–4 days	2.5	4.6	3.9
One week or more	4.0	5.5	9.0
Average deliberation	2.1	3.3	4.5
Number of cases	*618*	*406*	*167*

[JUDGES AND JURIES DO NOT DISAGREE MORE FREQUENTLY IN
DIFFICULT CASES]

We are now ready to take the final step and present the judge-jury disagreement figures for the easy and difficult cases. The hypothesis is that *if the jury has any propensity to misunderstand the case*, it will be more likely to disagree with the judge in those cases it perceives as difficult. Table 50 provides the relevant data.

TABLE 50

Judge–Jury Disagreement as Affected by Difficulty of Case

	Clear Cases		Close Cases	
	Easy	**Difficult**	**Easy**	**Difficult**
Judge and jury disagree	9%	8%	41%	39%
Number of cases	*618*	*57*	*406*	*110*

The result is a stunning refutation of the hypothesis that the jury does not understand. While, as we can see, jury disagreement is greater in close cases than in clear ones, there is virtually no difference between the frequency of disagreement when the case is easy and when the case is difficult; this holds true for the cases that are clear as well as for the close ones. * * *

[THE JURY GENERALLY CONFORMS ITS DECISIONS TO THE WEIGHT
OF THE EVIDENCE]

Reason assessment yielded almost no cases in which failure to understand was a reason for disagreement. The cross-tabulation presented in Table 50 yields the same result by revealing virtually identical frequencies of disagreement in easy and difficult cases. Thus, in our first try at confrontation we see that two methods of analysis— reason assessment and cross-tabulation—working independently of each other, yield congruent results. We conclude, therefore, that for the law's practical purposes the jury does understand the case.

The discussion turns now from consideration of the jury's understanding of the facts to a first look at what the jury does with them. What can be said of the degree to which the jury follows the weight and direction of the evidence? To what degree is the evidence a determinant of the jury's decision? If some way could be found to organize or map the evidence in terms of the evidentiary strength or weakness of the cases, one could test the jury's response by running its decisions across such an evidence map.

There is, of course, no ideal way of determining the strength of the evidence in each case, but we can make [an] approximation * * *. The simple approximation utilizes the judge's classification of cases as either clear or close. Using this distinction and adding as another dimension the way the judge himself decides the case, one can draw an evidential map in four gross categories:

1	2	3	4
Clear cases where the judge acquits	Close cases where the judge acquits	Close cases where the judge convicts	Clear cases where the judge convicts

This evidence map goes from the cases most favorable to the defendant to the cases least favorable to him. If the jury's judgment is in large part determined by the strength and direction of the evidence, one would predict that it would acquit most often in category 1 and least often in category 4, and that there would be a marked difference in its acquittal rate as we go from one category to the next. Table 51, which shows the jury's acquittal rate, indicates that this is indeed the case.

TABLE 51

Jury Acquittal in Clear and Close Cases

	1 Clear cases— judge acquits	2 Close cases— judge acquits	3 Close cases— judge convicts	4 Clear cases— judge convicts
Jury acquits	*95%*	*74%*	*46%*	*10%*
Number of Cases	*60*	*142*	*374*	*615*

In the strongest evidence category for the defendant, the jury acquits in 95 per cent of the cases; in the weakest category for the defendant it acquits in only 10 per cent of the cases; and in the middle categories, in terms of the strength of the case for the defendant, the jury, appropriately, acquits in 74 and 46 per cent of the cases, respectively. Thus, in these very broad terms, it is apparent that the jury's judgment does follow the direction of the evidence.

Questions

1. Judge Devitt shows no awareness of the findings of *The American Jury*. Judge Frank fails to see the need for empirical verification of his claims. Why have critics of the jury ignored scientific analysis?

2. The data upon which *The American Jury* is based were gathered in the late 1950s and early 1960s. Are these data a reliable guide to jury behavior in the 1980s and 1990s? Have jury cases become significantly more complex or controversial?

3. Kalven and Zeisel found that judges and juries agree 78 percent of the time in *criminal* cases (64 percent conviction and 14 percent acquittal). The jury acquits 19 percent of the time despite a contrary judicial inclination and convicts 3 percent of the time notwithstanding the judge's contrary evaluation. Why do jurors tend to acquit more frequently than judges? Is this a healthy phenomenon?

4. Although judges and jurors disagree in about 22 percent of all *civil* cases there is virtually no directionality to their disagreement. The jury

disagrees with the judge in the defendant's favor 12 percent of the time and in the plaintiff's favor 10 percent of the time. Why are the results so much more balanced in civil than in criminal litigation?

5. As observed in questions 3 and 4, judges and juries agree in about 78 percent of the cases that come before them. An important question is whether this level of agreement is satisfactory. For purposes of comparison note the following: Physicians faced with three patient-actors simulating a fixed set of symptoms on average achieved a single (and one might add, correct) diagnosis less than 72 percent of the time. A test group of experienced psychiatrists agreed on a single diagnosis of mental abnormality in only 70 percent of sample cases tested. Even the grant proposal evaluators of the National Science Foundation agreed on the merits of proposals only 75 percent of the time. See Diamond, *Order in the Court: Consistency in Criminal–Court Decisions,* in 2 The Master Lecture Series, Psychology and the Law (Sheirer & Hammonds eds.) (1982). Is the size of the rate of disagreement between judge and jury something about which to be alarmed?

3. THE MATTER OF DELAY

HARRY KALVEN—THE DIGNITY OF THE CIVIL JURY

50 Va.L.Rev. 1055, 1058–61 (1964).
Reprinted by permission of the publisher, copyright © 1964. University of Virginia Law Review Association and Fred B. Rothman & Co.

[In this article Professor Kalven reports on his empirical examination of the relation between delay and jury trial. He concludes that the evidence does not support a claim that jury trial is an overwhelming source of delay.]

* * * It is fashionable today to complain that the time costs of the jury trial have made it a luxury that hard-pressed urban court systems can no longer afford. Here, fortunately, our researches have advanced to the stage of publication, and in our volume, *Delay in the Court,* Hans Zeisel, Bernard Buchholz, and I made a careful analysis of the jury's role in causing delay. Our study was confined to a single court system, the Supreme Court of New York County (Manhattan), but the analysis was broad enough to make it relevant to the problem of court delay generally. Several points, more fully developed in the book, may be usefully recapitulated here.

Jury trials can contribute to delay only if it takes longer to try a case to a jury than to try the same case to a judge alone. The point, therefore, must be: If all cases now tried to juries were tried to judges, there would be a sufficient saving of trial time to make a significant contribution to the reduction of backlog and the elimination of delay.

* * *

How much longer is a jury trial than a bench trial? Estimates by experienced judges and lawyers have varied widely; and it is surprisingly difficult to arrive at a satisfactory answer since we cannot try *the same case* by each method with a stopwatch in hand. Further, since there is good reason to believe that cases tried to a jury are in many respects different and more complex than cases in which a jury is waived, we cannot arrive at an answer simply by comparing a sample of jury trials and a sample of bench trials. We were fairly successful in extricating ourselves from this methodological impasse. By using a series of estimates, we reached the conclusion that on the average a bench trial would be 40 per cent less time consuming than a jury trial of the same case. As far as I know, this 40 per cent figure remains the best estimate of the time savings.

The 40 per cent time cost is, to be sure, not trivial, and it will be weighed differently depending on one's view of the jury otherwise. However, this estimate, standing alone, does little to advance the discussion, regardless of its accuracy. A chief point of our study was to relate the impact on delay of abolishing the jury to the impact on delay of other remedies that were not being urged and thus to attempt to obtain a "price tag" for the civil jury system.

There are four alternative "remedies" to be compared with abolition of the jury:

(1) The New York court at the time of our survey had a total of twenty-six judges, nineteen of whom were sitting in the law division. It was our estimate that abolition of the jury in personal injury cases would have the same impact on court congestion as the appointment of 1.6 judges. The New York court is not in all respects typical, and the savings would be somewhat larger in many other courts. We would suggest, however, that before the jury is sacrificed on behalf of court congestion, a serious estimate be made of how many additional judges would be required to have the same impact on that delay.

(2) The second alternate remedy is more dramatic. In 1956 New York had experimented with a summer session as a way of increasing judicial manpower without adding judgeships. In effect the plan required that each judge surrender just two weeks of a three-month summer vacation. This scheme was abandoned after a one-year trial, due as much, perhaps, to the irritation of the trial bar as to that of the trial bench. However, we estimated that had New York continued with the summer session plan, the impact on delay would have been the same as that of 1.5 additional judges—or the same as the savings from abolition of the personal injury jury trial.

(3) A few years ago the Federal District Court for the Northern District of Illinois initiated use of the split trial—that is, separate trials of the liability and the damage issues. My colleagues, Hans Zeisel and Thomas Callahan, have made a careful study of the first two years of experience under the rule and conclude that its full use would save approximately 20 per cent of current trial time—or about half the saving to be expected from abolition of the jury.

These three comparisons make the 40 per cent estimate more meaningful and converge on a conclusion: If the case against the jury is that its abolition is to be considered a remedy for court congestion, then the proper topic is court congestion and what else can be done about it. When the price tag for the jury system is, as in New York, the appointment of 1.6 new judges, or the curtailing of summer vacations by two weeks per judge, or vigorous use of other remedies such as split trials, it seems that the jury is being sold for too low a price. In any event, responsible discussion of the jury's contribution to delay must confront these facts.

(4) There is a fourth set of figures that should be considered. We were able to compare a sample of New Jersey personal injury jury trial cases with a sample of New York personal injury jury trial cases; the two samples were made roughly comparable. Analysis showed that the New Jersey cases, on the average, were being tried 40 per cent faster than the New York cases. Analysis of a sample of trial transcripts, etc., was not very successful in unlocking the secret of New Jersey's speed, but the data strongly suggested that it is feasible to speed up the jury trial. It is arresting, indeed, that the time margin of New Jersey jury trials over New York jury trials is about equal to that of the New York bench trials over the New York jury trials, or the amount of time hoped to be saved by abolishing the jury.

The 40 per cent figure does not, to my mind, make out a persuasive case against the jury on grounds of court congestion alone. And there is a further point of some generality. It can well be argued that reduction of delay is a poor *ad hoc* reason for tampering with the jury system in any event. It is important that the pressures generated by the very real and stubborn problems of court congestion not be dealt with in a fashion which might permanently affect the quality of our justice. Delay is not a sufficient reason for altering the jury apart from consideration of the quality of the jury as an adjudicator. At most delay is an additional straw in the calculus of those already dissatisfied with the performance of the jury—and, as the New York study shows, the straw is not a very heavy one.

Questions

1. Isn't any delay a waste of resources that should be avoided if at all possible?

2. How likely is it that Kalven's 1950s research remains accurate and useful on the question of delay?

3. How much of a judge's time is spent actually trying lawsuits?

4. How strong is the delay argument in the debate over the jury?

4. THE NUMBER OF JURY TRIALS

RITA SIMON—THE JURY: ITS ROLE IN AMERICAN SOCIETY

3 (1980).
Reprinted by permission of the publisher, copyright © 1980.
Lexington Books, D.C. Heath and Company.

[Many critics have argued that the jury trial should be abolished because it is rarely used. Judge Marvin Frankel has called the jury an "ornament * * * reserved for a relative handful of cases." [a] Judge Frankel's view should be contrasted with the statistics gathered by Rita Simon in the following excerpt from her book about the jury in America.]

In the past quarter of a century, the jury has not only enjoyed popularity as a topic for research but it has also been called into service more frequently during this period than in the preceding two and a half decades. Johnson has argued that "over the last half-century, the jury's place in the American adjudicative process has been enormously diminished." Quoting from Chambliss and Seidman Johnson reported that "today less than two percent of all cases are so [jury] decided. "The jury," he continued, "retains mostly a symbolic significance." Johnson concluded that "the core of the twentieth century story is the destruction of the jury." But the data contained in the December 13, 1973 issue of *U.S. News and World Report* belie that contention. *U.S. News* reported that in 1973 two million citizens were called for jury duty and 150,000 jury trials were held in federal, state, and local courts combined. In federal district courts alone there were 9,251 jury trials. *U.S. News and World Report* claimed that the 1973 figures represented a 57 percent increase in jury trials over the past decade.

In 1955 Kalven and Zeisel estimated that there were 2,290 jury trials in federal district courts and 53,380 jury trials in state courts throughout the United States. If one considers the differences between 1955 and 1973, there has been almost two and a half times as many jury trials in 1973 than in 1955. In the federal district courts there has been over three times as many. These figures attest dramatically to the fact that the jury system is neither a dying, nor a symbolic institution. On the contrary, its usage has increased considerably in the last two decades.

HARRY KALVEN AND HANS ZEISEL—THE AMERICAN JURY

31–32 (1966).
Reprinted by permission of the authors, copyright © 1966.
Harry Kalven and Hans Zeisel.

Finally, we come back to the question of the significance of the jury in the criminal law, given the fact that, measured in percentages, the

a. Frankel, Partisan Justice 20 (1980).

jury trial constitutes but a small fraction of all criminal dispositions. It has become something of a commonplace to read the statistics on the impact of guilty pleas and jury waivers as gravely reducing the significance of the jury and transferring its power largely to the prosecuting attorney in the bargaining over guilty pleas. But we saw at every stage of this informal process of pre-trial dispositions that decisions are in part informed by expectations of what the jury will do. Thus, the jury is not controlling merely the immediate case before it, but the host of cases not before it which are destined to be disposed of by the pre-trial process. The jury thus controls not only the formal resolution of controversies in the criminal case, but also the informal resolution of cases that never reach the trial stage. In a sense the jury, like the visible cap of an iceberg, exposes but a fraction of its true volume.

5. JURY SIZE AND UNANIMOUS VERDICTS

VALERIE HANS AND NEIL VIDMAR—JUDGING THE JURY

165–76 (1986).
Reprinted by permission of the publisher, copyright © 1986.
Plenum Publishing Corp.

[In the 1970s the Supreme Court was confronted with an assault on the right to jury trial. The attack did not challenge the constitutional right directly but rather sought to reduce the size of the jury from 12 and to terminate the requirement that jury verdicts be unanimous. The court approved both these changes. Professors Valerie Hans and Neil Vidmar summarize the case law and social science findings that explored these issues.]

SIX VERSUS TWELVE, ALL VERSUS SOME

For hundreds of years, in both English and American courts, the jury was a twelve-person group whose members were required to agree unanimously on a verdict. In recent decades, two significant changes have altered the jury's form. Some jurisdictions now employ juries of six rather than twelve; others allow juries to reach majority decisions rather than unanimous ones. To conclude our study of jury decision-making, we need to explore the impact of these two changes on the functioning of the contemporary jury.

* * *

In 1973, Claude Davis Ballew managed the Paris Adult Theatre on Peachtree Street in Atlanta, Georgia. The theater showed the sexually explicit movie *Behind the Green Door* in November of that year. On November 9, two investigators from the Fulton County Solicitor General's office joined the regular patrons of the Paris Adult Theatre. After viewing *Behind the Green Door*, the investigators left to obtain a warrant for its seizure on the grounds that the movie was obscene. They took the warrant back to the theater and seized the film. Investigators returned to the theater later that month, again viewed *Behind the Green Door*, obtained yet another warrant, and seized a second copy of the film. Ballew was subsequently charged with two counts of distributing obscene material. Under Georgia law, material was obscene if, applying community standards, its predominant appeal was to prurient interests, it had no redeeming social value, and it went substantially beyond "customary limits of candor."

The charges against Ballew were misdemeanors. In the Criminal Court of Fulton County, where Ballew was to be tried, misdemeanor trials were heard before juries of five members, as required by the Georgia Constitution. Ballew argued that the Court should empanel a twelve-person jury in his case. Ballew pointed to the fact that a central function of the jury in an obscenity trial is the application of community standards to decide whether the material in question is obscene. Ballew maintained that a five-person jury would not adequately reflect the range of opinions of the community. The Court, however, denied his request. A five-person jury heard Ballew's case, and after 38 minutes of deliberation convicted him on both charges. The judge fined Ballew two thousand dollars and sentenced him to a year in prison, to be suspended upon payment of the fine.

Ballew then began the appeals process which would ultimately take his case to the U.S. Supreme Court. The Court of Appeals of the State of Georgia heard Ballew's claim that the five-member jury deprived him of his constitutional right to trial by jury, but they rejected his contention. The Supreme Court of Georgia refused to hear his case. Finally, in 1977, the U.S. Supreme Court agreed to consider his arguments, in part to review the issue of whether a five-person jury is unconstitutional.

* * *

Ballew's case was not the first time the Supreme Court had explored the constitutionality of juries of different sizes. In 1970, in *Williams v. Florida,* the Justices examined Florida's practice of using six-person juries in most criminal trials. The sole exception were death penalty cases, which were heard by twelve-member juries. Williams, charged with robbery, asked for a twelve-person jury instead of the usual six-person jury, but the judge denied the request. Williams was duly convicted and sentenced to life imprisonment. He appealed to the U.S. Supreme Court on several grounds, including the constitutionality of a six-person jury.

In their decision in *Williams,* the Supreme Court justices traced the history of the twelve-person jury and concluded that the number twelve appeared to be a "historical accident unrelated to the great purposes which gave rise to the jury in the first place." The key constitutional issue for jury size, they judged, was whether different sizes affected the jury's functioning. They held that a six-person jury did not undermine the jury's essential functions:

> [Jury performance] is not a function of the particular number of the body that makes up the jury. To be sure, the number should probably be large enough to promote group deliberation, free from

outside attempts at intimidation and to provide a fair possibility for obtaining a representative cross-section of the community. But we find little reason to think that these goals are in any meaningful sense less likely to be achieved when the jury numbers six, than when it numbers twelve.

The Court cited several "studies" as support for its conclusion that there were no discernible differences between six- and twelve-person juries. Scholars, however, devastatingly criticized the studies upon which the Court relied. One critic was Hans Zeisel, a coauthor of *The American Jury*. He reviewed the six articles the Court cited and concluded that they provided "scant evidence by any standards." For instance, one study was really only a report by a judge who had presided over certain trials in Washington, D.C. that used five-person juries; he wrote that he found them satisfactory. In another, a judge summarized the economic advantages of smaller civil juries. Another article reported the impressions of the court clerk and three lawyers that six-member juries in 43 Massachusetts trials seemed to produce about the same verdicts as twelve-person juries.

Zeisel went on to show through statistical analyses that there should be important consequences of a decision to employ a six- as opposed to a twelve-person jury. A central purpose of trial by jury is to represent the divergent views of the community. Zeisel demonstrated that the twelve-person jury will be better able to represent these different views than the six-person jury. His example: Suppose that 90% of the community holds one view and 10% holds a minority viewpoint. Further suppose that we draw 100 twelve-member juries and 100 six-member juries from this population randomly. Seventy-two of the 100 twelve-person juries would have at least one person with a minority viewpoint on the jury, while only 47 of the 100 six-person juries would have a minority representative.

Another important consequence of jury size is the variability of the decisions. The larger the sample of individuals from a community, the lower the margin of error is. Because six-person juries are smaller samples of the community, we can expect them to produce a wider variety of outcomes than twelve-person juries. Put another way, twelve-person juries are more likely to reach the same decision than are six-person juries. Zeisel showed how this principle would affect damage awards in personal injury cases. We know that jurors have very different ideas about how much injured claimants should be compensated, and that the ultimate award by the jury will be some-where around the average of its individual jurors. Suppose that the community is divided into six groups of equal size with differing beliefs about how much money a particular plaintiff should be awarded, with an average award of $3,500. Again, let's randomly select 100 six-person juries and 100 twelve-person juries from this "community" and calculate their average awards. A statistical analysis reveals that over two-thirds of the twelve-person juries will have average damage awards close to the community average, compared to just half of the six-person juries. The six-person juries are four times as likely to have extremely low or extremely high average damage awards. Hence, the twelve-person jury should provide a more accurate and a more reliable reflection of the community's assessment.

A final way that six- and twelve-person juries should differ, according to Zeisel, is in the number of deadlocked, or "hung," juries. Deadlocked juries should be *less* likely in six-person groups for several reasons. Almost inevitably, hung juries are found in groups which contain several dissenters at the beginning of the deliberation. Psychologically, jurors are able to hold out against a majority only when they have some initial support. There will be fewer minority jurors on six-person juries, and the likelihood that more than one dissenter will appear on a six-person jury is slimmer still. Zeisel compared the hung jury rate for twelve-person juries nationwide with the hung jury rate in Miami Circuit Court in which six-person juries were utilized. Hung juries were more than twice as frequent in the larger juries: 5.5% of the twelve-person juries hung while just 2.4% of the six-person juries hung. While the smaller size jury will thus be more economical, this reduction in hung juries, in Zeisel's words, "is but the combined result of less representative, more homogeneous juries and of a reduced ability to resist the pressure for unanimity."

* * *

The Supreme Court's next opportunity to confront the issue of jury size came just two years after Professor Zeisel's article was published. In *Colgrove v. Battin,* the Court considered jury size in federal civil cases rather than criminal cases. Justice Brennan, writing for the majority, sanctioned the use of the six-person jury in civil cases. Brennan wrote that the purpose of the jury trial in civil cases was to assure a fair and equitable resolution of factual issues. He stated that the key question, as in *Williams,* was whether jury size affected the jury's ability to do its job. Justice Brennan noted that much had been written about jury size since *Williams* had been decided. However, nothing persuaded the Justices to depart from their earlier conclusion that the reliability of the jury as a fact finder was unrelated to its size. Brennan cited Professor Zeisel's article, but countered it with another study showing that people in smaller juries discussed matters more openly. Brennan capped off his discussion of empirical work by stating, "In addition, four very recent studies have provided convincing empirical evidence of the correctness of the *Williams* conclusion that 'there is no discernible difference between the results reached by the two different-sized juries.'" Thus, the Court upheld the use of the six-person jury in federal civil trials.

Justice Marshall harshly dissented in the Colgrove decision:

> . . . my Brethren mount a frontal assault on the very nature of the civil jury as that concept has been understood for some seven hundred years. No one need be fooled by reference to the six-man

trier of fact . . . as a "jury." . . . We deal here not with some minor tinkering with the role of the civil jury, but with its wholesale abolition and replacement with a different institution which functions differently, produces different results, and was wholly unknown to the Framers of the Seventh Amendment.

Marshall focused primarily on constitutional issues and said that he thought that research studies were irrelevant to the issues of concern to him about six-person juries. Nevertheless, he cited the article by Professor Zeisel as indicating that changes in jury size did seem to produce variations in jury functioning and verdicts.

The *Williams* and *Colgrove* decisions had far-reaching consequences. Before 1970, only a handful of American courts used six-person juries. But after these two decisions, many jurisdictions across the nation embraced them. In part, this widespread adoption was related to a movement already under way to modernize and streamline the increasingly overburdened courts. Legislators and court administrators saw the reduction to the six-person jury as a measure that would simultaneously increase efficiency and reduce costs. To them, six-person juries meant fewer people to organize and less money required to pay jurors.

The response to the *Williams* and *Colgrove* decisions in the academic community was not nearly so favorable. The "convincing empirical evidence" that Brennan had cited so positively was evaluated and found wanting. Boston College psychology professor Michael Saks reviewed the studies and discovered that they suffered from a variety of research problems. For instance, two studies compared outcomes between six- and twelve-person juries in states where the attorney could choose the jury size. One of the studies found that six- and twelve-member civil juries in New Jersey Superior Court were no more likely to favor the plaintiff. However, the types of cases tried before juries of six and twelve were not the same; these differences may have hidden any effects of jury size. For instance, attorneys tended to choose smaller juries when the case was less complex and less costly. The twelve-person juries heard cases in which the damage awards were roughly triple those of the smaller juries. Attorneys may have been unwilling to take a gamble with smaller juries when the dollar amount at issue was large.

Another study cited by Justice Brennan examined the impact of a legal change in Michigan that reduced the size of the civil jury beginning in July of 1970. This study compared the outcomes of trials before that date with twelve-person juries and after that date with six-person juries, and found no differences in verdicts. However, several other important changes in the trial court also occurred at that time, and may have masked any effects of the change in jury size. Finally, a laboratory study with simulated jurors found no differences when jurors decided in groups of six or twelve. But the single case used in the simulation was an odd one. Not a single jury found for the plaintiff. The results, therefore, were essentially meaningless. Professor Saks and other scholars concluded that the four studies cited by Justice Brennan collectively were certainly not "convincing empirical evidence."

University of Michigan law professor Richard Lempert sounded another alarm. He argued persuasively that typical research strategies would not reveal differences between six- and twelve-member juries even if jury size had a significant impact in certain cases. Drawing on past jury research, he pointed out that in the majority of cases, the evidence in favor of one side or the other is clear, and would be decided similarly by juries of six, juries of twelve, or even judges deciding the case alone. Lempert calculated that six- and twelve-member juries could disagree over the verdict in no more than 14% of all cases. Even if jury size had a strong and important impact in most of these cases, the effects would be overshadowed and masked by the larger number of cases that would show no differences.

Many researchers, worried that the Court had overgeneralized from scanty and methodologically poor research, began to conduct better research studies comparing the performance of groups of different sizes. By the time that Claude Ballew's case was about to be heard by the U.S. Supreme Court, there was a considerable body of literature on differences between six- and twelve-person juries. Most of the literature supported the arguments of early critics that smaller juries provided poorer representation of community viewpoints and that the variability of six-person group decisions would be much greater than that of twelve-person groups. But recall that Ballew was not battling for a twelve-person jury over a six-person jury; rather, he was arguing that a *five*-person jury was unconstitutional.

* * *

The *Ballew* decision was in some ways gratifying and in other ways disturbing. Justice Blackmun wrote the majority opinion for the Supreme Court. After outlining Ballew's case and analyzing the constitutional issues, Blackmun wrote that the *Williams* and *Colgrove* decisions had generated a large quantity of research on the topic of jury size. He then carefully reviewed the myriad empirical studies, law review articles, and social science critiques, and concluded that the empirical data suggested that smaller juries were less likely to engage in effective group deliberation, to represent different views in the community, to counterbalance various biases, and to produce accurate verdicts. All but one of the studies Blackmun cited compared six- and twelve-person groups, and after Blackmun was through reviewing these studies and the deleterious effects of the six-person jury, one might have expected Blackmun to overrule the earlier decisions in *Williams* and *Colgrove* and declare the six-member jury unconstitutional. He did nothing of the kind. Instead, the Court reaffirmed the earlier decisions, while using the empirical data to justify drawing the line at six. As Blackmun put it:

While we adhere to, and reaffirm our holding in *Williams v. Florida*, these studies, most of which have been made since *Williams* was decided in 1970, lead us to conclude that the purpose and functioning of the jury in a criminal trial is seriously impaired, and to a constitutional degree, by a reduction in size to below six members. We readily admit that we do not pretend to discern a clear line between six members and five. But the assembled data raise substantial doubt about the reliability and appropriate representation of panels smaller than six.

Ballew's five-person jury was thus declared unconstitutional. Why did the Court fail to overturn its earlier decisions, in light of the new empirical evidence? Scholars speculated that because juries had been reduced from twelve to six throughout the nation after the Court's prior decisions, to reverse the earlier ruling would be very disruptive and no doubt unpopular. The safest, although somewhat illogical, decision in *Ballew* was to get off the slippery slope: to halt further reductions in the size of the jury while leaving the six-member jury intact. Thus, the line has been drawn; American juries must contain at least six persons.

In 1981, a Colorado man tested the limit. Charged with criminal mischief, he requested a jury of one person. A Colorado law stated that a criminal defendant may, with the approval of the judge, choose to be tried by a number of jurors less than the number to which he or she is otherwise entitled. The defendant's attorney reasoned that a lone juror would be very hesitant to convict. The trial judge granted the defendant's motion. But before the trial in front of a jury of one could proceed, an appellate court overruled the judge and said that six jurors was the lowest number a defendant could choose.

* * *

Another aspect of trial by jury that has undergone change in recent years is the requirement that jurors must unanimously agree on the verdict. The origin of the unanimity requirement is unknown, although the first report of a case in which it was required dates back to 1367. One explanation traces the unanimity requirement back to an earlier form of the jury trial—trial by compurgation. As we discussed earlier, in trial by compurgators, jurors were added to an original panel of twelve until twelve people voted for one of the parties. When the practice of adding jurors was discontinued, the requirement that the twelve jurors agree on a verdict was maintained. A second possibility is that jury unanimity developed to compensate the defendant for the inadequate legal and procedural rules which characterized trials in earlier times. Likewise, the penalties for offenses were extremely harsh in common law, and jury unanimity may have been viewed as some protection for the accused. Jury unanimity may also have developed because jurors originally were witnesses and had personal knowledge of the offense being tried. As noted earlier, in medieval times, it was presumed that there was only one correct view of the facts; if jurors did not agree, then they could be punished for perjury. This provided considerable incentive for unanimity. * * *

Landsman—Adversarial Justice ACB—7

In the United States, just two years after the Supreme Court justices had decided that state criminal trial juries need not consist of twelve persons in *Williams,* they concluded that unanimity was not constitutionally required for those juries either. In a pair of cases decided in 1972, *Johnson v. Louisiana* and *Apodaca v. Oregon,* the Court dealt a double blow to the unanimity requirement in state courts. However, it left intact the requirement that jurors agree unanimously in federal courts.

On January 20, 1968, Frank Johnson was arrested at his home. The victim of an armed robbery had identified Johnson as the culprit from photographs. Johnson then proceeded to a lineup, at which he was identified by still another robbery victim. At his trial on the second robbery charge, he pleaded not guilty, but a twelve-person jury convicted him by a nine-to-three vote. For crimes of robbery, Louisiana law specified that defendants be tried by a jury of twelve; moreover, a minimum of nine jurors had to agree on the verdict. Johnson appealed the majority verdict, arguing that because three of the jurors did not agree to convict, the prosecution had not proved the case beyond a reasonable doubt.

But Justice White, writing for the majority of the U.S. Supreme Court, said that just because some jurors dissented did not necessarily imply that the reasonable doubt standard had been violated. Justice White revealed some of the Court's assumptions about jury behavior when he stated:

> We have no grounds for believing that majority jurors, aware of their responsibility and power over the liberty of the defendant, would simply refuse to listen to arguments presented to them in favor of acquittal, terminate discussion and render a verdict. On the contrary it is far more likely that a juror presenting reasoned argument in favor of acquittal would either have his arguments answered or would carry enough other jurors with him to prevent conviction. A majority will cease discussion and outvote a minority only after reasoned discussion has ceased to have persuasive effect or to serve any other purpose— when a minority, that is, continues to insist upon acquittal without having persuasive reasons in support of its position.

Justice White suggested that at this point a minority juror should probably question whether his or her own doubts are reasonable, since they have failed to make an impression on the rest of the jurors.

Several other Justices, disagreeing with the majority opinion, cited a long line of Supreme Court cases upholding the right of all citizens, regardless of race, color, or creed, to participate on the jury. But under a majority rule like Louisiana's, nine jurors could ignore their fellow jurors of a different race or class. The dissenting Justices lamented that "today's judgment approves the elimination of the one rule that can ensure that such participation will be meaningful—the rule requiring the assent of all jurors before a verdict of conviction or acquittal can be returned." To these Justices, unanimity and impartial jury selection were complementary; they operated jointly to promote fairness and community confidence in the criminal justice system.

In the second case involving jury unanimity, *Apodaca v. Oregon*, three Oregon defendants convicted by less than unanimous juries challenged the constitutionality of the verdicts. The Court took the same approach to thinking about the importance of jury unanimity as it had taken when thinking about jury size in *Williams*. The Justices focused on the functions of the jury in contemporary society and inquired whether the requirement that jurors agree unanimously affected those functions. To fulfill its functions, the jury must interpose between the government and the accused the commonsense judgment of a group of laypeople. Justice White wrote for the majority that the exercise of this commonsense judgment was not significantly affected by jury unanimity, and he rejected the notion that jury unanimity was required to ensure meaningful participation of all segments of society.

Justice Douglas dissented strenuously. He maintained that eliminating jury unanimity would reduce the reliability of jury verdicts.

> The diminution of verdict reliability [in juries where unanimity is not required] flows from the fact that nonunanimous juries need not debate and deliberate as fully as must unanimous juries. . . . It is said that there is no evidence that majority jurors will refuse to listen to dissenters whose votes are unneeded for conviction. Yet human experience teaches that polite and academic conversation is no substitute for the earnest and robust argument necessary to reach unanimity.

Justice Douglas pointed out that jurors deliberated just 41 minutes in Robert Apodaca's trial before convicting him by a ten-to-two vote.

The Supreme Court's decisions about jury unanimity in the *Johnson* and *Apodaca* cases rested in part on the Justices' views about how unanimity would affect the quality and reliability of jury deliberation, and about equal participation in the jury room. Social scientists subsequently tested some of these assumptions in jury simulation experiments. For instance, one of us had six-person juries decide a case of robbery. At the beginning of the deliberation, all the groups had four members who favored a guilty verdict and two members who favored not guilty. Half of the groups deliberated knowing that they had to reach a unanimous decision. The other half were told instead that although it was desirable that they all agree, a majority verdict, involving just five out of six jurors, was acceptable. The group deliberations were videotaped. Later, law students scrutinized the videotapes and evaluated them. The law students agreed that, when there was a unanimity requirement, jurors trying to argue a minority position participated more actively and were more influential in the deliberations. Further analysis of the videotaped deliberations confirmed that minority members took a more active role in groups deliberating under a unanimous decision rule.

Psychologists Reid Hastie, Steven Penrod, and Nancy Pennington also conducted a jury simulation study to test the effects of the unanimity requirement. With the cooperation of local officials, they recruited members of the Superior Court jury pools in three Massachusetts counties to serve as subjects in their experiment. They presented all subject-jurors with a videotaped reenactment of an actual murder trial. Groups of twelve jurors were randomly assigned to one of three conditions. One-third of the juries were required to come to a unanimous decision, one-third had to reach a majority decision in which ten of the twelve agreed, and the final third had to reach a majority decision in which eight of the twelve agreed.

Although the ultimate verdicts were similar, under unanimous and majority rules the juries deliberated quite differently. Those required to come to a unanimous verdict spent a longer time deliberating, but their deliberations were not simply longer versions of those of majority juries. Professor Hastie characterized the unanimity juries as "evidence-driven" in contrast to the majority juries who engaged in "verdict-driven" deliberations. Unanimity juries were more thorough in their evaluation of the evidence and the law; jurors in the minority participated more actively in the discussion; and jurors were more satisfied with the final verdict under a unanimous decision rule.

These studies, as well as others, shed some doubt on assumptions underlying the majority opinions of the Supreme Court decisions in the jury unanimity cases. Jurors take a subtle message from the instruction that they need not be unanimous. They deliberate in a different manner, and the influence of jurors trying to argue a minority position is diluted, exactly as the dissenting Justices in *Apodaca* had feared. We will never know whether Ralph Johnson and Robert Apodaca would have been acquitted if their juries had been required to reach unanimous verdicts, but the research studies indicate that their juries would have deliberated more carefully and with greater attention to minority viewpoints.

*   *   *

As one pundit has noted, the Supreme Court is not last because it's supreme; rather, it's supreme because it is last. The Supreme Court has had, for the time being, the last word on the jury size and jury decision rule issues. In 1979, the Court decided *Burch v. Louisiana*, in which past jury size and jury unanimity decisions were combined to prohibit majority verdicts in six-person juries. The Court reasoned that since six is the absolute minimum number of jurors necessary to preserve the great functions of trial by jury, then a rule that allows just five of the six jurors to agree on a verdict is unconstitutional. If juries consist of six persons, they must reach unanimous verdicts; but if they consist of twelve, majority verdicts are acceptable.

Time will tell whether the important decisions to allow six-person juries and majority verdicts in larger juries have so fundamentally affected the functioning of the jury that, in Justice Marshall's words, the jury as we have known it has been replaced by an entirely new institution which functions differently and produces different results.

Questions

1. Is the dispute about the merits of 6 versus 12 member juries important? Why?

2. What is the value of hung juries? Can we afford them?

3. Why have judges been so keen to reduce the size of the jury?

4. What has been the result of shrinking the size of the jury? How has it affected jury performance and reliability?

5. Is unanimity important? Why?

6. How has terminating the unanimity requirement affected the performance of the jury? Is this good or bad?

Chapter 5

LAWYERS: THEIR USEFULNESS, ZEAL, AND CANDOR

The adversary system is based upon the premise that each litigant will forcefully and completely present his or her case. The forensic demands of such an approach led to the creation of a corps of professional advocates skilled in the arts of framing and prosecuting lawsuits. Obviously, the primary function of lawyers in such a system is to speak for those who employ them. Since early times, however, advocates have seen themselves as more than mere mouthpieces for hire. They have recognized that the nature of their work creates special obligations to the legal system they work in and the society that supports it. How to balance allegiance to clients and society has been a matter of constant debate. A small portion of that debate is reproduced below.

SECTION A. THE NEED FOR COUNSEL—TWO CONTRASTING VIEWS

POWELL v. ALABAMA
287 U.S. 45, 56–59, 68–73, 53 S.Ct. 55, 59–61, 64–65, 77 L.Ed. 158, 164–65, 170–71 (1932).

[*Powell* was the first in a series of cases involving nine young black men accused of raping two white women on a moving freight train in northern Alabama in March of 1931. The case was tried at Scottsboro, Alabama, less than two weeks after the alleged offense amidst the strongest sort of racial animosity. The case became a *cause célèbre* and the "Scottsboro boys" symbols of Southern injustice. The Supreme Court of the United States twice reviewed and reversed the convictions of the defendants. (For a superlative account of the case see Carter, *Scottsboro: A Tragedy of the American South.*)

It has been asserted that *Powell* was one of the first modern cases in which the Supreme Court sought to protect the rights of minority citizens. It is revealing that the court should have chosen the right to counsel as a means to achieve that end.]

Mr. Justice Sutherland delivered the opinion of the Court.

* * *

[U]ntil the very morning of the trial no lawyer had been named or definitely designated to represent the defendants. Prior to that time, the trial judge had "appointed all the members of the bar" for the limited "purpose of arraigning the defendants." Whether they would represent the defendants thereafter if no counsel appeared in their behalf, was a matter of speculation only, or, as the judge indicated, of mere anticipation on the part of the court. Such a designation, even if made for all purposes, would, in our opinion, have fallen far short of meeting, in any proper sense, a requirement for the appointment of counsel. How many lawyers were members of the bar does not appear; but, in the very nature of things, whether many or few, they would not, thus collectively named, have been given that clear appreciation of responsibility or impressed with that individual sense of duty which should and naturally would accompany the appointment of a selected member of the bar, specifically named and assigned. * * *

Nor do we think the situation was helped by what occurred on the morning of the trial. At that time, * * * Mr. Roddy stated to the court that he did not appear as counsel, but that he would like to appear along with counsel that the court might appoint; that he had not been given an opportunity to prepare the case; that he was not familiar with the procedure in Alabama, but merely came down as a friend of the people who were interested; that he thought the boys would be better off if he should step entirely out of the case. Mr. Moody, a member of the local bar, expressed a willingness to help Mr. Roddy in anything he could do under the circumstances. To this the court responded, "All right, all the lawyers that will; of course I would not require a lawyer to appear if—." And Mr. Moody continued, "I am willing to do that for him as a member of the bar; I will go ahead and help do any thing I can do." With this dubious understanding, the trials immediately proceeded. The defendants, young, ignorant, illiterate, surrounded by hostile sentiment, haled back and forth under guard of soldiers, charged with an atrocious crime regarded with especial horror in the community where they were to be tried, were thus put in peril of their lives within a few moments after counsel for the first time charged with any degree of responsibility began to represent them.

It is not enough to assume that counsel thus precipitated into the case thought there was no defense, and exercised their best judgment in proceeding to trial without preparation. Neither they nor the court could say what a prompt and thoroughgoing investigation might disclose as to the facts. No attempt was made to investigate. No opportunity to do so was given. Defendants were immediately hurried to trial. Chief Justice Anderson, after disclaiming any intention to criticize harshly counsel who attempted to represent defendants at the trials, said: ". . . the record indicates that the appearance was rather *pro forma* than zealous and active . . ." Under the circumstances disclosed, we hold that defendants were not accorded the right of counsel in any substantial sense. To decide otherwise, would simply be to ignore actualities. * * *

It is true that great and inexcusable delay in the enforcement of our criminal law is one of the grave evils of our time. Continuances are frequently granted for unnecessarily long periods of time, and delays incident to the disposition of motions for new trial and hearings upon appeal have come in many cases to be a distinct reproach to the administration of justice. The prompt disposition of criminal cases is to be commended and encouraged. But in reaching that result a defendant, charged with a serious crime, must not be stripped of his right to have sufficient time to advise with counsel and prepare his defense. To do that is not to proceed promptly in the calm spirit of regulated justice but to go forward with the haste of the mob. * * *

It never has been doubted by this court, or any other so far as we know, that notice and hearing are preliminary steps essential to the passing of an enforceable judgment, and that they, together with a legally competent tribunal having jurisdiction of the case, constitute basic elements of the constitutional requirement of due process of law. The words of Webster, so often quoted, that by "the law of the land" is intended "a law which hears before it condemns," have been repeated in varying forms of expression in a multitude of decisions. * * *

What, then, does a hearing include? Historically and in practice, in our own country at least, it has always included the right to the aid of counsel when desired and provided by the party asserting the right. The right to be heard would be, in many cases, of little avail if it did not comprehend the right to be heard by counsel. Even the intelligent and educated layman has small and sometimes no skill in the science of law. If charged with crime, he is incapable, generally, of determining for himself whether the indictment is good or bad. He is unfamiliar with the rules of evidence. Left without the aid of counsel he may be put on trial without a proper charge, and convicted upon incompetent evidence, or evidence irrelevant to the issue or otherwise inadmissible. He lacks both the skill and knowledge adequately to prepare his defense, even though he have a perfect one. He requires the guiding hand of counsel at every step in the proceedings against him. Without it, though he be not guilty, he faces the danger of conviction because he does not know how to establish his innocence. If that be true of men of intelligence, how much more true is it of the ignorant and illiterate, or those of feeble intellect. If in any case, civil or criminal, a state or federal court were arbitrarily to refuse to hear a party by counsel, employed by and appearing for him, it reasonably may not be doubted that such a refusal would be a denial of a hearing, and, therefore, of due process in the constitutional sense. * * *

In the light of the facts outlined in the forepart of this opinion—the ignorance and illiteracy of the defendants, their youth, the circumstances of public hostility, the imprisonment and the close surveillance of the defendants by the military forces, the fact that their friends and families were all in other states and communication with them necessarily difficult, and above all that they stood in deadly peril of their lives—we think the failure of the trial court to give them reasonable time and opportunity to secure counsel was a clear denial of due process.

But passing that, and assuming their inability, even if opportunity had been given, to employ counsel, as the trial court evidently did assume, we are of opinion that, under the circumstances just stated, the necessity of counsel was so vital and imperative that the failure of the trial court to make an effective appointment of counsel was likewise a denial of due process within the meaning of the Fourteenth Amendment. * * * In a case such as this, whatever may be the rule in other cases, the right to have counsel appointed, when necessary, is a logical corollary from the constitutional right to be heard by counsel. * * *

Let us suppose the extreme case of a prisoner charged with a capital offense, who is deaf and dumb, illiterate and feeble minded, unable to employ counsel, with the whole power of the state arrayed against him, prosecuted by counsel for the state without assignment of counsel for his defense, tried, convicted and sentenced to death. Such a result, which, if carried into execution, would be little short of judicial murder, it cannot be doubted would be a gross violation of the guarantee of due process of law; and we venture to think that no appellate court, state or federal, would hesitate so to decide. * * * The duty of the trial court to appoint counsel under such circumstances is clear, as it is clear under circumstances such as are disclosed by the record here; and its power to do so, even in the absence of a statute, can not be questioned. Attorneys are officers of the court, and are bound to render service when required by such an appointment. * * *

Questions

1. What is it that the court thinks an attorney can do for ignorant, illiterate, reviled defendants? Is the court right?

2. Why did the court choose the right to counsel as a vehicle to protect minority rights in this case? (Note that the haste with which the proceedings were conducted and the racially segregated composition of the jury panel were alternate available grounds of decision in the case.)

3. What sort of representation does the court expect of competent counsel? What if employed or assigned counsel fails to live up to this standard? Should cases generally be reversed for such failures? Why or why not?

4. Why do lawyers and clients need substantial time together? Aren't there serious risks of delay if this idea is carried too far?

5. Is the principle of the *Powell* case limited to criminal litigation? Should it have any bearing on the way civil cases are conducted?

6.　Why does the court go out of its way to find that the state must, in cases like *Powell*, provide counsel to the indigent defendant?　Who should pay for such representation?　What level of service should be provided to the indigent?

WALTERS v. NATIONAL ASSOCIATION OF RADIATION SURVIVORS

473 U.S. 305, 307, 320–21, 323–26, 330, 358–59, 362–63, 365, 368–72, 105 S.Ct. 3180, 3182, 3189–92, 3194, 3209, 3211–16, 87 L.Ed.2d 220 (1985).

[The recent decision of a seriously divided Supreme Court in the *Walters* case presents a striking contrast to the views expressed in *Powell*.]

JUSTICE REHNQUIST delivered the opinion of the Court.

Title 38 U.S.C. § 3404(c) limits to $10 the fee that may be paid an attorney or agent who represents a veteran seeking benefits for service-connected death or disability.　The United States District Court for the Northern District of California held that this limit violates the Due Process Clause of the Fifth Amendment, and the First Amendment, because it denies veterans or their survivors the opportunity to retain counsel of their choice in pursuing their claims.　＊　＊　＊

Appellees' first claim, accepted by the District Court, is that the statutory fee limitation, as it bears on the administrative scheme in operation, deprives a rejected claimant or recipient of "life, liberty or property, without due process of law," U.S.Const., Amdt. 5, by depriving him of representation by expert legal counsel.　Our decisions establish that "due process" is a flexible concept—that the processes required by the Clause with respect to the termination of a protected interest will vary depending upon the importance attached to the interest and the particular circumstances under which the deprivation may occur.　In defining the process necessary to ensure "fundamental fairness" we have recognized that the Clause does not require that "the procedures used to guard against an erroneous deprivation . . . be so comprehensive as to preclude any possibility of error," and in addition we have emphasized that the marginal gains from affording an additional procedural safeguard often may be outweighed by the societal cost of providing such a safeguard.　＊　＊　＊

The government interest, which has been articulated in congressional debates since the fee limitation was first enacted in 1862 during the Civil War, has been this: that the system for administering benefits should be managed in a sufficiently informal way that there should be no need for the employment of an attorney to obtain benefits to which a claimant was entitled, so that the claimant would receive the entirety of the award without having to divide it with a lawyer.　＊　＊　＊

There can be little doubt that invalidation of the fee limitation would seriously frustrate the oft repeated congressional purpose for enacting it.　Attorneys would be freely employable by claimants to veterans benefits, and the claimant would as a result end up paying part of the award, or its equivalent, to an attorney. But this would not be the only consequence of striking down the fee limitation that would be deleterious to the congressional plan.

A necessary concomitant of Congress' desire that a veteran not need a representative to assist him in making his claim was that the system should be as informal and nonadversarial as possible. This is not to say that complicated factual inquiries may be rendered simple by the expedient of informality, but surely Congress desired that the proceedings be as informal and nonadversarial as possible. The regular introduction of lawyers into the proceedings would be quite unlikely to further this goal. * * *

Knowledgeable and thoughtful observers have made the same point in other language:

"To be sure, counsel can often perform useful functions even in welfare cases or other instances of mass justice; they may bring out facts ignored by or unknown to the authorities, or help to work out satisfactory compromises. But this is only one side of the coin. Under our adversary system the role of counsel is not to make sure the truth is ascertained but to advance his client's cause by any ethical means. Within the limits of professional propriety, causing delay and sowing confusion not only are his right but may be his duty. The appearance of counsel for the citizen is likely to lead the government to provide one—or at least to cause the government's representative to act like one. The result may be to turn what might have been a short conference leading to an amicable result into a protracted controversy.

. . . . . .

"These problems concerning counsel and confrontation inevitably bring up the question whether we would not do better to abandon the adversary system in certain areas of mass justice . . .. While such an experiment would be a sharp break with our tradition of adversary process, that tradition, which has come under serious general challenge from a thoughtful and distinguished judge, was not formulated for a situation in which many thousands of hearings must be provided each month." Friendly, "Some Kind of Hearing," 123 U.Pa.L.Rev. 1267, 1287–1290 (1975).

Thus, even apart from the frustration of Congress' principal goal of wanting the veteran to get the entirety of the award, the destruction of the fee limitation would bid fair to complicate a proceeding which Congress wished to keep as simple as possible. It is scarcely open to doubt that if claimants were permitted to retain compensated attorneys the day might come when it could be said that an attorney might indeed be necessary to present a claim properly in a system rendered more adversary and more complex by the very presence of lawyer representation. It is only a small step beyond that to the situation in which the claimant who has a factually simple and obviously deserving claim may nonetheless feel impelled to retain an attorney simply because so many other claimants retain attorneys. And this additional complexity will undoubtedly engender greater administrative costs, with the end result being that less government money reaches its intended beneficiaries. * * *

Simple factual questions are capable of resolution in a nonadversarial context, and it is less than crystal clear why *lawyers* must be available to identify possible errors in *medical* judgment. * * *

JUSTICE STEVENS, with whom JUSTICE BRENNAN and JUSTICE MARSHALL join, dissenting.

The Court does not appreciate the value of individual liberty. It may well be true that in the vast majority of cases a veteran does not need to employ a lawyer and that the system of processing veterans benefit claims, by and large, functions fairly and effectively without the participation of retained counsel. Everyone agrees, however, that there are at least some complicated cases in which the services of a lawyer would be useful to the veteran and, indeed, would simplify the work of the agency by helping to organize the relevant facts and to identify the controlling issues. What is the reason for denying the veteran the right to counsel of his choice in such cases? The Court gives us two answers: First, the paternalistic interest in protecting the veteran from the consequences of his own improvidence; and second, the bureaucratic interest in minimizing the cost of administering the benefit program. I agree that both interests are legitimate, but neither provides an adequate justification for the restraint on liberty imposed by the $10-fee limitation. * * *

The Court's opinion blends its discussion of the paternalistic interest in protecting veterans from unscrupulous lawyers and the bureaucratic interest in minimizing the cost of administration in a way that implies that each interest reinforces the other. Actually the two interests are quite different and merit separate analysis.

In my opinion, the bureaucratic interest in minimizing the cost of administration is nothing but a red herring. Congress has not prohibited lawyers from participating in the processing of claims for benefits and there is no reason why it should. The complexity of the agency procedures can be regulated by limiting the number of hearings, the time for argument, the length of written submissions, and in other ways, but there is no reason to believe that the *agency's* cost of administration will be increased because a claimant is represented by counsel instead of appearing *pro se*. The informality that the Court emphasizes is desirable because it no doubt enables many veterans, or their lay representatives, to handle their claims without the assistance of counsel. But there is no reason to assume that lawyers would add confusion rather than clarity to the proceedings. As a profession, lawyers are skilled communicators dedicated to the service of their clients. Only if it is assumed that the average lawyer is incompetent or unscrupulous can one rationally conclude that the efficiency of the agency's work would be undermined by allowing counsel to participate whenever a veteran is willing to pay for his services. I categorically reject any such assumption.

The fact that a lawyer's services are unnecessary in most cases, and might even be counter-productive in a few, does not justify a total prohibition on their participation in all pension claim proceedings. * * *

The paternalistic interest in protecting the veteran from his own improvidence would unquestionably justify a rule that simply prevented lawyers from over-charging their clients. Most appropriately, such a rule might require agency approval, or perhaps judicial review, of counsel fees. It might also establish a reasonable ceiling, subject to exceptions for especially complicated cases. In fact, I assume that the $10–fee limitation was justified by this interest when it was first enacted in 1864. But time has brought changes in the value of the dollar, in the character of the legal profession, in agency procedures, and in the ability of the veteran to proceed without the assistance of counsel. * * *

[T]he statute is unconstitutional for a reason that is more fundamental than its apparent irrationality. What is at stake is the right of an individual to consult an attorney of his choice in connection with a controversy with the Government. In my opinion that right is firmly protected by the Due Process Clause of the Fifth Amendment and by the First Amendment.

The Court recognizes that the Veterans' Administration's procedures must provide claimants with due process of law, but then concludes that the constitutional requirement is satisfied because the appellees have not proved that the "probability of error under the present system" is unacceptable. In short, if 80 or 90 percent of the cases are correctly decided, why worry about those individuals whose claims have been erroneously rejected and who might have prevailed if they had been represented by counsel?

The fundamental error in the Court's analysis is its assumption that the individual's right to employ counsel of his choice in a contest with his sovereign is a kind of second-class interest that can be assigned a material value and balanced on a utilitarian scale of costs and benefits. It is true that the veteran's right to benefits is a property right and that in fashioning the procedures for administering the benefit program, the Government may appropriately weigh the value of additional procedural safeguards against their pecuniary costs. It may, for example, properly decide not to provide free counsel to claimants. But we are not considering a procedural right that would involve any cost to the Government. We are concerned with the individual's right to spend his own money to obtain the advice and assistance of independent counsel in advancing his claim against the Government.

In all criminal proceedings, that right is expressly protected by the Sixth Amendment. As I have indicated, in civil disputes with the Government I believe that right is also protected by the Due Process Clause of the Fifth Amendment and by the First Amendment. If the Government, in the guise of a paternalistic interest in protecting the citizen from his own improvidence, can deny him access to independent counsel of his choice, it can change the character of our free society. Even though a dispute with the sovereign may only involve property rights, or as in this case a statutory entitlement, the citizen's right of access to the independent, private bar is itself an aspect of liberty that is of critical importance in our democracy. Just as I disagree with the present Court's crabbed view of the concept of "liberty," so do I reject its apparent unawareness of the function of the independent lawyer as a guardian of our freedom.

In my view, regardless of the nature of the dispute between the sovereign and the citizen—whether it be a criminal trial, a proceeding to terminate parental rights, a claim for social security benefits, a dispute over welfare benefits, or a pension claim asserted by the widow of a soldier who was killed on the battlefield—the citizen's right to consult an independent lawyer and to retain that lawyer to speak on his or her behalf is an aspect of liberty that is priceless. It should not be bargained away on the notion that a totalitarian appraisal of the mass of claims processed by the Veterans' Administration does not identify an especially high probability of error.

Unfortunately, the reason for the Court's mistake today is all too obvious. It does not appreciate the value of individual liberty.

Questions

1. Who should decide on the need for counsel, the claimant or the government? Might the government have a pecuniary interest in blocking the appearance of counsel?

2. Did Congress literally prohibit the appearance of lawyers in Veterans Administration hearings? If not, why should the government be allowed to effectively exclude them from the process?

3. What is Justice Rehnquist's view of adversary proceedings? Why? What is his view of lawyers? Why?

4. Are modern government benefit programs run on an amicable and informal basis that liberally grants assistance and avoids injustice? Compare your answer with the recent observations of Senator Alan Cranston, Chairman of the Senate Veterans Affairs Committee that the Veterans Administration has a "cavalier attitude [which] suggests that some in the V.A. may consider the agency above the law," and the findings of at least three Veterans Administration auditors that incidents of unfairness have been occurring for years at many agency offices including, for example, the denial of benefits to a legless Korean war veteran because *he* failed to provide information *the agency* was obliged to supply. See *New York Times*, March 18, 1987, page 9 column 8.

5. What empirical evidence does Justice Rehnquist offer concerning the deleterious impact of lawyers on government benefit programs?

6. Are lawyers ever used to help determine errors in *medical* judgment? What are the implications of *Walters* for medical malpractice litigation?

7. How is liberty related to the retention of counsel in Justice Stevens' mind? Is he right?

8. Is Justice Stevens correct when he charges that Justice Rehnquist assumes the average lawyer "is incompetent or unscrupulous?"

9. Who has the better of the debate in the *Walters* case? Why?

SECTION B. REPRESENTATION OF A CLIENT'S INTERESTS—THE IMPLICATIONS OF THE ADVERSARIAL APPROACH

Zeal and confidentiality have come to be seen as the hallmarks of the adversarial advocate's duty to his client. Yet untempered zeal would require that lawyers disregard the dictates of the legal system and limitless confidentiality would invite fraud and chicane. That some limits are necessary is beyond doubt. But what those limits should be has engendered an intense and ongoing debate. The relation of zeal and confidentiality to basic adversarial principles is explored below. In subsequent sections the implications of zeal and confidentiality will be examined in greater detail.

1. FUNDAMENTAL PRINCIPLES

PROFESSIONAL RESPONSIBILITY: REPORT OF THE JOINT CONFERENCE

44 A.B.A.J. 1159, 1160–61, 1216–17 (1958).

Reprinted with permission of the *ABA Journal*, The Lawyer's Magazine, copyright © 1958. The American Bar Association Journal.

[In 1958 a conference composed of representatives of the American Bar Association and the Association of American Law Schools drafted the following statement concerning the lawyer's responsibilities. It was, in large measure, the product of Professor Lon Fuller whose description of the adversary system appears in Chapter II above. Here the focus is specifically on the lawyer's role in the process.]

THE LAWYER'S ROLE AS ADVOCATE IN OPEN COURT

The lawyer appearing as an advocate before a tribunal presents, as persuasively as he can, the facts and the law of the case as seen from the standpoint of his client's interest. It is essential that both the lawyer and the public understand clearly the nature of the role thus discharged. Such an understanding is required not only to appreciate the need for an adversary presentation of issues, but also in order to perceive truly the limits partisan advocacy must impose on itself if it is to remain wholesome and useful.

In a very real sense it may be said that the integrity of the adjudicative process itself depends upon the participation of the advocate. This becomes apparent when we contemplate the nature of the task assumed by any arbiter who attempts to decide a dispute without the aid of partisan advocacy.

Such an arbiter must undertake, not only the role of judge, but that of representative for both of the litigants. Each of these roles must be played to the full without being muted by qualifications derived from the others. When he is developing for each side the most effective statement of its case, the arbiter must put aside his neutrality and permit himself to be moved by a sympathetic identification sufficiently intense to draw from his mind all that it is capable of giving,— in analysis, patience and creative power. When he resumes his neutral position, he must be able to view with distrust the fruits of this identification and be ready to reject the products of his own best mental efforts. The difficulties of this undertaking are obvious. If it is true that a man in his time must play many parts, it is scarcely given to him to play them all at once. * * *

An adversary presentation seems the only effective means for combatting [the] natural human tendency to judge too swiftly in terms of the familiar that which is not yet fully known. The arguments of counsel hold the case, as it were, in suspension between two opposing interpretations of it. While the proper classification of the case is thus kept unresolved, there is time to explore all of its peculiarities and nuances. * * *

[I]n whatever form adjudication may appear, the experienced judge or arbitrator desires and actively seeks to obtain an adversary presentation of the issues. Only when he has had the benefit of intelligent and vigorous advocacy on both sides can he feel fully confident of his decision.

Viewed in this light, the role of the lawyer as a partisan advocate appears not as a regrettable necessity, but as an indispensable part of a larger ordering of affairs. The institution of advocacy is not a concession to the frailties of human nature, but an expression of human insight in the design of a social framework within which man's capacity for impartial judgment can attain its fullest realization.

When advocacy is thus viewed, it becomes clear by what principle limits must be set to partisanship. The advocate plays his role well when zeal for his client's cause promotes a wise and informed decision of the case. He plays his role badly, and trespasses against the obligations of professional responsibility, when his desire to win leads him to muddy the headwaters of decision, when, instead of lending a needed perspective to the controversy, he distorts and obscures its true nature.

THE LAWYER'S ROLE AS COUNSELOR

Vital as is the lawyer's role in adjudication, it should not be thought that it is only as an advocate pleading in open court that he contributes to the administration of the law. The most effective realization of the law's aims often takes place in the attorney's office, where litigation is forestalled by anticipating its outcome, where the lawyer's quiet counsel takes the place of public force. Contrary to popular belief, the compliance with the law thus brought about is not generally lip-serving and narrow, for by reminding him of its long-run costs the lawyer often deters his client from a course of conduct technically permissible under existing law, though inconsistent with its underlying spirit and purpose.

Although the lawyer serves the administration of justice indispensably both as advocate and as office counselor, the demands imposed on him by these two roles must be sharply distinguished. The man who has been called into court to answer for his own actions is entitled to a fair hearing. Partisan advocacy plays its essential part in such a hearing, and the lawyer pleading his client's case may properly present it in the most favorable light. A similar resolution of doubts in one direction becomes inappropriate when the lawyer acts as counselor. The reasons that justify and even require partisan advocacy in the trial of a cause do not grant any license to the lawyer to participate as legal adviser in a line of conduct that is immoral, unfair, or of doubtful legality. In saving himself from this unworthy involvement, the lawyer cannot be guided solely by an unreflective inner sense of good faith; he must be at pains to preserve a sufficient detachment from his client's interests so that he remains capable of a sound and objective appraisal of the propriety of what his client proposes to do. * * *

MAKING LEGAL SERVICES AVAILABLE TO ALL

If there is any fundamental proposition of government on which all would agree, it is that one of the highest goals of society must be to achieve and maintain equality before the law. Yet this ideal remains an empty form of words unless the legal profession is ready to provide adequate representation for those unable to pay the usual fees.

At present this representation is being supplied in some measure through the spontaneous generosity of individual lawyers, through legal aid societies, and—increasingly—through the organized efforts of the Bar. If those who stand in need of this service know of its availability, and their need is in fact adequately met, the precise mechanism by which this service is provided becomes of secondary importance. It is of great importance, however, that both the impulse to render this service, and the plan for making that impulse effective, should arise within the legal profession itself.

The moral position of the advocate is here at stake. Partisan advocacy finds its justification in the contribution it makes to a sound and informed disposition of controversies. Where this contribution is lacking, the partisan position permitted to the advocate loses its reason for being. The legal profession has, therefore, a clear moral obligation to see to it that those already handicapped do not suffer the cumulative disadvantage of being without proper legal representation, for it is obvious that adjudication can neither be effective nor fair where only one side is represented by counsel. * * *

The Representation of Unpopular Causes

One of the highest services the lawyer can render to society is to appear in court on behalf of clients whose causes are in disfavor with the general public.

Under our system of government the process of adjudication is surrounded by safeguards evolved from centuries of experience. These safeguards are not designed merely to lend formality and decorum to the trial of causes. They are predicated on the assumption that to secure for any controversy a truly informed and dispassionate decision is a difficult thing, requiring for its achievement a special summoning and organization of human effort and the adoption of measures to exclude the biases and prejudgments that have free play outside the courtroom. All of this goes for naught if the man with an unpopular cause is unable to find a competent lawyer courageous enough to represent him. His chance to have his day in court loses much of its meaning if his case is handicapped from the outset by the very kind of prejudgment our rules of evidence and procedure are intended to prevent.

Where a cause is in disfavor because of a misunderstanding by the public, the service of the lawyer representing it is obvious, since he helps to remove an obloquy unjustly attaching to his client's position. But the lawyer renders an equally important, though less readily understood, service where the unfavorable public opinion of the client's cause is in fact justified. It is essential for a sound and wholesome development of public opinion that the disfavored cause have its full day in court, which includes, of necessity, representation by competent counsel. Where this does not occur, a fear arises that perhaps more might have been said for the losing side and suspicion is cast on the decision reached. Thus, confidence in the fundamental processes of government is diminished.

The extent to which the individual lawyer should feel himself bound to undertake the representation of unpopular causes must remain a matter for individual conscience. The legal profession as a whole, however, has a clear moral obligation with respect to this problem. By appointing one of its members to represent the client whose cause is in popular disfavor, the organized Bar can not only discharge an obligation incumbent on it, but at the same time relieve the individual lawyer of the stigma that might otherwise unjustly attach to his appearance on behalf of such a cause. If the courage and the initiative of the individual lawyer make this step unnecessary, the legal profession should in any event strive to promote and maintain a moral atmosphere in which he may render this service without ruinous cost to himself. No member of the Bar should indulge in public criticism of another lawyer because he has undertaken the representation of causes in general disfavor. Every member of the profession should, on the contrary, do what he can to promote a public understanding of the service rendered by the advocate in such situations.

Questions

1. Why does the Joint Conference think that zealous advocacy is essential to an adversarial system of justice? Are they right?

2. Where must the advocate draw the line between zeal on a client's behalf and the public interest? For the Joint Conference that zeal is good which "promotes a wise and informed decision" and that zeal is bad which "mudd[ies] the headwaters of decision." How is the attorney to know the difference? Is there any cognizable standard here?

3. Can a lawyer effectively be both an advocate and a counselor?

4. What duty do lawyers owe to the unrepresented? How should this duty be discharged?

5. What duty do lawyers owe to the unpopular? Will lawyers actually risk their careers to represent social pariahs? What role might the organized bar play in this situation? See Kutler, *The American Inquisition: Justice and Injustice in the Cold War* 152–182 (1982) (detailing harassment faced by lawyers who represented Communists during the 1950s and salutory effect of efforts by organized bar in Cleveland, Ohio, and elsewhere to provide counsel to those being prosecuted.)

MONROE FREEDMAN—LAWYERS' ETHICS IN AN ADVERSARY SYSTEM

1–4 (1975).
Reprinted with permission of the author, copyright © (1975).
Monroe Freedman.

[Professor Monroe Freedman is one of the most outspoken supporters of the adversary system. His 1975 book, *Lawyers' Ethics in an Adversary System,*[a] has been viewed by both opponents and adherents as a seminal statement of the role of the adversarial lawyer. His work has fixed the terms of much of the modern debate about the attorney's proper function and behavior. Here he explores some of the fundamental values that undergird the adversarial approach to lawyering.]

In a recent case in Lake Pleasant, New York, a defendant in a murder case told his lawyers about two other people he had killed and where their bodies had been hidden. The lawyers went there, observed the bodies, and took photographs of them. They did not, however, inform the authorities about the bodies until several months later, when their client had confessed to those crimes. In addition to withholding the information from police and prosecutors, one of the attorneys denied information to one of the victims' parents, who came to him in the course of seeking his missing daughter.

There were interesting reactions to that dramatic event. Members of the public were generally shocked at the apparent callousness on the

a. Professor Freedman has elaborated his views in a number of articles, including "*Personal Responsibility in a Professional System,*" 27 Cath.U.L.Rev. 191 (1978) (Pope John XXIII Lecture), and in "*Legal Ethics and the Suffering Client,*" 36 Cath.U.L. Rev. 331 (1987).

part of the lawyers, whose conduct was considered typical of an un-
healthy lack of concern by lawyers with the public interest and with
simple decency. That attitude was encouraged by public statements by
the local prosecutor, who sought to indict the lawyers for failing to
reveal knowledge of a crime and for failing to see that dead bodies were
properly buried. In addition, the reactions of lawyers and law professors who were questioned by the press were ambivalent and confused,
indicating that few members of the legal profession had given serious
thought to the fundamental questions of administration of justice and
of professional responsibility that were raised by the case.

One can certainly understand the sense of moral compulsion to
assist the parents and to give the dignity of proper burial to the victims.
What seems to be less readily understood—but which, to my mind,
throws the moral balance in the other direction—is the obligation of
the lawyers to their client and, in a larger sense, to a system of
administering justice which is itself essential to maintaining human
dignity. In short, not only did the two lawyers behave properly, but
they would have committed a serious breach of professional responsibility if they had divulged the information contrary to their client's
interest. The explanation to that answer takes us to the very nature of
our system of criminal justice and, indeed, to the fundamentals of our
system of government.

Let us begin, by way of contrast, with an understanding of the role
of a criminal defense attorney in a totalitarian state. As expressed by
law professors at the University of Havana, "the first job of a revolu-
tionary lawyer is not to argue that his client is innocent, but rather to
determine if his client is guilty and, if so, to seek the sanction which
will best rehabilitate him".

Similarly, a Bulgarian attorney began his defense in a treason trial
by noting that: "In a Socialist state there is no division of duty between
the judge, prosecutor, and defense counsel. . . . The defense must
assist the prosecution to find the objective truth in a case." In that
case, the defense attorney ridiculed his client's defense, and the client
was convicted and executed. Sometime later the verdict was found to
have been erroneous, and the defendant was "rehabilitated".

The emphasis in a free society is, of course, sharply different.
Under our adversary system, the interests of the state are not absolute,
or even paramount. The dignity of the individual is respected to the
point that even when the citizen is known by the state to have
committed a heinous offense, the individual is nevertheless accorded
such rights as counsel, trial by jury, due process, and the privilege
against self-incrimination.

A trial is, in part, a search for truth. Accordingly, those basic
rights are most often characterized as procedural safeguards against
error in the search for truth. Actually, however, a trial is far more
than a search for truth, and the constitutional rights that are provided
by our system of justice may well outweigh the truth-seeking value—a

fact which is manifest when we consider that those rights and others guaranteed by the Constitution may well impede the search for truth rather than further it. What more effective way is there, for example, to expose a defendant's guilt than to require self-incrimination, at least to the extent of compelling the defendant to take the stand and respond to interrogation before the jury? The defendant, however, is presumed innocent; the burden is on the prosecution to prove guilt beyond a reasonable doubt, and even the guilty accused has an "absolute constitutional right" to remain silent and to put the government to its proof.

* * *

By emphasizing that the adversary process has its foundations in respect for human dignity, even at the expense of the search for truth, I do not mean to deprecate the search for truth or to suggest that the adversary system is not concerned with it. On the contrary, truth is a basic value, and the adversary system is one of the most efficient and fair methods designed for determining it. That system proceeds on the assumption that the best way to ascertain the truth is to present to an impartial judge or jury a confrontation between the proponents of conflicting views, assigning to each the task of marshalling and presenting the evidence in as thorough and persuasive a way as possible. The truth-seeking techniques used by the advocates on each side include investigation, pretrial discovery, cross-examination of opposing witnesses, and a marshalling of the evidence in summation. Thus, the judge or jury is given the strongest possible view of each side, and is put in the best possible position to make an accurate and fair judgment. Nevertheless, the point that I now emphasize is that in a society that honors the dignity of the individual, the high value that we assign to truth-seeking is not an absolute, but may on occasion be subordinated to even higher values.

The concept of a right to counsel is one of the most significant manifestations of our regard for the dignity of the individual. No person is required to stand alone against the awesome power of the People of New York or the Government of the United States of America. Rather, every criminal defendant is guaranteed an advocate—a "champion" against a "hostile world", the "single voice on which he must rely with confidence that his interests will be protected to the fullest extent consistent with the rules of procedure and the standards of professional conduct". In addition, the attorney serves in significant part to assure equality before the law. Thus, the lawyer has been referred to as "the equalizer", who "places each litigant as nearly as possible on an equal footing under the substantive and procedural law under which he is tried". * * *

Questions

1. How should a lawyer go about vindicating his or her client's dignitary interests? Where ought the line be drawn between these interests and the public interest?

2. Professor Freedman emphasizes the role of the attorney in *criminal* cases. Should the rules governing a lawyer's conduct be different in civil matters?

3. Isn't Professor Freedman's reference to Cuba and Bulgaria rhetorical overkill?

4. What should a lawyer do about the bodies hidden by his client? Is it clear that silence is the proper response in all circumstances?

2. THE PRINCIPLES CHALLENGED

DEBORAH RHODE—ETHICAL PERSPECTIVES ON LEGAL PRACTICE

37 Stan.L.Rev. 589, 589–591, 594–601, 617 (1985).
Reprinted with permission of the publisher, copyright © 1985.
The Board of Trustees of the Leland Stanford Junior University.

[Professor Deborah Rhode is one of a group of present-day critics who have sharply challenged the adversarial concept of lawyering. Here she focuses particular attention on the "formalist" argument that undivided partisanship is likely to lead to the production of all the evidence needed for a fair decision and the "individualist" argument that partisanship is essential to the protection of human dignity.]

The moral content of legal practice has never lacked for critics. Plato's condemnation of the lawyer's "small and unrighteous" soul has echoed for millenia across a wide variety of cultures. The invectives are familiar—attorneys are parasites on public disputes; their professional interest lies in amplifying rather than allaying controversy and in doing "for a guinea" what they would perceive "infamous to do for an empire." Throughout this century, innumerable variations have issued on the theme of Louis Brandeis' 1905 Harvard address: The bar has allied itself with business in opposition to the public interest.

From this historical perspective, the recent surge of animus towards lawyers seems unexceptional; the public assaults draw from a well-worn genre. What is unusual, however, is the extent of professional response. In the last decade, courts, commentators, and the organized bar have given unprecedented attention to legal ethics and etiquette.

Equally striking is the insular quality of that response. For the most part, the recent discourse on professional responsibility has evolved in a vacuum, inadequately illumined by moral theory and sociological research. Too often, the fundamental precepts of professionalism remain unexamined; arguments over candor, confidentiality, and client loyalty proceed without rigorous empirical or philosophical foundation. Most of the seminal work in legal ethics has focused on individual lawyer-client relationships that presuppose a considerable measure of personal autonomy, determinate objectives, and direct communication. That paradigm bears little resemblance to the daily practice of a growing percentage of the profession. Approximately two-thirds of the bar, including 95% of recent entrants, now work within organizations of some sort, and perform the bulk of their services for entities rather than individuals. In a substantial amount of legal practice, "the client" is not the "person with a problem" traditionally depicted in legal literature, but an organization with indeterminate or potentially conflicting interests. So too, the attorney often is not an independent moral agent but an employee with circumscribed responsibility, organizational loyalty, and attenuated client contact.

Under such circumstances, professional ideals that presuppose personal autonomy and public responsibilities may prove difficult to reconcile with the internal dynamics of employing institutions. Moreover, much of the bar's partisan ideology derives its primary force from individualist values. It is by no means self-evident, as the profession's codes and commentary generally assume, that concerns of individual dignity and trust are equally implicated in all legal practice, irrespective of the client's size, structure, and objectives * * *. For most attorneys, advancing client interests remains the primary means of securing financial success and professional status. A critical function of professional ideology is to make a virtue out of that necessity.

The following analysis explores the conventional justifications for lawyers' undivided partisanship—justifications that echo dominant communitarian and individualist strains in liberal political thought. The communitarian approach builds on societal interests in informed dispute resolution. It posits adversarial processes as the best available means to secure results in accordance with applicable law. From this formalist perspective, zealous client representation appears essential to a well-ordered legal system. An alternative approach justifies such advocacy by reference to individualist values. In this framework, lawyers' unqualified partisanship serves to safeguard private spheres of dignity and autonomy. These adversarial ideologies work both to legitimate professionally expedient choices and to deny moral responsibility for their consequences. Yet each form of argument, and the ethical norms it has spawned, rests on premises requiring closer scrutiny.

FORMALISM: THE ADVERSARY SYSTEM'S INVISIBLE HAND

Although most legal practice occurs outside any formal adversarial framework, justifications of partisanship often lean heavily on that paradigm. Underlying those justifications is a mixed formalist and free market conception of adjudicative processes. The bar seeks to resolve the contradiction between fidelity to a particular client and to the legal system as a whole by reference to a combative scheme of social ordering. The premise is that "truth" or the "right" result is attainable through competitive presentations of relevant factual and legal considerations. * * *

One of the strongest articulations of this claim appears in a report on professional responsibility by the Joint Conference of the American Bar Association and the Association of American Law Schools. The report's premise is that "[o]nly when [the trier of fact] has had the benefit of intelligent and vigorous advocacy on both sides can he feel fully confident of his decision." Moreover, only when each side undertakes full responsibility for preparing its case can the tribunal retain the neutrality essential for informed adjudication.

> Viewed in this light, the role of the lawyer as a partisan advocate appears not as a regrettable necessity, but as an indispensable part of a larger ordering of affairs. The institution of advocacy is not a concession to the frailties of human nature, but an expression of human insight in the design of a social framework within which man's capacity for impartial judgment can attain its fullest realization.

A substantial part of the profession doubtless shares a more modest vision. An institutional framework that tolerates competing perspectives may simply appear as the logical means of coping with ambiguity and regularizing disputes in a pluralist social order. Nonetheless, even these more pragmatic constituencies often retain the conviction, articulated by the ABA's General Practice Section, that the "adversary system provides the best method we have been able to devise to determine truth" or its reasonable approximation.

The most obvious difficulty with this premise is that it is neither self-evident nor supported by any empirical evidence. As Geoffrey Hazard, Reporter for the Model Rules Commission, candidly acknowledges, we have "no proof that the adversary system of trial yields truth more often than other systems of trial." Neither is it intuitively obvious that truth is more often revealed by self-interested, rather than disinterested, exploration. The virtues of private initiative and judicial passivity come at a cost. Lawyers are concerned with the production of belief, not of knowledge. Why assume, to paraphrase Macaulay, that the fairest results will emerge from two advocates arguing as unfairly as possible on opposite sides? That is not the way most countries adjudicate controversies, nor the way other professions conduct factual inquiry. Nor is it how the bar itself seeks truth in any setting outside the courtroom. In preparing for trial, for example, lawyers do not typically hire competitive investigators.

To retain plausibility, this defense of adversarial processes must proceed in a social and economic vacuum. The conventional paradigm presupposes combatants with roughly equal incentives, resources, and capabilities. How frequently those suppositions hold is open to question in a social order that tolerates vast disparities in wealth, renders most litigation enormously expensive, and allocates civil legal assistance almost entirely through market mechanisms. Under these circumstances, one would expect that the "haves" generally come out ahead. Commonplace as this point must be to any practicing attorney, it is conspicuous only by absence in most official explications of adversarial premises * * *.

The disparities in representation ignored by conventional paradigms are readily amplified under current practices. The adversary system's extensive procedural protections generate frequent opportunities for evasion, harassment, and delay. In large-scale litigation, principal pathologies include endless wrangling over peripheral issues, as well as over- and under-production of discoverable material. Pretrial proceedings too often give rise to casuistic constructions of discovery requests, disingenuous assertions of the attorney-client privilege, or "Hiroshima" responses to document demands (with any damaging items buried in a mass of trivia). Although the bar's conventional response to such problems has been that they "should be left to the procedural rules and sanctions of the court involved," these correctives have repeatedly proven inadequate. Sanctions are expensive to seek and administer, and judicial responses to adversarial imbalance or pretrial pugnacity are constrained by time, information, and perception of role. Although recent amendments to the Federal Rules encourage greater use of discovery sanctions, such formal mandates are likely to have limited effect on the incentive and information structures that impede judicial oversight.

These constraints on judicial governance are readily exploited by resourceful counsel. Many of the nation's most eminent law firms are noted for their skill in genteel procrastination. Among the most celebrated examples are Covington & Burling's 12–year delay of regulations governing peanut butter content, and Cravath, Swaine & Moore's 14–year defense of an antitrust case that, according to its chief litigator, involved thousands of exhibits, a 50,000–page record, and no real dispute about the facts. Nor is delay the only pretrial pathology. The adversarial framework has often generated an ethos in which truth becomes more an obstacle than an objective. In a national survey of 1500 large-firm litigators, half of those responding believed that unfair and inadequate disclosure of material information prior to trial was a "regular or frequent" problem. Similarly, 69% of surveyed antitrust attorneys had encountered unethical practices in complex cases; the most frequently cited abuses were tampering with witnesses' responses and destroying evidence.

As in Norman trial by combat, the prime objective in much contemporary litigation is to force the adversary to "cry craven" well before discovery of critical facts or adjudication by a neutral decisionmaker. The objective is frequently achieved. According to a survey of Chicago litigators, one in three cases was concluded without at least one party having discovered potentially significant information. Since close to 90% of all civil cases are settled prior to trial, and relatively little of lawyers' advocacy occurs in the presence of impartial adjudicators, the adversary paradigm offers an inadequate foundation for the partisanship role.

Even in full-dress hearings, it is questionable how often the invisible hand asserts itself. Bar ideology assumes that responsibility for ferreting out false testimony or for insuring "fair treatment" of unrepresented and inadequately represented opponents rests elsewhere. If an unmeritorious claim prevails, the fault lies with the judge, the jury, or the litigant who failed to secure adequate counsel. Yet such deflections of blame elide the inherent inadequacies of adversarial frameworks. Not all individuals have the information or resources to ensure an even contest, and neither the judge nor the jury may be well-situated to make appropriate adjustments. Carefully scripted court performances often bear limited resemblance to the actual facts triggering dispute. And conventional techniques of witness selection and preparation can easily yield guided tours down memory lane with predetermined destinations clearly in view.

Despite a long succession of scholarship identifying such difficulties, the organized bar remains firmly wedded to the adversary ethos. With rare exceptions, commentators * * * found no evidence "that the champion system has ill served us," and resisted all proposed rules that might "undermine," "abrogate," or "fundamentally change" adversarial norms * * *.

Fundamental difficulties remain in adversarial premises as well as practices. Under conventional formalist accounts, just results emerge through the rational application of law to fact in the course of competitive presentations * * * In effect, this perspective conflates substantive and procedural justice. Thus conceived, the perspective is vulnerable to all the critiques of formalism that have become standard fare in modern jurisprudential analysis.

Bar ideology makes no adjustment for the possibility that formalist application of legal rules may work injustice that other branches of government fail to redress. A recurring theme in bar rhetoric is that problems such as corporate immorality or adversarial imbalances are the responsibility of legislators, not lawyers. Ad hoc attorney paternalism is considered an inappropriate response to systemic failures. Publicly accountable officials, not privately appointed Platonic guardians, should determine the appropriate corrective. If counsel's zealous representation impedes the control of hazardous products or toxic substances, the fault rests not with the attorney but with those who failed to pass the requisite standards or to appropriate sufficient funds for enforcement.

Such genuflections to legislative process, however rhetorically reassuring, remain morally unpersuasive. Presumably, few lawyers are unaware of the inherent limitations in democratic procedures and regulatory solutions. Time lags in acquiring information and designing appropriate correctives are inevitable, and attorneys with access to confidential studies may often be more knowledgeable about injurious conduct far sooner than politicians or administrative officials. Even where problems are apparent, the costs of regulation may seem excessive, or interest group pressures and inadequate enforcement resources may prevent socially optimal resolutions. As long as disparities of wealth, knowledge, and power affect both the agenda and outcome of political debate, statutory solutions will imperfectly reflect societal values. Any legislative or administrative body may, as Duncan Kennedy notes, prove too "anaesthetized or simply overworked" to remedy obvious deficiencies in legal standards. Nonetheless, the bar's adversarial premise equates justice with the mechanical application of these standards.

This constricted view of legal processes yields a correspondingly myopic perception of professional responsibilities. Within this framework, counsel need not contemplate any broader notion of justice than that defined by existing legal norms * * *.

What is disquieting about this formalist approach is not simply its implicit hierarchy of values, but also the absence of any significant controversy over its terms. That of itself suggests the extent to which professional ideology has become detached from society's more general ethical norms. Relieved of any responsibility for substantive justice, lawyers can come to view it as peripheral to their own sense of achievement. Litigation becomes a game or ritual, and as William Simon notes, such perspectives relieve the process of any necessity to generate fair or rational results. Such a normative climate easily gives rise to the attitude expressed by one British barrister: "[I]t is sometimes more fun to have a bad case than a good one for it tests your powers of persuasion more severely. Certainly I have seldom felt better pleased than when I persuaded [the court] to come to a decision which I was convinced was wrong . . .."

This sporting theory of justice, however compatible with the profession's institutional incentives, fits poorly with its traditional ideals. Not only is such a perspective conducive to the procedural abuses described earlier, it seems fundamentally at odds with lawyers' aspirations to a public calling. To cope with that apparent contradiction, as well as with the vast range of representation in which adversarial safeguards are absent, bar ideology requires recourse to a second line of argument. This alternative approach legitimates partisanship norms not as instruments for achieving justice in particular cases, but as safeguards for values that are central to a just society.

INDIVIDUALISM: PRIVATE ENDS AS A PUBLIC CALLING

The second premise of adversarial ideology is that lawyers' undivided client allegiance serves fundamental interests of individual dignity, privacy, and autonomy. From this * * * perspective, justice depends not on the realization of substantively correct outcomes, but on the preservation of private rights. In Lord Brougham's classic formulation, the advocate "knows in the discharge of that office but one person in the world—[the] client and no other." From this premise follow two corollaries. First, lawyers should remain neutral partisans who defend, not judge, their clients. In addition, norms that assist that partisanship function, such as those governing confidentiality, should assume precedence over other societal concerns * * *.

The force of the bar's * * * claims derives in large measure from the criminal defense paradigm, where the case for undiluted partisanship is most compelling. When individuals' lives, liberties, or reputations are so immediately at risk, our constitutional tradition has sought to guarantee that they have advocates without competing loyalties to the state. The justifications for that guarantee have generated an extensive scholarly discourse that need not be rehearsed here. Given the small number of attorneys actively engaged in criminal defense work, the critical question is whether professional norms appropriate in that context should serve as the paradigm for all legal practice. Yet the bar's exaltation of individualism remains heavily parasitic on the criminal defense role. * * *

Such rhetoric is not smoothly transposed to the social and economic landscape of most legal practice. To be sure, in some civil matters, the disparity of power between the parties, the potential for abusive state or private action, or the possible constraints on fundamental rights may raise concerns analogous to those at issue in criminal proceedings. While the bar's contribution in those circumstances has been of enormous societal importance, such cases do not constitute the mainstay of legal work. Only a few lawyers are actively engaged in poverty, civil rights, civil liberties, or analogous litigation; a high percentage focus on problems of corporations and wealthy individuals. In those more typical cases, even if the state is involved, the balance of power is often rather different than the ABA's self-portrait assumes. When a Wall Street firm representing a Fortune 500 corporation squares off against a woefully understaffed state regulatory agency, it strains credulity to paint the corporate defender as a champion against official tyranny.

Moreover, as an explanation of the lawyer's role in private ordering, the appeal to tyranny seems rather forced. According to many commentators, any effort to place the "interests of society over the interests of the individual . . . [represents] a very significant move toward totalitarianism. It makes the lawyer an agent of the state." Not only does this logic confuse social responsibility with social control, it condemns one form of domination only to license another. The specter of the "collectivist" state serves to justify undivided partisanship in pursuit of private power, no matter how abusive. To assume that clients are entitled to assistance in any action not plainly prohibited collapses moral and legal rights. Only the most uninformed faith in legislative processes and unrefined concept of moral responsibility could sustain such a vision.

The individualist rationale retains force through a rarified conception of legal practice and a reified view of professional role. By assimilating all forms of legal assistance to a David and Goliath paradigm, the argument avoids testing its value assumptions against more realistic social and economic backdrops. From a rhetorical perspective, that assimilation makes eminent sense. It is far easier to defend a highly privatistic vision of the social good and the profession's responsibilities when the lawyer appears as protector of the persecuted rather than friend of the finance company. Yet highly abstracted encomiums to individualism fail to explain the wholesale appropriation of adversarial norms in the defense of organizational interests.

Among private practitioners, the traditional consensus has been that lawyers' societal responsibilities should be identical whether they represent institutions or individuals. Yet no serious efforts have been made to justify that position or to confront its discontinuity with values underpinning the partisanship role. In much contemporary legal practice, it is by no means clear who constitutes the corporate "client." Nor is it self-evident that concerns of human dignity and autonomy are best served by lawyers' undivided commitment to organizational objectives, whatever the consequences to individual third parties, such as consumers, employees, or victims of environmental violations. The less adequately those individual interests are represented, the less convincing becomes the defense of undiluted client allegiance.

In any event, however persuasive one finds the abstract appeal to dignitary values, its status as justification for particular professional standards is far more questionable. When rules governing access to the legal system and fidelity to client interests are examined in social context, it is difficult to defend their formulation by reference to individualist concerns.

An obvious threshold difficulty with that defense involves the financial underpinnings of advocacy, a point on which most proponents of the adversary ethos are diplomatically silent. Almost without exception * * * commentators who invoked fundamental values simply ignored the vast array of civil matters in which the stakes do not justify or the claimant cannot secure a "champion against a hostile world."
* * *

In fact, numerous, frequently bar-sponsored, empirical studies reflect a vast universe of unrepresented individual and public interests and woefully inadequate pro bono contributions by the private bar. One ABA study estimated that individuals consulted lawyers on far less than one-third of "all the problems encountered that reasonably [could be] called legal problems." Even before the Reagan administration cutbacks substantially reduced the Legal Services operating budget, its lawyers were handling at most 2 million of the 6 to 132 million legal problems annually encountered by persons below the poverty line. According to the most comprehensive survey available, some three-fifths of sampled attorneys devoted less than five percent of their billable hours to pro bono pursuits, and almost one-third made no contribution at all. The average investment of the bar as a whole was about six percent of billable hours, and much of that assistance was designed to accommodate existing or potential clients. The vast majority of nonbillable services were rendered not to indigent individuals or public interest causes, but to friends, relatives, and organizations such as hospitals, Jaycees, and garden clubs. * * *

Like its formalist counterpart, the individualist premise of partisanship enshrines an impoverished view of professional obligations. The premium placed on client loyalty and confidentiality affords maximum insulation from third-party claims or oversight. Yet the parochialism of these concerns is easily masked with an appealing individualist rhetoric. By invoking deeply rooted liberal values, the adversarial ethos retains force as the dominant vision of professional responsibility. But that vision, in conflating clients' legal and moral rights, sanctifies a form of private partisanship not readily reconciled with societal concerns or professional aspirations. * * *

Questions

1. Why does Professor Rhode choose to address what she calls the "more modest" vision that the adversary system "determine[s] truth" rather than the proposition put forward by the Joint Conference that adversarial advocacy helps realize the goal of "impartial judgment?" Isn't this the setting up of a straw man to facilitate her arguments? Isn't the Joint Conference's proposal the more modest and important?

2. Is it fair for Professor Rhode to cite Professor Hazard as if he were a spokesman on behalf of the adversary method when he has been one of its most outspoken critics? See generally Hazard and Rhode, *The Legal Profession: Responsibility and Regulation* (1985).

3. Is it true that adversarial argumentation is used only in the courtroom? Aren't disputatious techniques used in many scholarly and scientific disciplines?

4. Compare Professor Rhode's view of the distinctness of the criminal process with that of Professor Stephen Saltzburg in *Lawyers, Clients, and the Adversary System*, 37 Mercer Law Review 647, 659–60 (1986):

> Any assertion that the goal of the adversary process in a criminal case is different from its goal in civil litigation must be rejected. The goal of criminal trials is to impose liability on those whom the substantive law indicates have committed crimes. The goal of civil cases is to permit liability to be imposed according to substantive principles. To say that the criminal case is unique is to confuse the goals of the process with some of its elements.
>
> It is true that the burden of persuasion is the highest in criminal cases, that prison and sometimes even the death penalty may be used as penalties only in criminal cases, and that certain constitutional provisions have unique applicability in criminal cases. It is also true that some aspects of civil and criminal cases are very similar. The role of counsel * * * is little different in civil and criminal cases. The role of juries is virtually the same in all cases.
>
> That incidents of trial may differ somewhat in civil and criminal cases does not mean that the goals of the process also differ. Because of concern for the individual and realization of the power of the state to stigmatize and punish criminal offenders in special ways, the American legal system gives the benefit of uncertainty to the criminal defendant. This means that the government bears the risk of an

erroneous decision in a very special way, but it does not mean that the goal of the criminal trial is different from the goal of a civil trial. The difference is nothing more than an expression of an understanding that courts may assign the risks of error unequally when there is good reason to do so.

Who has the better of the argument?

5. Should organizations and corporations get a different sort of legal representation than individuals? Should corporate conduct be scrutinized more carefully by the lawyers working for them? What standards should the lawyers apply? How should each lawyer's judgments be communicated to the corporation and society at large?

SECTION C. THE PROPER SCOPE OF ZEAL

IN RE McCONNELL

370 U.S. 230, 230–36, 82 S.Ct. 1288, 1289–92, 8 L.Ed.2d 434, 435–39 (1962).

[The more zealous a lawyer is on behalf of a client the more likely he or she is to come into conflict with the trial judge. In *McConnell* the United States Supreme Court addressed such a clash and the consequent use of the contempt power by the trial judge.]

Mr. Justice Black delivered the opinion of the Court.

The petitioner Thomas C. McConnell, a lawyer, was summarily found guilty of contempt of court for statements made while representing the Parmelee Transportation Company in an antitrust suit for treble damages and an injunction. The complaint charged that a number of defendants had unlawfully conspired to destroy Parmelee's business by restraining and monopolizing trade in violation of the Sherman Act. Petitioner and his co-counsel, Lee A. Freeman, had done extensive pretrial preparation on the issue of conspiracy which was the heart of their case. At the very outset of the trial, however, the district judge on his own motion refused to permit counsel to try to prove their conspiracy charge, holding that they must first prove in a wholly separate trial that defendants' actions had resulted in an economic injury to the public—an erroneous holding since we have held that the right of recovery of a plaintiff in a treble damage antitrust case does not depend at all on proving an economic injury to the public.

Cut off by the judge's erroneous ruling from trial of the basic issue of conspiracy and wishing to provide a record which would allow this ruling to be reviewed by the Court of Appeals, counsel for Parmelee asked counsel for defendants to stipulate that plaintiff would have introduced certain evidence of conspiracy had it been allowed to do so. Defense counsel refused to stipulate, however, insisting that Parmelee's counsel prepare their record by following the procedure set out in Rule 43(c) of the Federal Rules of Civil Procedure, which requires that before an offer of proof is made questions upon which the offer is based must first be asked in the presence of the jury. Unwilling to risk dismissal of their appeal for failure to follow Rule 43(c), Parmelee's counsel proceeded to produce and question witnesses in the presence of the jury in order to lay the proper foundation for their offers of proof of conspiracy. But during the process of this questioning the judge ordered it stopped and directed that any further offers of proof be made without first having asked questions of witnesses in the presence of the jury. This ruling placed Parmelee's counsel in quite a dilemma because defense counsel was still insisting that all offers of proof be made in strict compliance with Rule 43(c) and there was no way of knowing with certainty whether the Court of Appeals would treat the trial court's order to dispense with questions before the jury as an excuse for failure to comply with the Rule. Petitioner therefore not only sought to make clear to the court that he thought defense counsel's objection was "right" but also repeatedly insisted that he be allowed to make his offers of proof in compliance with the Rule. Following the trial the judge charged petitioner and his co-counsel Freeman in a number of specifications with being guilty of contemptuous conduct during the course of the trial. * * *

[In the court of appeals five of the six findings of contempt made by the district court were reversed. One specification against petitioner McConnell was, however, sustained.]

That specification reads:

"On April 27, 1960, in the presence and hearing of the jury, after the Court had instructed the attorneys for plaintiff to refrain from repeatedly asking questions on subjects which the Court had ruled [were] not admissible, in the presence of the jury as distinguished from an offer of proof outside the presence of the jury, the following occurred:

" 'By Mr. McConnell: Now you are trying to tell us we can't ask these questions. We have a right to ask these questions, and until we are stopped from asking these questions we are going to ask them, because it is in our prerogative in doing it.

" 'By the Court: I am now stopping you from asking the questions about conversations with Mr. Cross, because I have ruled specifically, definitely and completely that it is not an issue in this case.

" 'By Mr. McConnell: We have a right to ask them.

" 'By the Court: You can offer proof on it.

" 'By Mr. McConnell: We have a right to ask questions which we offer on this issue, and Your Honor can sustain their objection to them. *We don't have a right to read the answers, but we have a right to ask the questions, and we propose to do so unless some bailiff stops us.'* " (Emphasis added.)

The record shows that after this colloquy petitioner's co-counsel asked for a short recess, that following this recess petitioner did not continue to ask questions which the judge had forbidden and that in fact he did not ask any more such questions again throughout the remainder of the trial. We agree with Judge Duffy who dissented below that there was nothing in petitioner's conduct sufficiently disruptive of the trial court's business to be an obstruction of justice. It is true that petitioner stated that counsel had a right to ask questions that the judge did not want asked and that "we propose to do so unless some bailiff stops us." The fact remains, however, that the bailiff never had to interrupt the trial by arresting petitioner, for the simple reason that after this statement petitioner never did ask any more questions along the line which the judge had forbidden. And we cannot agree that a mere statement by a lawyer of his intention to press his legal contention until the court has a bailiff stop him can amount to an obstruction of justice that can be punished under the limited powers of summary contempt which Congress has granted to the federal courts. The arguments of a lawyer in presenting his client's case strenuously and persistently cannot amount to a contempt of court so long as the lawyer does not in some way create an obstruction which blocks the judge in the performance of his judicial duty. The petitioner created no such obstacle here.

While we appreciate the necessity for a judge to have the power to protect himself from actual obstruction in the courtroom, or even from conduct so near to the court as actually to obstruct justice, it is also essential to a fair administration of justice that lawyers be able to make honest good-faith efforts to present their clients' cases. An independent judiciary and a vigorous, independent bar are both indispensable parts of our system of justice. To preserve the kind of trials that our system envisages, Congress has limited the summary contempt power vested in courts to the least possible power adequate to prevent actual obstruction of justice, and we think that that power did not extend to this case.

Reversed.

Questions

1. How active was the trial judge in this litigation? Was any of the conflict in the case caused by this activism?

2. How should counsel deal with a trial judge who is clearly wrong about the law and insists on procedures that jeopardize a client's rights?

3. Should courts have summary contempt powers? How might they be abused?

4. In *Offutt v. United States,* 348 U.S. 11, 75 S.Ct. 11, 99 L.Ed. 11 (1954) the Supreme Court held that judges must use "self-restraint" when exercising the contempt power. How is this ruling related to the concept of zealous advocacy?

5. Why were the appellate judges who reviewed the *McConnell* case so inclined to overrule findings of contempt?

6. After *McConnell,* how "strenuously and persistently" can a lawyer argue his or her case?

MONROE FREEDMAN—LAWYERS' ETHICS IN AN ADVERSARY SYSTEM

9–16 (1975).
Reprinted with permission of the author, copyright © 1975.
Monroe Freedman.

[Here Professor Freedman considers the nature and scope of zealous advocacy.]

[T]he adversary system assumes that the most efficient and fair way of determining the truth is by presenting the strongest possible case for each side of the controversy before an impartial judge or jury. Each advocate, therefore, must give "entire devotion to the interest of the client, warm zeal in the maintenance and defense of his rights and the exertion of his utmost learning and ability". The classic statement of that ideal is by Lord Brougham, in his representation of the Queen in *Queen Caroline's Case*. Threatening to defend his client on a ground that would, literally, have brought down the kingdom, Brougham stated:

> . . . An advocate, in the discharge of his duty, knows but one person in all the world, and that person is his client. To save that client by all means and expedients, and at all hazards and costs to other persons, and, amongst them, to himself, is his first and only duty; and in performing this duty he must not regard the alarm, the torments, the destruction which he may bring upon others. Separating the duty of a patriot from that of an advocate, he must go on reckless of the consequences, though it should be his unhappy fate to involve his country in confusion.

Let justice be done—that is, for my client let justice be done—though the heavens fall. That is the kind of advocacy that I would want as a client and that I feel bound to provide as an advocate. The rest of the picture, however, should not be ignored. The adversary system ensures an advocate on the other side, and an impartial judge over both. Despite the advocate's argument, therefore, the heavens do not really have to fall—not unless justice requires that they do.

The attorney's obligation of entire devotion to the interests of the client, and warm zeal in the maintenance and defense of the client's rights, would seem to be beyond serious controversy. From time to time, however, a critic with a particular ideological commitment will insist that there are public interest limits on how zealous the advocate should strive to be in a particular case or area of law. For example, Chief Judge George Hart of the United States District Court for the District of Columbia has complained that criminal defense lawyers, in their zealous defense of people accused of crimes, are forgetting the public interest in controlling crime. In a debate before a group of law students, Judge Hart castigated lawyers for filing "frivolous" motions on behalf of their clients—although, when questioned, he was compelled to admit that motions he had denied on the ground that they were frivolous had subsequently been upheld by the Court of Appeals.

Coming from a rather different ideological viewpoint, Ralph Nader some years ago led a group of law students in the picketing of a major Washington, D.C., law firm, Wilmer, Cutler & Pickering. Mr. Nader's complaint was that the law firm, in representing General Motors in a case in which the company had been charged with practices harmful to the environment, had negotiated with the Justice Department to obtain a consent decree on terms favorable to the company, and thereby avoided a lengthy hearing at which evidence damaging to the company might have been adduced by the government. Mr. Nader's view was that it was in the public interest to have the adverse information made public (and thereby available to private parties who might want to sue the company), and that the lawyers had therefore violated their professional responsibilities in negotiating the consent decree. Yet another illustration is provided by the efforts of the State of Virginia to limit the effectiveness of the advocacy of NAACP lawyers in school desegregation cases, by charging that the solicitation of clients for those cases violated public interest restrictions on advertising by lawyers and therefore warranted disciplinary action. * * *

One of the great ironies about the various suggestions that public interest limits should be imposed upon zealous advocacy is that few, if any, of the proponents of such limits in specific areas would agree with those making the same proposal with respect to other areas of the law. For example, I doubt that * * * Mr. Nader would approve of the efforts of the State of Virginia to restrict the effectiveness of the advocacy of the NAACP. Nor, of course, would Judge Hart have much sympathy with Mr. Nader's denunciation of General Motors' attorneys * * *.

Unfortunately, attacks upon lawyers representing disfavored clients and causes have gone beyond verbal abuse. As stated in an article in the *Harvard Civil Rights–Civil Liberties Law Review:* "It has become both professionally and legally dangerous to be a lawyer representing the poor, minorities, and the politically unpopular." The article refers to the increasing tendency during the latter 1960's (continued into the early 1970's) to institute disciplinary proceedings and criminal contempt charges against lawyers representing unpopular clients and causes. That tendency has been encouraged by Chief Justice Burger, who also has been concerned that zealous advocacy has gone beyond the bounds of the public interest as he sees it. Thus, the Chief Justice has charged that "all too often" overzealous advocates commit a variety of improprieties, ranging from disruption of proceedings to seeing "how loud [they] can shout" or how many people, "including the judges", they can insult. According to the Chief Justice: "At the drop of a hat—or less—we find adrenalin-fueled lawyers cry out that theirs is a 'political trial'," with the result that "rules of evidence, canons of ethics and codes of professional conduct—the necessity for civility—all become irrelevant." In response to that alarming circumstance, the Chief Justice has called for severe measures—"strict regulation and public accountability" of lawyers in order to safeguard the public interest.

In the light of the actual facts, however, Chief Justice Burger's repeated attacks on "adrenalin-fueled lawyers", who must be strictly controlled lest the judicial system be overwhelmed by courtroom disruption, have an air of unreality. For example, in 1971, the *New York Times* conducted a survey and independent interviews with legal authorities around the country and reported that courtroom disorder was "not a serious or growing problem". Similarly, in an extensive study conducted by the Association of the Bar of the City of New York, it was found that "there is no serious quantitative problem of disruption in American courts". It is, of course, questionable whether it comports with civility to make sweeping and unsubstantiated charges against lawyers representing unpopular clients and causes. The real threat to the proper administration of justice is in the effort to restrict the advocacy of such lawyers, on whatever ground.

Since the most strident attacks have related to alleged misconduct in the courtroom, particularly with reference to disrespect to the bench, it might be useful to consider some excerpts from actual transcripts. The first comes from a case in which the judge remarked that a particular item of evidence was "extremely vulgar". Counsel retorted that he had no doubt that His Honor was a better judge of vulgarity than was counsel. The second trial incident involved the following exchange between court and counsel:

> **Judge:** . . . You know that is a most improper question to ask.
>
> **Attorney:** I know when a person has his mind made up, it is not easy to change it.
>
> **Judge:** I do not want you to make a speech now.
>
> **Attorney:** I am going to make a speech—that is what I am paid for.

In the third transcript excerpt, the dialogue between attorney and judge went this way:

> **Attorney:** I stand here as an advocate for a brother citizen, and I desire that the [record in this case be complete and accurate].
>
> **Judge:** Sit down, Sir! Remember your duty or I shall be obliged to proceed in another manner [i.e., referring to disciplinary proceedings].
>
> **Attorney:** Your [Honor] may proceed in any manner you think fit. I know my duty as well as Your [Honor] knows yours. I shall not alter my conduct.

Those incidents are of particular interest for two reasons. First, neither involved a modern American lawyer; in each instance the attorney was a highly respected English barrister. Second, far from resulting in disciplinary proceedings against the lawyers, each of those episodes has been cited by eminent authorities in the most favorable terms.

The comment on the judge's expertise in vulgarity was made by Sir Marshall Hall, a noted barrister of the earlier part of this century, and has been quoted by his biographer as illustrative of Sir Marshall's courtroom wit. The second exchange also involved Marshall Hall, and his biographer relates that having insisted upon making a speech, Hall did so and "won the day".

The lawyer in the third instance was no less a figure in English law than Lord Erskine. According to Lord Campbell, Erskine's defiance of the court was "a noble stand for the independence of the bar". Similarly, one of the most highly regarded of American jurists, Judge Roger Traynor of the California Supreme Court, has used Erskine's statement as illustrative of the attorney's duty to assert the client's rights in a forthright manner. And Professors Louisell and Hazard introduce the incident with the following comment: "So much emphasis is currently placed upon avoidance of improper argument that it seems amiss not to remind today's young lawyer of his duty of effective representation of his client in an adversary system."

Questions

1. Does Lord Brougham go too far? Should a lawyer feel free "to involve his country in confusion" in the course of representing a client?

2. Is it fair of Professor Freedman to label critics of "warm zeal" as ideology-mongers of the right or left? Does Professor Rhode appear to fit Professor Freedman's categorization?

3. Is there ever a case in which Professor Freedman would agree that a lawyer should restrict his or her representation?

4. Are the limits of frivolity the only ones that should guide a lawyer's selection of arguments? Why or why not?

5. When is a lawyer's defiance of a judge a "noble stand" and when is it improper? Can a lawyer go too far? What is the appropriate measure of propriety?

GEOFFREY HAZARD—ETHICS IN THE PRACTICE OF LAW

132–35 (1978).
Reprinted with permission of the publisher, copyright © 1978.
Yale University Press.

[Professor Hazard has, for many years, focused his attention on questions of lawyers' ethics in the adversarial framework. He is a leading critic of the adversary system and was Reporter to the American Bar Association Commission (the so-called Kutak Commission) that in 1980 recommended sweeping anti-adversarial amendments to the lawyers' ethical code. The following excerpt is drawn from a book he prepared to summarize the proceedings of a conference held in 1976 to discuss the ethical practice of law.]

* * *

In the American system * * * the advocates' relationship to his client's cause is * * * dependent and intimate. In litigation involving "repeat business" clients, the advocate or his firm usually is also counsel under retainer to the client. In litigation involving "one shot" clients, such as plaintiff's injury claims, the lawyer's fee is usually contingent on the outcome. In any event, the advocate is expected and permitted to investigate the facts and interrogate witnesses before trial, thus becoming a party to the evidence before its presentation in court. A * * * [wide] range of harassing tactics is indulged in American litigation. Hence, the advocate's situation in our version of the adversary system is fairly defined by Shaw's description of marriage: it "combines the maximum of temptation with the maximum of opportunity." It is not difficult to see why the lawyer may be relatively ineffective as a source of restraint on his client.

The advocate who represents large corporations rarely confronts the problems of client perjury or fabrication or destruction of evidence. But he faces problems that are similar if more subtle. What does a lawyer do with the client who wants to fight the case to the bitter end, even though the advocate thinks that the other side's case is substantially just and that the matter should be settled? What does he do in a case where he is convinced that the other side is wrong on the merits but also convinced that the judge or jury or administrative hearing officer will be prejudiced against his corporate client? Does this justify the use of harassing tactics? If the case has a political aspect, may he delay its progress in the hope that there will be a change in administration? If so, within what limits? Legitimate and illegitimate techniques shade into each other—vigorous maneuver into harrassment, careful preparation of witnesses into subornation of perjury, nondisclosure into destruction of evidence. At some point in deterioration of rules of form, an expert in rough and tumble becomes simply a thug.

This brings in view another serious problem of the adversary system. The trial lawyer can become completely immersed in his lawsuits, to the point where they become his identity and their outcome the sole criterion of his professional stature. Indeed, it is often only with difficulty that a modern trial specialist can maintain distance between himself and his craft. The whole tendency of his work leads him to hold, with Vince Lombardi, that winning is not the most important thing but the only thing. And the result can be that he becomes incapacitated to give his client detached advice about the prospects of ultimate victory and the advisability of settling through compromise. The problem can be especially severe in "big" cases for and against big corporations, because one such case can for several years be the vocation of a good part of a firm or agency's litigation staff. But it is inherent in the system. An English barrister is reported to have remonstrated, upon the prospect of compromising a bitter suit between heirs to a large fortune, "What? And allow that magnificent estate to be frittered away among the beneficiaries?"

If it is possible that the adversary system can work satisfactorily, and necessary that it must do so because no other system of adjudication is likely to be any better, it remains true that the system in its present form is pretty sick. The problem can be posed in terms of the attitude with which the advocate should approach a case. One approach, whether in reality or in idealized form we cannot be entirely sure, is that of the English barrister. In this approach, the advocate undertakes a dispassionate analysis of the facts and a magisterial consideration of the law with the aim of establishing common ground with his opposite number and thereupon settling the case on the basis of truth and legal justice, or at worst, isolating for trial the issues of fact or law that prove intractable. A lot of litigation in this country is actually determined this way, when the advocates trust each other's competence, integrity, and judgment. But a lot of litigation is conducted otherwise. In the other approach the advocate is a streetfighter—aggressive, guileful, exploitive. Some clients seem to want it that way, at least until they find out that two can play the game. At any rate many clients suppose that is the way litigation inevitably must be conducted and approach their counsel with a corresponding set of expectations. The advocate in turn can confirm and exploit these expectations, providing fulfillment of the prophecy if he wishes. As the institution of adversary adjudication now stands, the advocate has very strong inducements to oblige.

If the adversary system is to be changed, it will not be a simple undertaking. The system as it exists expresses a number of strongly held beliefs and ideals. One is that justice should be free. It is this proposition that supports the rule that the loser in litigation does not have to pay the winner's expenses. From this in turn follows the contingent fee system and the lack of inhibitions on running up an opposing party's costs, with the corresponding impairment of the advocate's gatekeeper function. Another belief is that entry into the legal profession should be relatively democratic. From this proposition it follows that admission is relatively easy, levels of training uneven, and professional esprit de corps weak. From this it follows that the images of professional lawyers are fuzzy and the potential for self-policing correspondingly low. Another is that litigation should secure not only justice under law but natural and popular justice. From this it follows that litigation often has inherently political, redistributive, and sometimes subversive characteristics, which infuse not only the merits of the controversies but the way they are prosecuted or defended. The "Chicago Seven" trial is an illustration. Still another belief is the notion that militant advocacy is an especially genuine and efficacious expression of social conscience. Exemplars of this style are the relentless prosecutor, the fearless vindicator of the oppressed, the wiley strategist for the establishment. It would be better if there were a larger constituency that understood, with Judge Learned Hand, that being in litigation, whatever its outcome, can justly be compared with sickness and death.

Perhaps the problem is this: We can have a system that does not charge user fees, lets everyone play, seeks both law and common justice, and is subject to few inhibitions in style. We can also have a system in which a trial is a serious search for the truth or at least a ceremony whose essential virtue is solemnity. But we probably cannot have both. So long as the advocate in the American system is supposed to be at once a champion in forensic roughhouse and a guardian of the temple of justice, he can fulfill his responsibilities only if he combines extraordinary technical skill with an unusually disciplined sense of probity. That seems to be asking too much of any profession.

Questions

1. Are American lawyers at risk of becoming thugs?

2. Was Vince Lombardi wrong? If so, why? How might a lawyer with Lombardi's view be a liability to a client? To the legal system?

3. Should costs be shifted to losing litigants? What would be the effect upon those with limited means? On litigation in general? Who would be available to address the concerns of those excluded in this way?

4. Should admission to the bar be made more difficult? Should the bar be more exclusive? What would be the effect of a more exclusive bar on the provision of service to injured parties?

5. Should advocates serve as gatekeepers responsible for discouraging litigation?

6. What empirical proof does Professor Hazard offer that we cannot have a system that effectively balances factfinding and full client representation?

SECTION D. THE LIMITS OF CONFIDENTIALITY

MONROE FREEDMAN—LAWYERS' ETHICS IN AN ADVERSARY SYSTEM

4–8 (1975).
Reprinted with permission of the author, copyright © 1975.
Monroe Freedman.

[Professor Freedman here examines the question of confidentiality from the adversarial lawyer's point of view. He focuses much of his argument on the case of *People v. Belge,* 83 Misc.2d 186, 372 N.Y.S.2d 798 (Onondaga County Court 1975) aff'd 50 A.D.2d 1088, 376 N.Y.S.2d 771 (Appellate Division, Fourth Department 1975). There two lawyers in Lake Pleasant, New York, were informed by their murder-suspect client that he had killed several other people. The client told his lawyers where the bodies were buried and one of the attorneys verified this information by digging up the remains of one of the victims. The attorneys did not inform the authorities of their discovery until it was tactically advantageous in the original murder prosecution. The lawyers were eventually prosecuted on a number of charges and exonerated of any wrongdoing.]

The lawyer can serve effectively as advocate * * * "only if he knows all that his client knows" concerning the facts of the case. Nor is the client ordinarily competent to evaluate the relevance or significance of particular facts. What may seem incriminating to the client, may actually be exculpatory. For example, one client was reluctant to tell her lawyer that her husband had attacked her with a knife, because it tended to confirm that she had in fact shot him (contrary to what she had at first maintained). Having been persuaded by her attorney's insistence upon complete and candid disclosure, she finally "confessed all"—which permitted the lawyer to defend her properly and successfully on grounds of self-defense.

Obviously, however, the client cannot be expected to reveal to the lawyer all information that is potentially relevant, including that which may well be incriminating, unless the client can be assured that the lawyer will maintain all such information in the strictest confidence. "The purposes and necessities of the relation between a client and his attorney" require "the fullest and freest disclosures" of the client's "objects, motives and acts". If the attorney were permitted to reveal such disclosures, it would be "not only a gross violation of a sacred trust upon his part", but it would "utterly destroy and prevent the usefulness and benefits to be derived from professional assistance". That "sacred trust" of confidentiality must "upon all occasions be inviolable", or else the client could not feel free "to repose [confidence] in the attorney to whom he resorts for legal advice and assistance". Destroy that confidence, and "a man would not venture to consult any skillful person, or would only dare to tell his counselor half his case". The result would be impairment of the "perfect freedom of consultation by client with attorney", which is "essential to the administration of justice". Accordingly, the * * * Code of Professional Responsibility provides that a lawyer shall not knowingly reveal a confidence or secret of the client, nor use a confidence or secret to the disadvantage of the client, or to the advantage of a third person, without the client's consent.

It must be obvious at this point that the adversary system within which the lawyer functions, contemplates that the lawyer frequently will learn from the client information that is highly incriminating and may even learn, as in the Lake Pleasant case, that the client has in fact committed serious crimes. In such a case, if the attorney were required to divulge that information, the obligation of confidentiality would be destroyed, and with it, the adversary system itself. Even so, it is occasionally suggested that a lawyer who does not divulge a client's self-incriminatory information would be guilty of such crimes as obstruction of justice, misprision of a felony, or becoming an accomplice after the fact. Such statutes, however, cannot be understood as applying to lawyers who have learned incriminating information after the crime has already been committed. First, criminal statutes should be strictly construed to avoid applying them more broadly than the legislature intended or to those who may not have been adequately on notice that their conduct was unlawful. Second, a statute should be strictly construed to avoid unnecessarily raising constitutional issues, particularly when there is a likelihood that the statute would have to be found constitutionally invalid. Finally, to construe an ordinary obstruction-of-justice statute or other criminal law in a way that would destroy the traditional lawyer-client relationship would violate the constitutional rights to counsel, trial by jury, and due process, and the privilege against self-incrimination.

That is not to say, of course, that the attorney is privileged to go beyond the needs of confidentiality imposed by the adversary system, and actively participate in concealment of evidence or obstruction of justice. For example, in the *Ryder* case, which arose in Virginia several years ago, the attorney removed from his client's safe deposit box a sawed-off shotgun and the money from a bank robbery and put them, for greater safety, into the lawyer's own safe deposit box. The attorney, quite properly, was suspended from practice for 18 months. (The penalty might well have been heavier, except for the fact that Ryder sought advice from senior members of the bench and bar, and apparently acted more in ignorance than in venality.) The important difference between the *Ryder* case and the one in Lake Pleasant lies in the active role played by the attorney in *Ryder* to conceal evidence. There is no indication, for example, that the attorneys in Lake Pleasant attempted to hide the bodies more effectively. If they had done so, they would have gone beyond maintaining confidentiality and into active participation in the concealment of evidence.

The distinction should also be noted between the attorney's knowledge of a past crime (which is what we have been discussing so far) and knowledge of a crime to be committed in the future. Thus, a major exception to the strict rule of confidentiality is the "intention of his client to commit a crime, and information necessary to prevent the crime". Significantly, however, even in that exceptional circumstance, disclosure of the confidence is only permissible, not mandatory. Moreover, a footnote in the Code suggests that the exception is applicable only when the attorney knows "beyond a reasonable doubt" that a crime will be committed. There is little guidance as to how the lawyer is to exercise the discretion to report future crimes. At one extreme, it seems clear that the lawyer should reveal information necessary to save a life. On the other hand, * * * the lawyer should not reveal the intention of a client in a criminal case to commit perjury in his or her own defense.

It has been suggested that the information regarding the two bodies in the Lake Pleasant case was not relevant to the crime for which the defendant was being prosecuted, and that, therefore, that knowledge was outside the scope of confidentiality. That point lacks merit for three reasons. First, an unsophisticated lay person should not be required to anticipate which disclosures might fall outside the scope of confidentiality because of insufficient legal relevance. Second, the information in question might well have been highly relevant to the defense of insanity. Third, a lawyer has an obligation to merge other, unrelated crimes into the bargained plea, if it is possible to do so. Accordingly, the information about the other murders was clearly within the protection of confidentiality.

The suggestion has also been made with respect to the Lake Pleasant case that the obligation of confidentiality was destroyed because the defendant had authorized disclosure to the prosecutor insofar as it might be helpful in plea bargaining. Plea bargaining is, unfortunately, an integral part of the criminal justice system and, as noted above, the lawyers had an obligation to attempt to dispose of the other murder charges in the same plea. Therefore, a defendant would be deprived of important rights if disclosure could not be authorized for the limited but crucial purpose of plea bargaining, without forfeiting confidentiality in general. A significantly different situation was presented in the case of a lawyer representing a figure in the Watergate investigations. There the client had authorized the lawyer to sell the client's story to a newspaper columnist. Since the authorized disclosure in that case went beyond the needs of effective representation in the judicial proceeding, the client forfeited the right to confidentiality, and the attorney was properly directed to testify before a grand jury. Similarly, if the attorney in the Lake Pleasant case had been authorized to inform the victims' parents, confidentiality would have been jeopardized.

It has also been suggested that the attorneys in Lake Pleasant were not bound by confidentiality once they had undertaken to corroborate the client's information through their own investigation. It is the duty of the lawyer, however, to conduct a thorough investigation of all aspects of the case, and that duty "exists regardless of the accused's admissions or statements to the lawyer of facts constituting guilt. . . ." For example, upon investigation, the attorneys in the Lake Pleasant case might have discovered that the client's belief that he had killed other people was false, which would have had important bearing on an insanity defense.*

In summary, the Constitution has committed us to an adversary system for the administration of criminal justice. The essentially humanitarian reason for such a system is that it preserves the dignity of the individual, even though that may occasionally require significant frustration of the search for truth and the will of the state. An essential element of that system is the right to counsel, a right that would be meaningless if the defendant were not able to communicate freely and fully with the attorney.

* The suggestion has also been made that the attorneys might have revealed the information through an anonymous telephone call. I do not believe that the proposal merits serious discussion—that a breach of the client's trust can be legitimated by carrying out the breach in a surreptitious manner.

In order to protect that communication—and, ultimately, the adversary system itself—we impose upon attorneys what has been called the "sacred trust" of confidentiality. It was pursuant to that high trust that the lawyers acted in Lake Pleasant, New York, when they refrained from divulging their knowledge of where the bodies were buried.

Questions

1. Why does a lawyer need to know "all that his client knows"? Does confidentiality really ensure that he or she will get all the necessary information? Is there any empirical support for this argument?

2. Why can't a lawyer hide the fruits of a crime? Is this really any different from reburying the body in the Lake Pleasant case?

3. Why shouldn't lawyers be required in all cases to disclose a client's intent to commit a crime?

4. Is it really clear that one should not report a client's intent to commit perjury? The United States Supreme Court has taken the opposite view. See *Nix v. Whiteside,* 475 U.S. 157, 106 S.Ct. 988, 89 L.Ed.2d 123 (1986).

5. Should the rules governing confidentiality be different in criminal and civil cases? If so, why? If not, why not?

ALBERT ALSCHULER—THE PRESERVATION OF A CLIENT'S CONFIDENCES: ONE VALUE AMONG MANY OR A CATEGORICAL IMPERATIVE?

52 U.Colo.L.Rev. 343, 349–55 (1981).
Reprinted with permission of the publisher, copyright © 1981.
University of Colorado Law Review.

[Professor Alschuler is a thoughtful observer of the American justice system. He has focused much of his work on the failings of our criminal process because of its excessive reliance on plea bargaining and inadequate insistence on vigorous courtroom inquiry. Here he responds to Judge Marvin Frankel's argument that the rules protecting the confidentiality of communications between lawyer and client unduly inhibit the search for truth.]

I take as my text the following passage from Judge Marvin E. Frankel's masterful critique of the adversary system, *Partisan Justice:*

> The theory of the [attorney-client] privilege is powerful: the client can be effectively represented only if the lawyer has an accurate account of what the client knows, believes, and has done. Accordingly, to obtain effective representation, the client must feel free and safe in making full and frank disclosures to counsel . . ..
>
> It will be seen without surprise that a privilege fashioned by lawyers has substantial benefits for lawyers . . . .. It is difficult enough to extract information from a client in the best of circumstances; a wary and mistrustful client would be unmanageable.

For these benefits, to attorney and client and the public interest in effective legal service, there is, as for everything, a price. The effect of every evidentiary privilege, every grant in the law of a right to withhold information, is an added barrier to the search for truth. The lawyer is authorized and required by the privilege to cover up what may be evil and needed facts. The interests injured by the cover-up may be precious ones.[1]

This passage poses the issue of delimiting the attorney-client privilege as a straightforward problem of balancing two obviously opposing values. Once this balancing formulation is accepted, it is not difficult to conclude, as Judge Frankel does, that a lawyer should be permitted and indeed required to reveal a client's confidences in a number of situations—for example, that in which the client has presented perjured testimony, that in which he has disclosed to the lawyer the place where the bodies of some murder victims lie mouldering, and even that in which the client has disclosed information that "would probably have a substantial effect on the determination of a material issue." This paper contends, however, that Judge Frankel's conventional formulation of the problem as one of choosing between effective legal representation and effective truth determination is oversimplified and misleading. For one thing, the choice posed by Judge Frankel often may be illusory. The privilege may not seriously impair the search for truth. For another, the value served by the preservation of a client's confidences is not merely the promotion of effective representation. Apart from this instrumental value, fundamental ethical values of loyalty, honesty and fair treatment are at stake—values that cannot properly be "balanced" against truth determination on an unweighted utilitarian scale.

Consider initially the "price" that, in Judge Frankel's view, the attorney-client privilege exacts. His analysis assumes an affirmative answer to an unresolved empirical question: does the privilege pose a significant barrier to the search for truth? As Judge Frankel recognizes, the privilege is grounded on the view that it promotes a client's frank disclosures to his lawyer, something that Judge Frankel says is difficult enough to secure even with the privilege intact. To the extent that the privilege truly is necessary to insure a client's frank disclosures, it does not impede the search for truth. A lawyer cannot reveal to a tribunal (or to the family of a murder victim or to anyone else) information that his client has successfully hidden from him; and if the effect of withdrawing or limiting the privilege were merely to cause a client to withhold his confidences, the effectiveness of the lawyer's representation might be impaired while the search for truth would not be advanced in the slightest. Judge Frankel has apparently assessed the costs of the attorney-client privilege at the time at which a lawyer has secured his client's confidences so that the issue is merely whether he should reveal them. At this point, with the relevant information already within the lawyer's control, the privilege does seem to impair

1. M. Frankel, Partisan Justice 64 (1980).

the search for truth, but this view of the problem disregards the very stage of the process that the privilege is designed to influence.

Of course one may imagine that even without the privilege some clients would "level" with their lawyers, revealing not only facts that they wish their lawyers to present in courts and other forums but facts that they wish to keep hidden. On this assumption, the privilege often would seem both unnecessary and a barrier to the search for truth. It plainly would shield information that could have been secured in its absence. To resolve the empirical issue in the manner that Judge Frankel's analysis suggests, however, would bring a much more basic ethical issue into focus. When a client's disclosures to his lawyer are, in effect, disclosures to others and when the client makes these disclosures to the lawyer despite the fact that he is unwilling to make them to others, he apparently does not "know the score." He may well have been "snookered" by the lawyer's explicit and implicit assurances of loyalty into parting with information that he did not expect the lawyer to divulge. The central question is not whether this means of gathering information to promote accurate adjudication might sometimes be effective—whether it might sometimes aid the search for truth—but whether it is fair to induce a person to part with information in this fashion. To obtain information by implicit or explicit deception ordinarily cannot be justified simply by showing that the information is useful. Not only does deception in any form pose a clear ethical issue, but an attorney's representation serves important functions that make it especially inappropriate for him to serve as a governmental information-gathering agent.

Judge Frankel seems to view the attorney-client privilege solely as a means of promoting effective legal service after a client's disclosures have been made; but apart from this objective, the privilege plays a central role in promoting a sense that our legal system is fair. People with legal problems need help; they often do not understand the complicated legal system in which they are enmeshed. Their sense of fairness (as well as ours) is enhanced when they need not fend for themselves—when they are entitled to the services of other people who understand the system and whose function within the system is to be on their side. This simple and powerful ideal of legal representation is obviously sacrificed when a client senses that his attorney's loyalties are divided.

Without a broad attorney-client privilege, a client must consider what disclosures to make to his attorney, and no expert can guide him in making this early, important decision. The client must view his attorney as another part of the legal establishment, and he must remain unrepresented before his representative. The system becomes substantially more just when a client can rely on his attorney without question or doubt—when he can know as well as he is likely ever to know the future that giving the truth to his attorney will not hurt him. Accordingly, a relationship of confidence between attorneys and their clients is essential to a sense of fair treatment on the part of the clients themselves.

In the world of Judge Frankel, it is unclear whether an attorney would promise to preserve a client's confidences and then violate this pledge if the client revealed where the bodies were buried or, indeed, if the client provided any information "that would probably have a substantial effect on the determination of a material issue." Rather than betray his client in this fashion, the attorney might describe the Frankelian limits of confidentiality before asking for information. Both of these alternatives, however, would be unsatisfactory.

When a client has relied on an attorney's pledge of confidentiality, violation of that pledge is no trivial thing. The inherent dishonesty of this course of conduct may be aggravated by the attorney's special authority in what is likely to be a psychologically troublesome situation; by the fact that both the attorney's license to dispense legal advice and (under Judge Frankel's proposals) the requirement of disclosure would proceed from the state; by the fact that the lawyer's basic function is to serve his client's interests, not retard them; and by the fact that the lawyer customarily accepts his client's money for providing his services. As this paper will indicate, rare and extreme situations may arise in which even the deliberate betrayal of a client's confidences may be justified. Nevertheless, a lawyer's betrayal of his client cannot simply be "balanced" against whatever utilitarian gains this betrayal might provide.

The second alternative—that of giving each client Judge Frankel's list of exceptions to the obligation of confidentiality before asking for his story—would almost certainly destroy any significant sense of confidentiality within the attorney-client relationship. Indeed, it might be viewed by many clients as a veiled invitation to perjury. Among other things, the attorney would say in effect, "I am about to ask you for the facts, and basically I am required by law and by the ethics of my profession not to reveal what you tell me. Nevertheless, if you reveal adverse facts that probably would have a substantial effect on the determination of a material issue, I will be bound to disclose them. Now please tell me the whole truth. In particular, do not omit adverse, material facts merely because, as an officer of the court as well as your loyal confidant, I will insure that those facts are used against you."

Judge Frankel, like the Kutak Commission of which he is a member, emphatically condemns the client interviewing technique illustrated in *Anatomy of a Murder*—that of "telling the client 'the law' before eliciting the facts," so that the client, if he likes, can present facts that will match the legal requirements for a successful claim or defense. A "truth in interviewing" disclaimer of the sort suggested above, however, would be similar in effect. Many clients surely would view it as a lawyer's strange and guarded way of saying, "Now is the time to make up a good story, and for heaven's sake do not tell me too much." It savors of the "horseshedding" of witnesses that Judge

Frankel mentions with distaste and indeed of subornation. The alternative both to this "horseshedding" and to the betrayal of one's clients is, of course, for a lawyer to assure his clients of confidentiality and then to keep his promise.

Of course the principles advanced in this paper can be strained by extreme cases. Perhaps a lawyer should not violate a client's confidences by revealing the location of his victims' dead bodies; but the obligation of confidentiality might well yield if, as the lawyer viewed the bodies, one of them moved a bit and moaned. Certainly the lawyer ought to secure medical assistance for this victim even at the cost of betrayal of his client's secrets. Similarly, when a client has confessed that he is guilty of a crime and has given his lawyer information that he would not have known unless he were guilty in fact, the lawyer ought at least attempt to prevent the imprisonment or execution of another person for this crime. And one cannot reasonably deny that similar exceptions might be warranted for other very extreme cases.

In short, and in answer to the question posed in the title to this paper, the obligation of confidentiality is not a categorical imperative. Hardly anything is. Nevertheless, it comes close, and to view it merely as an "interest" to be balanced against all other interests seems too easily to countenance dishonesty and the betrayal of clients by members of the legal profession. The customary formulation of the issue to be resolved in determining the scope of the attorney-client privilege cheapens what is probably the most basic obligation of any lawyer, an obligation that gives his work great dignity and purpose—the obligation to serve his clients rather than to become part of the official machinery that judges them.

Questions

1. Lawyers have arranged for themselves the broadest privilege against compelled disclosure of information. No one else in our society gets as much protection from judicial inquiry. Is this a proper balancing of the needs inherent in the lawyer/client relationship and those of society at large? Are lawyers sufficiently disinterested to make such a judgment?

2. Is Alschuler correct in doubting the social costs of confidentiality?

3. What does fairness have to do with maintaining the confidentiality of a client's communications with his or her lawyer? Do you agree with Alschuler's argument about the importance of fairness?

4. According to Alschuler what would be the practical consequences of substantially limiting the scope of the lawyer/client privilege? Is he correct?

DEBORAH RHODE—ETHICAL PERSPECTIVES ON LEGAL PRACTICE

37 Stan.L.Rev. 589, 612–17 (1985).
Reprinted with permission of the publisher, copyright © 1985.
The Board of Trustees of the Leland Stanford Junior University.

[Professor Rhode here turns her attention to the social costs of confidentiality especially in the corporate context.]

*   *   *

[T]he *Rules* require disclosure by an attorney only where necessary to avoid assisting a client's criminal or fraudulent act in proceedings before a tribunal. Lawyers may, but need not, reveal confidences in only two other circumstances: to prevent crimes likely to result in imminent death or substantial bodily harm, or to assert their own claims in a controversy with the client. Thus official ideology not only permits but may require counsel to remain a silent witness to highly asocial conduct.

Absolving lawyers from disclosure obligations under such circumstances is not easily reconciled with individualist premises. Casting the lawyer's office as a secular "confessional for the troubled individual" scarcely justifies its status as a haven for corporate prerogative. Particularly where the tradeoff is between shareholder profit and human safety, it is by no means obvious why organizational interests should occupy such a preferred position in defining counsel's ethical responsibilities.

The profession's conventional defense of its limited disclosure obligations is too familiar to warrant extended exegis here. Nonetheless, the core arguments are readily summarized and reduced to two essential propositions: first, that any risk of disclosure would deter clients from freely confiding in counsel; and second, that the costs of such a chill on clients' access to legal assistance would outweigh any societal benefits. Such claims are not without some intuitive force. The public's distaste for tattling reflects deeply rooted convictions about the value of trust and candor in human relationships. The critical issue, however, is not whether those values are worth preserving, but to what extent they are reconcilable with fundamental interests in protecting innocent third parties. On this point, most professional discourse has been utterly unilluminating.

Defenders of broad confidentiality protections almost invariably assume what is to be proven, namely that *any* disclosure responsibilities would dismember lawyer-client relationships. *   *   * The common assumption was that any qualification of confidentiality protections would "chill all client communications"; lawyers' access to "potentially sensitive information would be virtually eliminated," uprooting "a fundamental cornerstone of our legal system." Only where lawyers enjoyed a relationship of "total trust [and] candor" could they effectively assist clients in conforming their conduct to legal mandates.

Although rarely made explicit, the empirical basis for such assertions appears to be that attorneys' obligations are well known and that any qualification would induce clients to suppress critical facts that they now divulge. Neither supposition is self-evident * * *. [D]isclosure standards have been riddled with exceptions and indeterminacies, with which few laymen are familiar. Moreover, many clients will withhold evidence of compromising conduct, regardless of the bar's formal rules or clients' perceptions of them. What knowledge their counsel acquires will often be the product of paper trails and external corroboration rather than voluntary revelations. In any event, concerns about personal as well as organizational liability frequently leave clients with no practical alternative but to consult attorneys, and it is unclear how often some risk of disclosure would materially alter the terms of counsel's involvement. From a historical and cross-cultural perspective, it appears that most professionals, including American lawyers, have managed to discharge confidential counseling functions without the absolute freedom from third-party obligations that the organized bar now claims.

Thus, claims predicated on the lawyer's role as an institutional superego by no means justify the breadth of modern confidentiality protections. Given the scope of the attorney-client privilege, little is known about the extent to which lawyers have managed to channel patrons along "proper paths." Yet certainly the current incidence of illegal or hazardous corporate conduct suggests room for improvement. It is at least conceivable that some qualified third-party responsibilities might incline attorneys toward greater activism in their prophylactic role.

Finally, it bears note that even the most fervent defenders of unqualified confidentiality have seldom pursued the logic of their position when attorneys' own interests are at issue. Few * * * *Rules* evoked greater consensus than the provision allowing lawyers to reveal information necessary to collect fees or to establish their own position in a dispute with the client. Yet nothing * * * explains why disclosures to protect lay victims will erode client trust, while revelations to secure attorneys' financial interests will not. In effect, the bar's selective endorsement of confidentiality exceptions concedes the empirical point at issue. Once one acknowledges that clients' general expectation of confidentiality can be maintained despite some limited risk of betrayal, it is unclear why the pecuniary concerns of lawyers should assume priority over the potentially more significant claims of third-party victims.

In short, the profession is scarcely well situated to make a disinterested assessment of the societal risks and benefits of less categorical confidentiality protections * * *. Had a less parochial constituency been passing on these issues, it might well have reached a different accommodation of the competing public concerns. When self-interest is not at issue, many professionals, including lawyers, have concluded that "the uncertain and conjectural character" of threats to client confidence should not take precedence over concrete risks to innocent third party victims.

This is not, of course, to imply that tinkering with disclosure standards would in itself effect major changes in lawyers' perceived societal responsibilities. Whatever the bar's codified rules, avid policemen will not emerge among those whose salary and status flow directly from the targets of surveillance. In the face of strong economic, social, and cultural barriers to tattling, attorneys will inevitably resolve doubts in expedient directions. But it by no means follows that professional ideology should help to suppress those doubts by elevating prudential interests to ethical mandates.   *   *   *

Questions

1. Professor Rhode suggests that allowing corporate clients the same sort of confidentiality assured to individuals may produce seriously negative social consequences. Do you agree? Should the rules with respect to confidentiality be different for corporate clients? For a negative answer to this question from the United States Supreme Court see *Upjohn Co. v. United States,* 449 U.S. 383, 101 S.Ct. 677, 66 L.Ed.2d 584 (1981). (Holding that a corporation has the same right to the attorney/client privilege as an individual.)

2. What is the effect of Professor Rhode's referring to breaches of confidentiality as "tattling"? For a very different view of the seriousness of betrayal of confidences see Navasky, *Naming Names* (1980). (Discussing the disastrous consequences suffered by many Americans during the 1950s when their prior political affiliations were disclosed.)

3. Does Professor Rhode recognize and deal with the fairness and practicality arguments developed by Professor Alschuler?

4. Doesn't Professor Rhode make a telling point concerning the dissolution of confidentiality when attorneys enter into disputes with former clients? What ought to be done in such cases? Does this mean that confidentiality ought to be abandoned?

*

Index

†